Foreign Language Teachers and Intercultural Competence

LANGUAGES FOR INTERCULTURAL COMMUNICATION AND EDUCATION
Editors: Michael Byram, *University of Durham, UK*
Alison Phipps, *University of Glasgow, UK*

The overall aim of this series is to publish books which will ultimately inform learning and teaching, but whose primary focus is on the analysis of intercultural relationships, whether in textual form or in people's experience. There will also be books which deal directly with pedagogy, with the relationships between language learning and cultural learning, between processes inside the classroom and beyond. They will all have in common a concern with the relationship between language and culture, and the development of intercultural communicative competence.

Other Books in the Series

Developing Intercultural Competence in Practice
Michael Byram, Adam Nichols and David Stevens (eds)
Intercultural Experience and Education
Geof Alred, Michael Byram and Mike Fleming (eds)
Critical Citizens for an Intercultural World: Foreign Language Education as Cultural Politics
Manuela Guilherme
How Different Are We? Spoken Discourse in Intercultural Communication
Helen Fitzgerald
Audible Difference: ESL and Social Identity in Schools
Jennifer Miller
Context and Culture in Language Teaching and Learning
Michael Byram and Peter Grundy (eds)
An Intercultural Approach to English language Teaching
John Corbett
Critical Pedagogy: Political Approaches to Language and Intercultural Communication
Alison Phipps and Manuela Guilherme (eds)
Vernacular Palaver: Imaginations of the Local and Non-native Languages in West Africa
Moradewun Adejunmobi

Other Books of Interest

Age, Accent and Experience in Second Language Acquisition
Alene Moyer
The Good Language Learner
N. Naiman, M. Fröhlich, H.H. Stern and A. Todesco
Language Learners as Ethnographers
Celia Roberts, Michael Byram, Ana Barro, Shirley Jordan and Brian Street
Language Teachers, Politics and Cultures
Michael Byram and Karen Risager
Focus on French as a Foreign Language: Multidisciplinary Approaches
Jean-Marc Dewaele (ed.)

For more details of these or any other of our publications, please contact:
Multilingual Matters, Frankfurt Lodge, Clevedon Hall,
Victoria Road, Clevedon, BS21 7HH, England
http://www.multilingual-matters.com

LANGUAGES FOR INTERCULTURAL COMMUNICATION AND EDUCATION 10
Series Editors: Michael Byram and Alison Phipps

Foreign Language Teachers and Intercultural Competence

An International Investigation

Lies Sercu *with* Ewa Bandura, Paloma Castro, Leah Davcheva, Chryssa Laskaridou, Ulla Lundgren, María del Carmen Méndez García and Phyllis Ryan

MULTILINGUAL MATTERS LTD
Clevedon • Buffalo • Toronto

Library of Congress Cataloging in Publication Data
Sercu, Lies.
Foreign Language Teachers and Intercultural Competence: An International Investigation/Lies Sercu, with Ewa Bandura ... [et al.].
Languages for Intercultural Communication and Education: 10
Includes bibliographical references and index.
1. Language and languages–Study and teaching. 2. Intercultural communication.
3. Multicultural education. 4. Communicative competence.
I. Bandura, Ewa. II. Title. III. Series.
P53.45.S473 2005
418'.0071'1–dc22 2005009569

British Library Cataloguing in Publication Data
A catalogue entry for this book is available from the British Library.

ISBN 1-85359-844-5/EAN 978-1-85359-844-9 (hbk)
ISBN 1-85359-843-7/EAN 978-1-85359-843-2 (pbk)
ISBN 1-85359-845-3/EAN 978-1-85359-845-6 (ebook)

Multilingual Matters Ltd
UK: Frankfurt Lodge, Clevedon Hall, Victoria Road, Clevedon BS21 7HH.
USA: UTP, 2250 Military Road, Tonawanda, NY 14150, USA.
Canada: UTP, 5201 Dufferin Street, North York, Ontario M3H 5T8, Canada.

Typeset by Techset Ltd.
Printed and bound in Great Britain by the Cromwell Press Ltd.

Contents

Foreword

This book is part of the cultural turn in language teaching, which has taken place since the 1980s in various forms in different parts of the world. A common point of departure has been the assertion that foreign language teaching should not only focus on language (and/or literature at later stages), but also include a cultural dimension in a broader sense. Language teaching should demonstrate that there are connections between language and culture.

Foreign Language Teachers and Intercultural Competence is the result of a large empirical investigation that seeks to explore the cultural dimension in terms of intercultural communicative competence (of teachers and learners). In so doing, it positions itself among the approaches that have been developed in the European context, especially through the multifaceted work of Michael Byram. The main point of departure of this approach is the conviction that language teaching has two sides: a language side and a culture side, and that one of the greatest pedagogical challenges consists in integrating these two sides so that students get a sense of their interconnectedness. The approach is characterized by a dualism and an assertion of an intimate relationship between the two. Such compounds as the following are typical: language-and-culture, language-culture, culture-and-language, and as pointed out below, this is a way of thinking which is becoming familiar to language teachers in schools.

There are also other ways of conceptualizing the relationship between language and culture, the most important being the conviction that language *is* culture, that the focus should be on defining and teaching the cultural dimension of language itself, or of discourse. One example is work with literature, which may be seen as working with language/discourse as a cultural practice. Another example is the interest in defining cultural areas of language use, such as politeness norms, and non-verbal communication accompanying and enriching verbal communication. These approaches do not base themselves on a language-culture dualism, but prefer to coalesce language and culture into a single unity dominated by language. It remains to be seen if language teachers also take an interest in this way of conceptualizing the language-culture relationship in their professional practice.

Furthermore, the book reports an investigation that focuses on intercultural competence rather than cultural competence. Though there are many ways of understanding these concepts, one possible distinction is that cultural competence involves knowledge, skills and attitudes concerning a specific cultural area such as that associated with (one of the) target language countries, whereas intercultural competence involves knowledge, skills and attitudes at the interface between several cultural areas including the students' own country and a target language country. The development of intercultural competence is thus seen as a process that includes the students' experiences and competencies from their own cultural backgrounds, a process that allows them to reflect on their own cultural assumptions as an integral part of the further development of their skills and knowledge of the world.

Among the many players in language teaching and learning, the authors of *Foreign Language Teachers and Intercultural Competence* have chosen to focus on the teacher, and in doing that they highlight a border area in the professional identity of language teachers. Though more and more teachers see themselves as teachers of language and culture (whatever the relationship), the education of language teachers is often not organized in a way that helps them to accomplish this task in a professional way. It is still mostly up to the individual teacher to introduce elements of culture learning, or to develop the topics of textbook materials, in a pedagogically satisfactory way that allows for discussion, reflection and personal development. The book relates this issue to the issues of teacher cognition in general: how do teachers think about their own practice and about the preconditions for that? How can one describe their metacognitive awareness?

The investigation is a quantitative, comparative study that comprises questionnaire answers received during the summer of 2001 from foreign language teachers in seven countries: Belgium, Bulgaria, Poland, Mexico, Greece, Spain and Sweden. Thus it is a rather broad investigation. There is no specific reason for the choice of countries; it is the countries that the already existing network of researchers had contact with. The basic unit of the comparative analysis is the individual country, and the general purpose of the broad investigation has been to find out if it is possible to describe *an average profile for foreign language teachers.* Thus the aim is to define mainstream attitudes to the cultural dimension of language teaching among ordinary teachers. The group of researchers conclude that it is possible to define such an average profile.

The book does not pretend to be a work about theory; the authors do not, for example, delve into the complexities of the relationships between language, literature, culture and globalization. The focus is on data about how teachers perceive the cultural dimension of foreign language teaching and learning, how they perceive their students' knowledge of and attitudes to target language countries, their reports on their own teaching, the significance of study trips and exchanges, and their own experiences with target language countries via travel and the use of media of different kinds.

Foreign Language Teachers and Intercultural Competence thus provides a good basis for the further development of this field of study with regard to theories, methods and practices. The authors suggest in-depth qualitative studies of teachers and their perception of their overall situation, and they suggest innovations in initial and in-service teacher education. The investigation gives rise to many interesting questions that might be included in follow-up studies, such as: What are teachers' attitudes to the aspects of intercultural competence that focus on critical cultural awareness and the development of students as citizens (Guilherme, 2002)? What is intercultural competence today, taking into consideration actual political and cultural developments on the global scene? What is the role of language learning for students' (and teachers') general identity development in a complex world?

Last, but not least, this book is rewarding because teachers will be able to recognize themselves in the results and in the discussions of them. Because the researchers asked teachers questions that focus on the practical reality of their classes and on the concrete teaching and learning processes and conditions, they received reactions that reflect everyday perceptions of teachers located in the conflict between pedagogical ideals and practical possibilities. The book thus gives us a picture of the foreign language teacher that is both more concrete and more comprehensive than what we knew hitherto.

Karen Risager
Roskilde University, Denmark

Preface

This book results from an international research project, in which eight researchers from seven different countries were involved. The data for the project were collected in the course of May 2001. All researchers are members of CULTNET, a network of researchers of interculture in foreign language education (http://millennium.arts.kuleuven.ac.be/cultnet). Lies Sercu (K.U.Leuven, Belgium) initiated and coordinated the project. The other project partners were Ewa Bandura (Jagiellonian University, Poland), Paloma Castro (University of Valladolid, Spain), Leah Davcheva (The British Council, Bulgaria), Chryssa Laskaridou (Directorate for primary education in Western Thessaloniki, Greece), Ulla Lundgren (Jönköping University, Sweden), María del Carmen Méndez García (University of Jaén, Spain) and Phyllis Ryan (UNAM: Universidad Nacional Autonóma de México, México).

The cooperation has been a stimulating and exciting experience for all of us. The book presented here is much more than a collection of individual papers. Though the different chapters in which we present our research results have been jointly written by two researchers only, they could not have been produced without the preparatory work of all eight researchers involved in the project. In the first stage of the project, each researcher collected the data on which these research results are based in her own country and provided a description of these data. These per country descriptions served as the basis for writing the cross-country research reports presented here.

We want to express our gratitude to a number of people here. First of all, we want to thank Mike Byram, who started CULTNET and who continues to be a source of inspiration for many of us. We are grateful for his comments at intermediate stages in the research process.

We are much obliged to Jan De Baere, too, who helped us transform a paper questionnaire into a web-based questionnaire, and who processed the data for us.

We also want to thank the editors of the series in which this volume is published, Alison Phipps and Mike Byram, for their valuable feedback and comments. We also want to thank the editorial staff at Multilingual Matters for their professionalism and support.

Finally, our warmest thanks are due to the many others, who do not appear as 'authors', but without whom the book and the project would not have been possible: to the teachers who volunteered to take part in the project. We hope we have done justice to their views.

Lies Sercu
Leuven, 1 May 2004

Chapter 1

Teaching Foreign Languages in an Intercultural World

LIES SERCU

There is no doubt that we are living in times of great change. As we educators prepare our students for the 21st century, we are aware of many changes occurring globally. Population mobility continues throughout the world at an all-time high in human history, bringing extensive cross-cultural contact among diverse language and cultural groups. Predictions focus on an increasingly interconnected world, with global travel and instant international communications available to more and more people. Businesses and professions seek employees fluent in more than one language, to participate in the international marketplace as well as to serve growing ethnolinguistic minorities living within each community. Employers increasingly want their employees to be interculturally competent. They want them to be skilful negotiators in increasingly intercultural work situations.

Change is not exclusive or selective in terms of the sectors of society which it affects. Industry, health, politics and business are affected, but also education. In different parts of Europe, just as elsewhere in the world, the presence of ethnic and linguistic minority children in schools is becoming an everyday phenomenon. Policy makers include intercultural objectives in curricula, and teachers find themselves faced with the challenge of promoting the acquisition of intercultural competence through their teaching. This is true for teachers of a diversity of subjects. It is definitely true for teachers of foreign languages. Foreign language education is, by definition, intercultural. Bringing a foreign language to the classroom means connecting learners to a world that is culturally different from their own. Therefore, all foreign language educators are now expected to exploit this potential and promote the acquisition of intercultural competence in their learners. The objective of language learning is no longer defined in terms of the acquisition of communicative competence in a foreign language. Teachers are now required to teach intercultural communicative competence.

In this book, we report on a research project which focused specifically on foreign language teachers' perceptions regarding the teaching of intercultural communicative competence in foreign language education and on how current teaching practices in foreign language education relate to those expected of a 'foreign language and intercultural competence teacher' (FL&IC teacher).

Intercultural Communicative Competence in Foreign Language Education

Being able to cope with intercultural experiences requires that a person possesses a number of intercultural competencies and characteristics. These characteristics and competencies have been identified as the willingness to engage with the foreign culture, self-awareness and the ability to look upon oneself from the outside, the ability to see the world through the others' eyes, the ability to cope with uncertainty, the ability to act as a cultural mediator, the ability to evaluate others' points of view, the ability to consciously use culture learning skills and to read the cultural context, and the understanding that individuals cannot be reduced to their collective identities (see e.g. Sen Gupta, 2002).

In the literature on the subject, the intercultural experience tends to be described as an uncomfortable one, requiring the revision of beliefs, concepts and attitudes that one has hitherto taken for granted. The process includes changes in attitudes, beliefs, identity and values (Berry *et al.*, 1992). It requires people to revise their social identity, to reconsider the ideas they have held about out-groups, and to reconsider their position towards these out-groups since they have now themselves become members of the out-group. The range of feelings experienced varies from anger and anxiety to excitement and relief. The emotions come from many sources: fear of encountering something new, excitement at the discovery of new and different ways of thinking, relief through self-expression, anger that a deeply held belief may have been challenged. The common factor is the element of surprise which is the cornerstone of the intercultural experience. There are those who may respond with envy or embarrassment, others with pleasure and appreciation. One of the consequences of intercultural experiences may be that individuals retrench themselves in their pre-exposure beliefs and resist attempts to

Table 1.1 Components of intercultural competence

Knowledge	*Skills/behaviour*	*Attitudes/traits*
• Culture specific and culture general knowledge • Knowledge of self and other • Knowledge of interaction: individual and societal • Insight regarding the ways in which culture affects language and communication *Savoirs*	• Ability to interpret and relate *Savoir-comprendre* • Ability to discover and/or interact • Ability to acquire new knowledge and to operate knowledge, attitudes and skills under the constraints of real-time communication and interaction • Metacognitive strategies to direct own learning *Savoir-apprendre/ savoirs-faire*	• Attitude to relativize self and value others • Positive disposition towards learning intercultural competence *Savoir-être* • General disposition characterized by a critical engagement with the foreign culture under consideration and one's own *Savoir-s'engager*

look at their own cultural systems from the point of view of 'the other'. They may experience a high level of what is called acculturative stress, and experience feelings of marginality and alienation, identity confusion and heightened psychosomatic symptoms, high levels of anxiety and depression (Sen Gupta, 2002).

What, then, do people need to learn in order to be able to cope with intercultural contact situations? In the context of foreign language education, intercultural competence is linked to communicative competence in a foreign language. Communicative competence refers to a person's ability to act in a foreign language in a linguistically, sociolinguistically and pragmatically appropriate way (Council of Europe, 2001: 9). Intercultural communicative competence, then, builds on communicative competence and enlarges it to incorporate intercultural competence. So as to clarify the concept of intercultural competence to educators and teachers in the domain of foreign language education, the knowledge, skills and attitudes which together make up intercultural competence have been organized in a conceptual framework comprising five *savoirs* (Byram, 1997). These five *savoirs* should not be considered as isolated components, but rather as components that are integrated and intertwined with the various dimensions of communicative competence. Communicative competence itself can in fact be considered a sixth *savoir*, namely *savoir communiquer.* In Table 1.1, we present the different components of intercultural competence under three main headings; namely knowledge, skills/behaviour and attitudes/traits.

- The first *savoir, savoirs* with a plural 's', constitutes the knowledge dimension of the conceptual framework. It has been defined as 'knowledge about social groups and their cultures in one's own country, and similar knowledge of the interlocutor's country on the one hand, and similar knowledge of the processes and interaction at individual and societal levels, on the other hand' (Byram, 1997: 35). These *savoirs* together constitute the frame of reference of the people living (in) a particular culture. The words and gestures which people use, the behaviours they display, the values they believe in, the symbols they cherish, etc. are always culture-bound and carry meaning within a particular cultural frame of reference. Therefore, in intercultural communication it is important always to be sensitive to potential referential differences. Apart from culture-specific knowledge, the interculturally competent person also needs to acquire a certain amount of culture-general knowledge, which will allow him/her to deal with a large diversity of foreign cultures.
- *Savoir-apprendre* and *savoir-comprendre* together constitute the skills dimension of the conceptual framework. *Savoir-apprendre* refers to 'the capacity to learn cultures and assign meaning to cultural phenomena in an independent way' (Byram & Zarate, 1997: 241). *Savoir-comprendre* is related to *savoir-apprendre,* and refers to the capacity to interpret and relate cultures. These two *savoirs* are clearly in line with the answers that theorists of education have formulated in response to the changing and expanding nature of the world in which people will need the knowledge, skills (and attitudes) to continue learning throughout their lifetime. Thus, the terms reflect constructivist theories of autonomous learning, as they have been formulated in, for example, Scardamalia and Bereiter (1991, 1994), Wood and Wood (1996) or Richardson (1997).
- *Savoir-faire* refers to the overall ability to act in an interculturally competent way in intercultural contact situations, to take into account the specific cultural identity of one's interlocutor and to act in a respectful and co-operative way.
- *Savoir-être* and *savoir-s'engager* are best considered together since they refer to a general disposition that is characterised by 'a critical engagement with the foreign culture under consideration and

one's own' (*savoir-s'engager*) (Byram, 1997: 54) and 'the capacity and willingness to abandon ethnocentric attitudes and perceptions and the ability to establish and maintain a relationship between one's own and the foreign culture (*savoir-être*)'.

Foreign Language and Intercultural Competence Teacher

From the above descriptions of the intercultural experience, the intercultural person and intercultural communicative competence in foreign language education, it is clear that, in order to support the intercultural learning process, foreign language teachers need additional knowledge, attitudes, competencies and skills to the ones hitherto thought of as necessary and sufficient for teaching communicative competence in a foreign language. This insistence on the development of learners' intercultural skills, attitudes and knowledge requires a revision of professionalism in foreign language teaching. Teachers need an adequate sociocultural knowledge of the target language community, frequent and varied contacts with it and a thorough command of the pragmatic rules of use of the foreign language in contexts that may be considered to belong to their professional sphere (e.g. staying with a foreign colleague to organise class exchanges and/or e-mail contacts). They understand that cultural models differ and that they pervade our outlook on life and communication with others. They are familiar with the levels of communication (e.g. notions, speech acts, non-verbal communication) at which intercultural misunderstandings may arise, and are able and willing to negotiate meaning where they sense cross-cultural misunderstanding. They define the objectives of foreign language education in terms of language learning and of intercultural competence acquisition. In addition, they are skilful creators of (cross-curricular) learning environments that promote their learners' acquisition of intercultural communicative competence. They can employ teaching techniques that promote the acquisition of *savoirs, savoir-apprendre, savoir-comprendre, savoir-faire, savoir-s'engager* and *savoir-être.* They can help pupils relate their own culture to foreign cultures, to compare cultures and to empathise with foreign cultures' points of view. They are knowledgeable about their pupils' perceptions of and attitudes towards the foreign peoples and cultures associated with the foreign language they teach. They are willing to start from them when designing the learning process and know how to choose input materials with a view to modifying any wrongful perceptions learners may have. To that end, they know how to assess learning materials from an intercultural perspective and how to adjust these materials should they not allow them to achieve the aims of intercultural competence teaching. Next to being skilful classroom teachers, teachers are able to use experiential approaches to language-and-culture teaching. With respect to attitudes, FL&IC teachers ought to be favourably disposed towards the integration of intercultural competence teaching in foreign language education and willing to actually work towards achieving that goal. In sum, teachers of intercultural communicative competence also need to be acquainted with basic insights from cultural anthropology, culture learning theory and intercultural communication. They need to be willing to teach intercultural competence and need to know how to do so (Edelhoff, 1993; Felberbauer, 1997; Willems, 2000).

The above suggests an important shift in emphasis in professionalism in foreign language teaching. Till recently, teachers could meet the demand to broaden their pupils' minds through familiarising themselves with culture-specific information and passing that information on to their pupils. The expectations in the intercultural domain currently voiced towards foreign language teachers require them to acquire quite a different and more substantial body of cultural knowledge and develop a range of new skills that will allow them to promote their learners' acquisition of intercultural competence.

The assumption seems to be that teachers are already moving in the advocated direction and are willing to support the new objectives put forward. Teachers are supposed to already have left the traditional foreign-culture teaching approach far behind, and to have moved well in the direction of multicultural and intercultural teaching. The observation that this belief remains largely intuitive with little rigorous evidence to support it, constituted the rationale for the research project reported on here.

Language Teachers as Teachers of Intercultural Communicative Competence: A Research Project

The study's aim was threefold. First, it wanted to inquire into how foreign language teachers' current professional self-concepts relate to the envisaged profile of the intercultural foreign language teacher. Second, it wanted to investigate to what extent current teaching practice can be characterised as directed towards the attainment of intercultural communicative competence instead of towards communicative ('linguistic') competence. Third, the study wanted to determine teachers' degree of willingness to interculturalise foreign language education, and identify the factors that appear to affect their readiness.

Because similar expectations towards teachers are voiced in many national curricula and on the European level, the research topic was viewed in international perspective. We collected data with respect to foreign language teachers' perceptions and teaching practices in seven countries, namely Belgium, Bulgaria, Poland, Mexico, Greece, Spain and Sweden.[1] Via the international set-up, we wanted to find out whether it is possible to describe an average foreign language-and-culture teacher in terms of perceptions and attitudes regarding intercultural competence teaching and actual teaching practice, irrespective of the country in which s/he teaches.

We were interested in the way in which teachers describe themselves, in what they say they do, in who they say they are, in who they say their pupils are, etc. In other words, we were interested in teachers' thinking, in their perceptions, beliefs, attitudes, and knowledge.

In research on teachers' thinking, 'conceptions' is the general term used to describe beliefs, knowledge, preferences, mental images, and other similar aspects of teachers' mental structures. When taken as a whole, the body of research on teachers' conceptions suggests that these conceptions, to a large extent, shape teachers' instructional behaviour. They determine how teachers respond to reality, organise new information, and define and interpret tasks (Knowles & Holt-Reynolds, 1991; Pajares, 1992; Nespor, 1987). Teachers' general conceptions regarding teaching, learning and education shape the development of context-specific conceptions, which directly lead to choice of specific teaching activities. When teachers have conflicting conceptions regarding particular aspects of their profession and teaching job, this direct link between conceptions and actual instruction is less clear. The body of research also suggests that it is very difficult to influence the conceptions or the practices of either experienced or beginning teachers. General and context-specific conceptions are largely implicit and arise primarily from a teacher's experience as both a student and a teacher. Moreover, teachers with considerable experience teaching in a particular class have developed routines for many common aspects of instruction and no longer give instructional decisions much conscious thought. Their conceptions can be expected to be quite robust and strongly influence a teacher's evaluation of new instructional goals and techniques (Henderson, 2002). These insights gained from research on teacher thinking are crucial for understanding the way in which teachers currently perceive the advocacy to integrate intercultural competence teaching in foreign language education, or the reasons why they appear hesitant or unwilling to change their actual instructional behaviour and teaching practice.

At the end of the book, we will consider how our findings which pertain to intercultural competence teaching in foreign language education relate to these research findings on teachers in general.

Teachers' beliefs were elicited by means of an English-medium web-based questionnaire, with mainly closed and some open questions. The questionnaire has been included in Appendix 1. This approach allowed us to compare different national data sets in a relatively straightforward manner. In the final chapter of this book, we will discuss our research methodology in detail, highlighting strengths and limitations and suggesting areas for further research. For now, we only want to point out that we considered more qualitative research methodologies, frequently employed in research on teacher thinking, less appropriate in view of the fact that the research was international in set-up and that one of the aims of the research was to compare teachers' profiles in the different countries participating in the research. Using unstructured interviews, journals, collaborative data collection techniques and the like would have yielded more in-depth data, but would have made international comparison next to impossible.

The questionnaire inquired into teachers' perceptions of their profession and teaching practice. In our study, 'teaching practice' refers to both inside classroom and outside classroom activities to promote the acquisition of intercultural competence. We asked teachers to report on how frequently they practise teaching activities such as 'ask learners to independently explore an aspect of the foreign culture' or 'talk to learners about their own experiences in the foreign country', or how frequently they address particular cultural topics, such as 'daily life and routines' or 'norms, values and beliefs' in the foreign language classroom. We also asked them to estimate how they divide their teaching time over culture teaching and language teaching. As regards outside classroom activities, we invited teachers to report on their school's policy regarding school trips and exchange projects, and on whether or not they believed in the effect of such experiential activities on their learners' knowledge and attitudes regarding the foreign cultures associated with the foreign language they are learning. We also collected indirect information on teachers' views about intercultural competence teaching through asking them to clarify how they perceive the objectives of foreign language education, of culture teaching, and of intercultural competence teaching.

The questionnaire was offered to an opportunity sample in May 2001. In each of the participating countries, we invited an equal number of respondents to participate in the research. They were not randomly chosen, but purposefully selected. Purposeful sampling is based on the assumption that the investigator wants to discover, understand, and gain insight and therefore must select a sample from which the most can be learned (Merriam, 1998; Creswell, 1994). The criteria we used to select the respondents were: language taught (English, German, French, other language) and sector of education (secondary).

Four-hundred and twenty-four teachers participated, with Belgium having the largest sample (151) and Bulgaria the smallest (30), a number that still allows statistical analyses to be run on the data. Of all respondents, 20.03% are male, 79.97% female. The average respondent is 40-years old. The Swedish average teacher is the oldest (48) and the Polish the youngest (35). Seventy-nine percent of the respondents reported to be primarily teachers of English, 9% to be teachers of German, 7% to be teachers of French and 2% to be teachers of Spanish. Two percent mentioned still other languages to be the main language(s) they teach. Two-thirds of the respondents teach in general secondary education, one-third in technical, vocational or artistic secondary education. The average length of experience of language teaching is 15 years.

Though the samples are opportunity samples, statistical analyses on the data revealed that the different country samples are more comparable than different with respect to the respondents' sex, age, degrees obtained, main languages taught, other languages taught, number of years of teaching experience, percentage of ethnic minority community children in school and foreign languages taught in school. The number of teaching periods and the kind of education offered at the various schools, however, appeared to differ significantly. The Poles, Mexicans and Bulgarians teach most hours (23 teaching hours/week) and the Swedes fewest (15 teaching hours/week), with a Swedish teaching period, however, lasting a full hour, not 50 or 40 minutes. As regards the type of education offered, some country samples are largely composed of respondents teaching in secondary education (e.g. Spain, Greece, Poland), while other country samples show a more even spread over different kinds of education, notably vocational education, artistic education or still other kinds of education.

Except in Poland, the questionnaire was not translated and this has affected the composition of the sample in all countries, except in Sweden and Belgium. In Mexico, Greece, Bulgaria and Spain next to all respondents are teachers of English. In Sweden and Belgium larger numbers of teachers of French, German or Spanish participated. In Poland, where the questionnaire was translated, one-fifth of the respondents were teachers of German.

Finally, we want to point out that the fact that the questionnaire was offered in electronic (web-based) format entailed some difficulties in some countries, but not in others. In Sweden, about one-third of the respondents completed a paper version of the questionnaire. In Poland, next to all respondents completed the paper version. A small number of Mexican teachers experienced difficulty in accessing the questionnaire, but could be helped by telephone. In Spain, most teachers completed the questionnaire electronically. In Belgium, Greece, Mexico, Spain and Bulgaria, next to all teachers completed the electronic version of the questionnaire.

Main Research Findings

Below we summarise our main research findings. They reflect the main aims of our study. This summary will orient the reader while reading the following chapters in which we present the findings specific to the different dimensions which together constitute teachers' conceptions of their profession and of its intercultural dimension. These specific dimensions concern the teachers' perceptions of the objectives of foreign language education, their degree of familiarity with the foreign culture primarily associated with the foreign language they teach, their perceptions of their pupils' culture-and-language learning profile, their perceptions of their culture teaching practices and of the cultural component of the teaching materials they use, their views regarding experiential culture learning activities (school trips and exchange projects) and, finally, their opinions regarding different facets of intercultural competence teaching. Here, we merely list the main results of our study. In the final chapter, we will draw the different components of the picture together and comment on them, discussing their meaning and implications.

The respondents' foreign language and culture teaching profiles

The study's first aim was to describe foreign language teachers' current professional self-concepts and to relate these to the envisaged profile of the intercultural foreign language teacher. The second aim was to determine teachers' degree of willingness to interculturalise foreign language education, and identify the factors that appear to affect their readiness.

Our findings reveal that we can speak of two clearly distinct teacher profiles when trying to map teachers' beliefs regarding the integration of intercultural competence in foreign language education. We labelled these profiles 'the favourably disposed foreign language teacher' and 'the unfavourably disposed foreign language teacher'. Each profile can be identified by means of a number of characteristics. Teachers who are not in favour believe that it is impossible to integrate language and culture teaching. They also believe that intercultural skills cannot be acquired at school, let alone in the foreign language classroom. On the whole, these teachers do not believe in the positive effect of intercultural competence teaching on pupils' attitudes and perceptions. The only effect they see is a negative one: intercultural competence teaching reinforces pupils' already existing stereotypes. In addition, these teachers believe that it is only when there are ethnic minority community children in one's classes that one should teach intercultural competence. Teachers who are, by contrast, favourably disposed towards integration share a number of convictions too. They believe that teaching culture is as important as teaching the foreign language, and that it is possible to integrate both. In their opinion, intercultural competence teaching makes pupils more tolerant. These teachers prefer an approach that is cross-curricular and are convinced that teachers of every subject should teach intercultural competence, not only foreign language teachers. In addition, they do not think intercultural competence should only be taught in schools with ethnic minority community children; it should be taught to all pupils.

Our data also reveal that no clear relationship appears to exist between teachers' beliefs regarding integration and the way in which they actually shape their teaching practice. Teachers who are clearly willing to interculturalise foreign language education are not yet teaching towards the acquisition of intercultural competence. Their willingness does not necessarily imply more extensive culture teaching in terms of the frequency with which culture-teaching activities are practised or particular cultural topics are addressed. In only three out of seven countries do teachers who are favourably disposed towards integration appear to teach culture more extensively than their colleagues who are less favourably disposed. Moreover, the overall impression is that in actual teaching practice, teachers prefer traditional teacher-directed approaches geared towards the enhancement of pupils' familiarity with the foreign culture, not approaches directed towards the full attainment of intercultural competence, with its cognitive, attitudinal and skills components. They tend not to take account of their pupils' perceptions and attitudes regarding the foreign cultures when shaping their teaching practice. Experiential learning activities, such as school trips or exchange programmes, feature no more than peripherally in teachers' overall conceptions of what it is they want to achieve in foreign language education. Interestingly, the extent of teachers' familiarity with the foreign cultures appeared to affect the extent to which teachers touch upon different aspects of the foreign culture in the foreign language classroom.

Relationship between the actual and envisaged FL&IC teaching profile

Towards the beginning of this chapter, we described what knowledge, attitudes and skills a foreign language and intercultural competence teacher (FL&IC teacher) should possess in order to be able to promote the acquisition of intercultural competence in the foreign language classroom. Our findings suggest that teachers are moving towards becoming FL&IC teachers, but that at present their profile does not meet all the expectations regarding knowledge, skills and attitudes desirable in the 'foreign language and intercultural competence teacher'. Individual teachers may already possess the envisaged FL&IC teacher profile. The majority of teachers in all participating countries, however, either have what could be labelled 'a foreign language teacher profile', focusing primarily and almost exclusively on the acquisition of communicative competence in the foreign language, or a 'foreign language and culture teaching profile', focusing primarily on the acquisition of communicative competence in the foreign language, but also teaching culture so as to enhance pupils' familiarity with the foreign culture as well as their motivation to learn the foreign language.

As regards knowledge, we said that foreign language teachers should be sufficiently familiar with the foreign cultures associated with the foreign language they teach, and that the contacts they have should be both varied and frequent. Our findings reveal that teachers from the seven countries regard themselves as being sufficiently familiar with the culture of the foreign language(s) they teach. As far as contacts are concerned, they show that tourist contacts in Belgium, Greece, Spain and Sweden are more frequent than in Poland, Bulgaria and Mexico, and that media contacts are equally frequent in all seven countries.

From the kinds of teaching activities most frequently practised in the foreign language classroom, we can conclude that teachers tend to employ techniques that aim to enlarge learners' knowledge of the foreign culture (*savoirs*), and not to encourage learners to search for information in different sources (*savoir-apprendre*), analyse it independently and critically (*savoir-comprendre, savoir-s'engager*) and present their findings in order to discuss them with others. Though 'comparison of cultures' appears to be an activity frequently practised, other activities aiming at the acquisition of intercultural skills, such as 'reflect critically on one's sources of information', 'explore an aspect of the foreign culture', 'practise skills useful in intercultural contact situations' are not.

As regards skills, we stated that teachers should be able to employ teaching techniques that promote the acquisition of *savoirs, savoir-apprendre, savoir-comprendre, savoir-faire, savoir-s'engager* and *savoir-être.* Teachers should be able to help pupils relate their own culture to foreign cultures, to compare cultures and to empathise with foreign cultures' points of view. They should be able to select appropriate teaching materials and to adjust these materials should they not allow the aims of intercultural competence teaching to be achieved. Next to being skilful classroom teachers, teachers should also be able to use experiential approaches to language-and-culture teaching. The description above of the kinds of teaching activities, which teachers tend to practise in their foreign language classroom, suggests that teachers are not yet practising intercultural teaching skills.

As regards the demand that FL&IC teachers should be able to select teaching materials appropriate for intercultural competence teaching, our data suggest that teachers are definitely able to comment critically on the cultural contents of foreign language teaching materials, pointing out good and less satisfactory sides. Care has to be taken, however, not to equal this ability with the ability to assess teaching materials with respect to their potential for teaching intercultural competence. The teachers who commented on the cultural dimension of their teaching materials did so from the perspective of the traditional 'foreign cultural approach', pointing out where the information regarding the foreign culture had been faultily selected or represented. Individual teachers also point to the need to revise the textbook's approach to the teaching of culture, and demand more intercultural tasks. The number of teachers doing so is very small, and does not allow the conclusion that teachers are able to assess the culture teaching approaches adopted by their textbooks from the perspective of 'intercultural approach'. Neither do our data allow us to state that teachers are able to adjust the materials they use in order to enhance their potential for promoting the acquisition of intercultural competence.

Next to being skilful classroom teachers and assessors of foreign language teaching materials, FL&IC teachers should also be able to use out-of-classroom experiential approaches to language-and-culture teaching, it was said. Our data reveal that school trips and exchange programmes tend to not be considered activities that take place in the context of foreign language education. Only a minority of the teachers devote time to preparing or following-up on this kind of activity in the foreign language classroom. Our findings allow the conclusion that teachers are convinced school trips and exchange programmes have positive effects on learners' perceptions and attitudes regarding foreign cultures. Yet, despite teachers' beliefs in the positive effects on learners, they also think of these activities as the responsibility of the school, of other teachers or of all teachers. Teachers who do devote teaching time to following-up on experiential learning activities appear to use activities that assist learners to reflect on their experiences and on cultural differences between their own and the foreign culture, which can thus be said to be typical of intercultural approaches to foreign language education.

Finally, when comparing the current foreign language teachers' profile and the envisaged FL&IC teacher profile from the point of view of attitudes, our data reveal that a very large proportion of teachers are clearly willing to integrate intercultural competence teaching in foreign language education. They also show that this willingness is not reflected in the way in which they currently shape their teaching practice or define the objectives of foreign language education. These objectives continue to be defined mainly in linguistic terms, though teachers in some countries, notably Bulgaria and Greece, clearly give greater prominence to cultural objectives than teachers in other countries. As regards the way in which teachers attend to their pupils' perceptions and attitudes, it is clear they take their decisions as to how to shape their culture teaching practice largely independently of their pupils' current knowledge and disposition. In this sense, they do not meet the expectations of the FL&IC teacher.

Average profile

With respect to our final research question, namely 'Is it possible to speak of an "average culture-and-language teaching profile", that applies to teachers in a number of different countries?', our data allow the conclusion that it is possible to speak of such a profile with respect to many of the facets of teachers' self-concepts and teaching practices investigated in this research. Our data do not allow the conclusion, however, that teachers in the different countries approach foreign language and culture teaching in the same way. In the following chapters we will point out quite a number of differences between countries. It is self-evident that the specific context in which one teaches affects one's teaching approach. This context is constituted by the pupils with whom one works and the school where one is based, but also by factors at the macro level of education, such as national (curricular) guidelines or stipulations of attainment targets.

Significance of the Study

Before sharing the results we obtained with respect to the specific dimensions of teachers' professional self-concept we investigated, we want to point out in which respects we consider our results to be significant. Like with the summary of our main findings, we will not enter into detail here, but leave comments and discussion till the final chapter of this book.

In this book, we focus on teachers' beliefs regarding intercultural competence teaching in foreign language education and we do so in an international perspective. Our findings will be of interest to anyone wanting to find out how foreign language teachers in a number of different countries view intercultural competence in foreign language education and how their views impact on their teaching. Both the country-specific and comparative reports will help individual teachers to reflect on their own perceptions and teaching practice, on where they stand on the 'favourably disposed–unfavourably disposed' continuum in comparison with other teachers in their own country or with foreign language teachers in general. The findings may serve as a starting point for discussions with colleagues, for exchange of ideas regarding the integration of an intercultural dimension in one's foreign language teaching and for initiatives to reconsider jointly, in one's teaching team, existing teaching practices.

Understanding teachers' perceptions and the reasons why they embrace or reject intercultural competence teaching is crucial for teacher educators who want to design (international) teacher education programmes which can clarify and exemplify to foreign language teachers how they can promote the acquisition of intercultural competence in their classes. Our findings highlight important differences and commonalities in teachers' perceptions. Both national and international teacher education programmes can build on these commonalities and have teachers from different countries cooperate, knowing that they all share a common body of knowledge, skills and convictions. They can also exploit differences between teachers to enhance teachers' understanding of intercultural competence.

Apart from being significant from a practical educational point of view, our findings are also significant from a scientific point of view. We believe we have, for the first time, shown the variability, but also relative consistency, of language teachers' views regarding their profession in a considerable number of countries. By doing so, we have touched upon a host of questions which call for further investigation, and in that sense have set a research programme for the years to come. Until now, much of the research on teachers' beliefs has focused on the areas of science and maths education or on reading (see e.g. Bell *et al.*, 2000; Prosser & Trigwell, 1999). These investigations have frequently been concerned with understanding how teacher beliefs impact on practice. Our study differs from these past studies in several ways. Our focus has been on teachers of foreign languages, and more specifically on teachers' beliefs regarding the cultural dimension of foreign language education and the teaching of intercultural competence. Though some studies have investigated foreign language teachers' conceptions (see e.g. Borg, 1998a, 1998b, 2003; Freeman & Richards, 1993; Green, 1996; Markee, 1997), far fewer have focused on foreign language teachers' perceptions of the intercultural dimension of foreign language education, with the notable exceptions of Byram and Risager (1999), Ryan (1997, 1998) and Sercu (2001). The present study also differs from other studies of teachers' beliefs by its international set-up and its emphasis on commonalities in teachers' beliefs, rather than on the idiosyncrasies of individual teachers' mental processes. Though an international perspective lay at the basis of Byram and Risager's study, comparing British and Danish teachers (Byram & Risager, 1999), a far larger number of countries were involved in our study, which makes it unique.

Overview of the Book

In the next eight chapters, we present our research findings. The findings are presented in answer to the different subquestions we used to investigate our main research concept, namely 'teachers' conceptions regarding foreign language-and-culture teaching'. These questions are:

(1) How do teachers perceive of the objectives of foreign language education?
(2) How familiar do teachers consider themselves with the foreign cultures of which they teach the foreign language?
(3) How do teachers perceive their pupils' knowledge and attitudes regarding the foreign cultures associated with the foreign languages they teach?
(4) How do teachers describe their culture teaching practices?
(5) How do teachers perceive the cultural dimension of teaching materials?
(6) How do teachers perceive the effect of school trips and exchange projects on pupils' intercultural competence?

(7) What attitude do teachers have vis-à-vis different aspects of intercultural competence teaching in foreign language education?
(8) To what extent are teachers willing to interculturalise foreign language education and what factors appear to affect their willingness?

Each chapter focuses on one of the above questions and starts with a brief description of the chapter's topic and a justification of why the topic was included. This justification makes it clear how the chapter's topic is related to our overall research topic, namely to provide a state of the art overview of teachers' perceptions regarding intercultural foreign language education, and of current culture teaching practices in a number of countries. The focus is mainly on general tendencies, but whenever interesting and relevant, we present the research findings pertaining to individual countries. The data for each chapter were collected by the different researchers involved in the project. Each chapter can thus be viewed the result of the collective effort of a group of people.

In Chapter 9, we view the different components of teachers' perceptions and teaching practice, and consider to what extent the different facets appear to build a coherent teacher profile. Using statistical techniques, we make patterns in teachers' beliefs visible which would otherwise have remained hidden. We consider which factors affect a teacher's willingness to teach intercultural competence in foreign language education, explore to what extent actual culture teaching appears consistent, and draw these two components together, considering to what extent teachers' obvious willingness to teach intercultural competence is reflected in their current teaching. In the final part of the chapter, we will reflect on the extent to which teachers' actual teaching profile corresponds to the envisaged profile of the intercultural competence teacher we have described in the introductory chapter to this book.

The concluding chapter, Chapter 10, starts with a discussion of what we think our findings mean and how they relate to previous research findings. It proceeds with a discussion of our research methodology and, reflecting on its strengths and weaknesses, provides suggestions for further research. The chapter concludes with recommendations for teacher education and educational policy which we believe arise from our research findings.

We hope our study has adduced strong evidence that teachers of language-and-culture need a more complex and enriching education than foreign language teachers have enjoyed till now. In both its academic and its pedagogic dimensions, teacher education needs to provide opportunities for learning which are both cognitive and experiential, and promote both personal and professional development. The responsibilities of the foreign language teacher for introducing learners, whether young or old, to learning which challenges and modifies their perspective on the world and their cultural identity as members of a given social and national group, are enormous. To be able to promote the acquisition of intercultural competence, teachers themselves need to revisit their common sense notions of what it means to teach and learn a foreign language in the light of a new teaching philosophy, that truly recognises the intercultural nature of all encounters between speakers originating from different cultural backgrounds.

Their belief that teaching and learning a foreign language is always an intercultural process will provide them with a firm basis for reshaping their teaching practice in such a way that it adequately prepares learners for the intercultural world in which they are living.

Note

1. These countries are the countries where the researchers who participated in the project are working.

Chapter 2

Objectives of Foreign Language Teaching and Culture Teaching Time

PALOMA CASTRO and LIES SERCU

'Communicative language teaching' has become part of the familiar landscape of language teaching in the last three or four decades. It may be interpreted differently in different countries and by different teachers, but it is a concept which most probably is familiar to the foreign language teachers who participated in our study. It betrays a focus on communication skills and on language competence, in contrast to a concern for intercultural skills and competence. In this chapter we explore the ways in which teachers define the objectives of foreign language education. We inquire into the extent to which their conceptions of communicative language teaching incorporate culture teaching, and to what extent culture teaching is defined in terms of intercultural communicative competence rather than in terms of a traditional culture teaching approach. Such a foreign culture teaching approach aims to familiarise learners with the facts and figures regarding the foreign country primarily associated with the foreign language they are learning, but pays little, if any, attention to reflection on one's own cultural identity, on cultural differences or on how cultures relate to and affect each other. Neither does it include an element of autonomous exploration of cultures. Rather, the foreign culture approach mainly aims to present 'the truth' about a particular country, which learners are to accept and acquire.

The way in which teachers define the objectives of their teaching is likely to affect their teaching practice. It is likely that teachers who perceive the objectives of foreign language education also in terms of teaching intercultural competence will be more willing to interculturalise foreign language education than teachers who perceive the objectives in terms of the acquisition of communicative competence only. Their teaching practice may also come closer to intercultural communicative competence teaching than that of the latter group. In this chapter, we start our exploration of teachers' teaching practices via an analysis of the balance of time they attribute to 'culture' in contrast to 'language' in their lessons, an exploration which will be continued in subsequent chapters. It is likely that teachers who perceive the objectives also in terms of teaching intercultural competence will devote more time to culture teaching than teachers who perceive the objectives in terms of the acquisition of communicative competence only. Teachers who say they integrate language and culture teaching for 100% of teaching time may come closer to the ideal of the FL&IC teacher than teachers who show no awareness of the relationship between language and culture or of the need to teach language and culture in an integrated way.

Teachers' Perceptions of the Objectives of Foreign Language Education

The respondents were asked to rank eight possible objectives of foreign language education. These are given in Table 2.1 below. The objectives have been ordered here according to whether they can be considered culture learning objectives, language learning objectives or objectives aimed at the acquisition of (language) learning skills. In the questionnaire, they appeared in random order.

Figure 2.1 presents the results obtained for all respondents considered together.[1] We see a clear preference for language learning objectives. Teachers who prioritise linguistic competence aim to promote in their pupils the acquisition of a level of proficiency in the foreign language so they can use it for practical purposes (mean score 5.90). They are also interested in enthusing their pupils to learn foreign languages (mean score 5.74). The language learning objective relating to developing proficiency to read literary works, an objective that is connected to the culture learning objectives, is ranked last (mean score 3.20).

With respect to culture learning objectives, teachers relate the idea of culture teaching and learning primarily to the teaching of civilisation, that is, to increasing learners' knowledge of the facts and events of the target culture (mean score 5.05). Second in importance is promoting an open mind and a positive disposition towards the unfamiliar (mean score 4.66). The objective ranked last is to assist pupils in developing a better understanding of their own identity and culture (mean score 3.77). Teachers perceive the objectives of foreign language education more in terms of enhancing familiarity with what is foreign, and less in

Table 2.1 Possible objectives of foreign language education

Culture learning objectives	
(1)	Promote pupils' familiarity with the culture, and the civilisation of the countries where the language, which they are learning, is spoken.
(2)	Promote the acquisition of an open mind and a positive disposition towards unfamiliar cultures.
(3)	Assist pupils to develop a better understanding of their own identity and culture.
Language learning objectives	
(4)	Assist pupils to acquire a level of proficiency in the foreign language that will allow them to read literary works in that foreign language.
(5)	Enthuse pupils to learn foreign languages.
(6)	Promote the acquisition of a level of proficiency in the foreign language that will allow the learners to use the foreign language for practical purposes.
General skills/language skills learning objectives	
(7)	Assist pupils to acquire the skills that will be useful in other subject areas in life (such as memorise, put into words, formulate accurately, give a presentation, etc.).
(8)	Promote the acquisition of learning skills that will be useful for learning other foreign languages.

terms of promoting reflection on one's own culture and identity or on intercultural relationships.

These findings suggest that teachers above all try to develop communicative competence in their pupils and not so much intercultural communicative competence. Looking at how the different countries ranked the culture, language and skills learning objectives, we can observe to what extent this general tendency applies to the different national groups. As Figure 2.2 reveals, Belgian, Mexican, Polish, Spanish and Swedish teachers define the objectives of foreign language education primarily in linguistic terms, and thus reflect this general tendency. Only Bulgarian and Greek teachers appear to prioritise culture learning objectives over language learning objectives.

A detailed study of the order in which teachers in the different countries ranked the eight objectives, again confirms this tendency, and indeed reveals a picture that is largely similar in the different countries, as evident in Figure 2.3. Teachers appear to define the objectives of

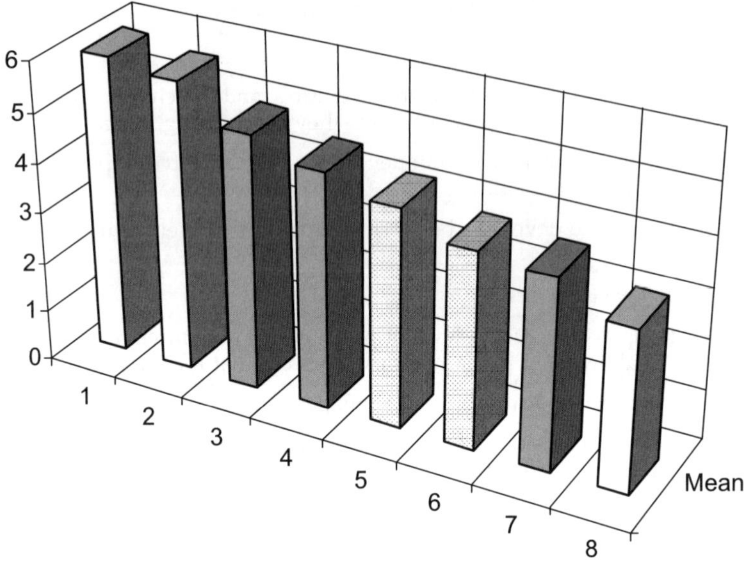

Figure 2.1 Teachers' perceptions of the objectives of foreign language education. Objectives grouped. All respondents considered together. Mean scores ranging between 0.00 and 8.00.

(1) Promote the acquisition of a level of proficiency in the foreign language that will allow the learners to use the foreign language for practical purposes.
(2) Enthuse my pupils for learning foreign languages.
(3) Promote my pupils' familiarity with the culture, the civilisation of the countries where the language which they are learning is spoken.
(4) Promote the acquisition of an open mind and a positive disposition towards unfamiliar cultures.
(5) Assist my pupils to acquire skills that will be useful in other subject areas and in life (such as memorise, summarise, put into words, formulate accurately, give a presentation, etc.).
(6) Promote the acquisition of learning skills that will be useful for learning other foreign languages.
(7) Assist my pupils in developing a better understanding of their own identity and culture.
(8) Assist my pupils to acquire a level of proficiency in the foreign language that will allow them to read literary works in the foreign language.

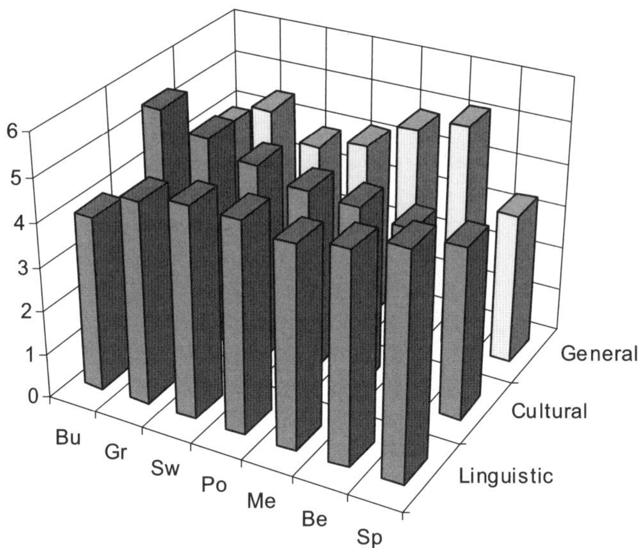

Figure 2.2 Teachers' perceptions of the objectives of foreign language education. Objectives grouped. Respondents considered per country. Mean scores ranging between 0.00 and 8.00. Be = Belgium, Bu = Bulgaria, Gr = Greece, Me = Mexico, Po = Poland, Sp = Spain and Sw = Sweden.

foreign language education above all in terms of the acquisition of the ability to use the foreign language for practical purposes and in terms of motivating pupils to learn foreign languages. Still, three countries slightly deviate from this order of priorities, with Bulgarian teachers putting relatively more emphasis on the promotion of an open mind, Greek teachers on promoting familiarity with the foreign culture and Mexican teachers on promoting the acquisition of general learning skills. This is an interesting finding, which is difficult to interpret at present. It may be that Bulgarian and Greek pupils are not motivated for learning foreign languages and that their teachers consider culture teaching a way to make language learning more motivating, tangible and realistic. It may also be that teachers in these countries focus on culture learning because they value it in its own right and want to educate their pupils to become more interculturally competent human beings. The Mexican case suggests that teachers deem general learning skills, which will be useful in other subject areas and in life, relatively

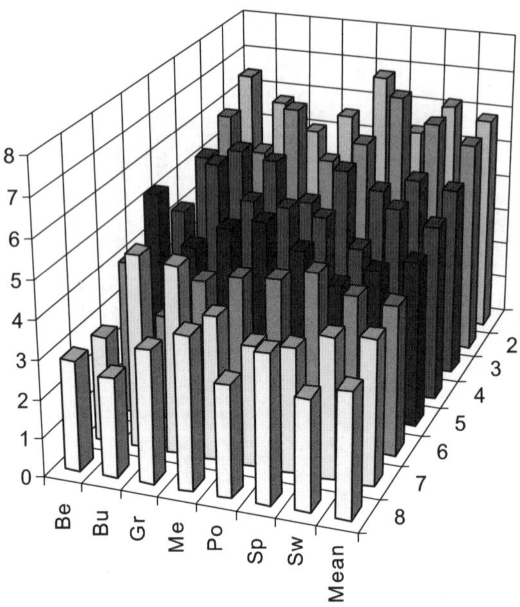

Figure 2.3 Teachers' perceptions of the objectives of foreign language education. Objectives and countries considered individually. Mean scores ranging between 0.00 and 8.00. Be = Belgium, Bu = Bulgaria, Gr = Greece, Me = Mexico, Po = Poland, Sp = Spain and Sw = Sweden.

(1) Promote the acquisition of a level of proficiency in the foreign language that will allow the learners to use the foreign language for practical purposes.
(2) Enthuse my pupils for learning foreign languages.
(3) Promote my pupils' familiarity with the culture, the civilisation of the countries where the language which they are learning is spoken.
(4) Promote the acquisition of an open mind and a positive disposition towards unfamiliar cultures.
(5) Assist my pupils to acquire skills that will be useful in other subject areas and in live (such as memorise, summarise, put into words, formulate accurately, give a presentation, etc.).
(6) Promote the acquisition of learning skills that will be useful for learning other foreign languages.
(7) Assist my pupils in developing a better understanding of their own identity and culture.
(8) Assist my pupils to acquire a level of proficiency in the foreign language that will allow them to read literary works in the foreign language.

more important. This suggests that Mexican teachers consider themselves to be primarily subject teachers, but, more so than in other countries, as teachers who have a role to play in the attainment of cross-curricular learning objectives. Finally, it is interesting to note that Bulgarian and Greek teachers are the only two groups which consider foreign language education also in terms of assisting pupils to develop a better understanding of their own identity and culture. The implication of this could be that they consider culture teaching in a truly intercultural perspective, in which learners have to relate cultures and not merely acquire knowledge regarding a foreign culture. Mexican, Swedish, Spanish, Polish and Belgian teachers (in this order) do not express clear support for this objective, which suggests that they view culture teaching more in the traditional sense of passing on knowledge about the foreign cultures usually associated with the foreign language they teach.

Teachers' Perceptions of 'Culture Teaching' in a Foreign Language Teaching Context

Teachers' perceptions were further investigated by asking them to rank nine possible culture teaching objectives in order of importance. These are listed below in Table 2.2, with an indication of whether the statement addressed the knowledge dimension, the attitudinal dimension or the skills dimension of intercultural competence. The information in brackets also shows that some statements define culture in terms of small c culture (relating to interactions in daily life) and others in terms of highbrow, capital C Culture (relating to the Arts).

All teachers[2] ranked the nine objectives of 'culture teaching' in foreign language education as shown in Figure 2.4.

It is clear from their responses that teachers support the development of attitudes of openness and tolerance and define culture teaching more in terms of passing on knowledge than providing intercultural skills. The knowledge they favour is 'providing information about daily life and routines' rather more than information about the foreign Culture, history, geography and political conditions. The implications of this could be that they associate cultural information with communication and this may be a trace of the relationship between intercultural competence and communication competence being dominated by communicative skills rather than the general educational objectives, which might be associated with Culture, history, geography and political issues.

The skills objective that enjoys highest support amongst teachers is to 'promote reflection on cultural differences'. Interestingly, teachers do not

Table 2.2 Possible culture teaching objectives

Knowledge dimension
• Provide information about the history, geography and political conditions of the foreign culture(s) (culture/Culture).
• Provide information about daily life and routines (culture).
• Provide information about shared values and beliefs (culture/Culture).
• Provide experiences with a rich variety of cultural expressions (literature, music, theatre, film, etc.) (Culture).
Attitudinal dimension
• Develop attitudes of openness and tolerance towards other peoples and cultures.
Skills dimension
• Promote reflection on cultural differences.
• Promote increased understanding of students' own culture (+ also knowledge of own culture/Culture).
• Promote the ability to empathise with people living in other cultures.
• Promote the ability to handle intercultural contact situations.

express a similarly strong support for a clearly related objective, namely 'assist pupils to develop a better understanding of their own culture and identity'. Perhaps teachers consider this a responsibility of mother tongue and arts teachers, or even teachers of religion, rather than of foreign language teachers. This dissociation of reflection on cultural differences and one's own cultural identity suggests that teachers define 'reflection on cultural differences' foremost in terms of 'familiarising pupils with aspects of the foreign culture'. Though they may ask pupils to compare these aspects in both cultures, the emphasis is above all on improving the learners' understanding of the foreign culture, not of their own cultural identity. This again confirms the general impression that teachers define culture teaching in terms of passing on knowledge rather than promoting intercultural skills. The fact that 'promote the ability to handle intercultural contact situations', or 'promote the ability to empathise with people living in a foreign culture' receive low support corroborates this finding.

A detailed study of the order in which teachers in the different countries ranked the nine objectives of culture teaching (see Figure 2.5)

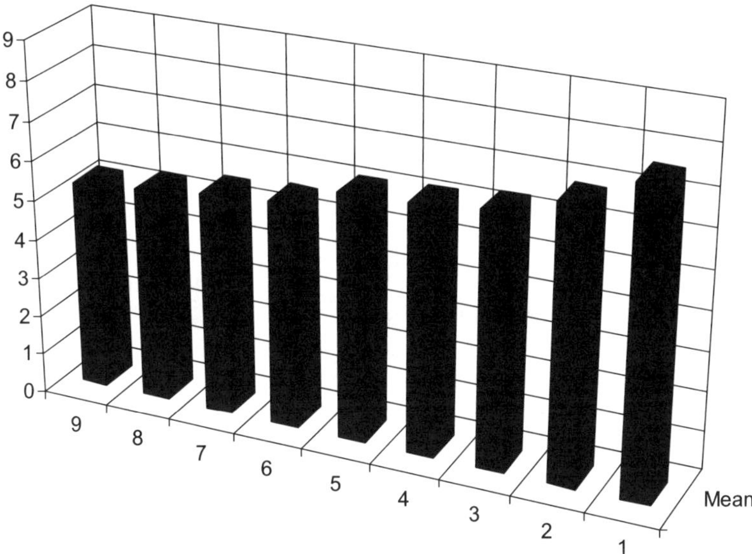

Figure 2.4 *Teachers'* perceptions of culture teaching. Objectives grouped. Respondents considered as one group. Mean scores ranging between 0.00 and 8.00.

(1) Develop attitudes of openness and tolerance towards other peoples and cultures.
(2) Provide information about daily life and routines.
(3) Promote reflection on cultural differences.
(4) Provide information about shared values and beliefs.
(5) Provide experiences with a rich variety of cultural expressions (literature, music, theatre, film, etc.).
(6) Promote the ability to handle intercultural contact situations.
(7) Provide information about the history, geography and political conditions of the foreign culture(s).
(8) Promote the ability to empathise with people living in other cultures.
(9) Promote increased understanding of students' own culture.

revealed that teachers are in agreement that the two most important objectives are to increase learners' familiarity with aspects of daily life and to promote openness and tolerance in pupils' attitudes. The largest support for the promotion of an open mind in pupils exists amongst Bulgarian, Greek and Swedish teachers. They put this objective before increasing learners' familiarity with aspects of daily life and routines.

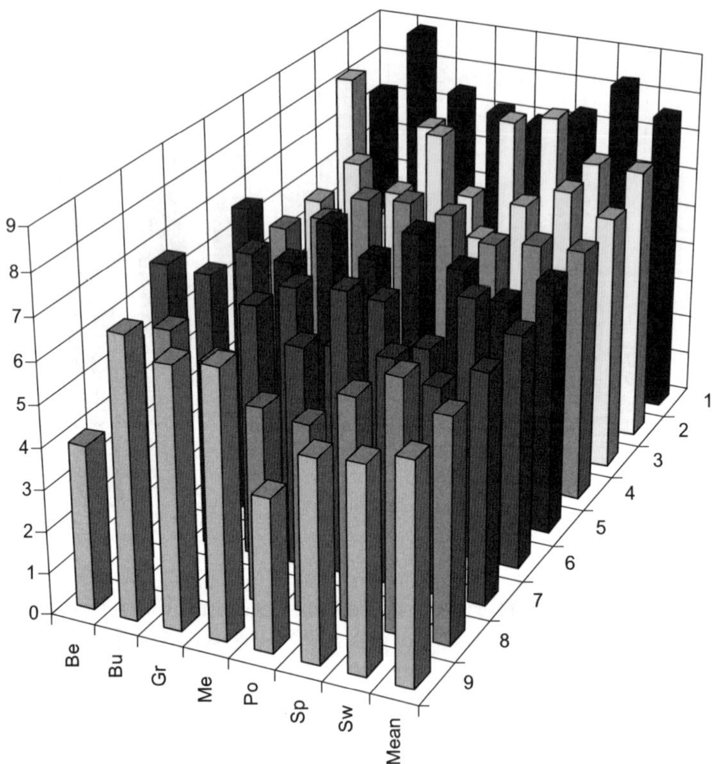

Figure 2.5 Teachers' perceptions of culture teaching in foreign language education. Per country presentation. Scores ranging between 0.00 and 9.00. Be = Belgium, Bu = Bulgaria, Gr = Greece, Me = Mexico, Po = Poland, Sp = Spain and Sw = Sweden.

(1) Develop attitudes of openness and tolerance towards other peoples and cultures.
(2) Provide information about daily life and routines.
(3) Promote reflection on cultural differences.
(4) Provide information about shared values and beliefs.
(5) Provide experiences with a rich variety of cultural expressions (literature, music, theatre, film, etc.).
(6) Promote the ability to handle intercultural contact situations.
(7) Provide information about the history, geography and political conditions of the foreign culture(s).
(8) Promote the ability to empathise with people living in other cultures.
(9) Promote increased understanding of students' own culture.

Teachers in Spain, Poland and Belgium, by contrast, deem the provision of information more important. Mexican teachers stand out somewhat, since they give greatest importance to promoting reflection on cultural differences. These findings confirm what we said earlier when commenting on the weight teachers give to either language learning objectives, culture learning objectives or general learning skills objectives. Bulgarian and Greek teachers were then found to put relatively more emphasis on the promotion of an open mind than teachers in other countries. We also pointed out that Mexican teachers expressed an unusually strong support for objectives relating to the promotion of general learning skills. In the context of culture teaching in foreign language education, Mexican teachers appear to rephrase this overall objective of their teaching in terms of promoting reflection on cultural differences. One could indeed say that this ability to compare cultures will help learners, not only within the context of a specific language learning course, but also when learning other languages and cultures as well as in the context of other subject areas where this skill is needed.

Teachers' Perceptions of the Time They (Want to) Devote to Culture Teaching

This section focuses on how teachers distribute their teaching time over language teaching and culture teaching, on the extent of their willingness to teach culture and on the reasons they mention for not getting round to culture teaching more often. Information regarding these issues will shed additional light on the way in which they perceive the objectives of foreign language education and, in particular, on the importance they give to culture teaching.

Table 2.3 provides an overview of teachers' perceptions of the percentage of their teaching time they devote to either language teaching or culture teaching.

From Table 2.3, it can be observed that the majority of the sample dedicates more time to language teaching than to culture teaching. As a matter of fact, the large majority of teachers in all participating countries either picked the option '80% language teaching–20% culture teaching' or '60% language teaching–40% culture teaching'. Spain appears to be the country where teachers are in agreement most. 91.43% of all participating teachers ticked the second option, namely '80% language teaching–20% culture teaching'. In other countries, teachers' answers appear more varied. These findings confirm what teachers said in relation to the objectives of their teaching, opting clearly for language teaching rather

Table 2.3 Distribution of teaching time over language teaching and culture teaching. All countries considered separately. Percentages indicate the percentage of the teaching time devoted to either language teaching (L.T.) or culture teaching (C.T.)

	BE	*BUL*	*GRE*	*MEX*	*POL*	*SPA*	*SWE*	*MEAN*
100% integration L.T.–C.T.	4.08%	3.23%	10.26%	17.78%	0.00%	2.86%	10.00%	6.89%
20% L.T.–80% C.T.	1.36%	3.23%	0.00%	2.22%	0.00%	0.00%	0.00%	0.97%
40% L.T.–60% C.T	2.04%	9.68%	0.00%	6.67%	4.08%	0.00%	0.00%	3.21%
60% L.T.–40% C.T	41.50%	41.94%	33.33%	33.33%	28.57%	5.71%	35.00%	31.34%
80% L.T–20% C.T	51.02%	41.94%	53.85%	40.00%	67.35%	91.43%	55.00%	57.23%
100% L.T.	0.00%	0.00%	2.56%	0.00%	0.00%	0.00%	0.00%	0.37%
	100%	100%	100%	100%	100%	100%	100%	100%

Table 2.4 Teachers' degree of willingness to devote more time to culture teaching

	BE	*SWE*	*POL*	*MEX*	*GRE*	*SPA*	*BUL*	*MEAN*
No opinion	2.04%	3.39%	0.00%	0.00%	0.00%	0.00%	0.00%	0.78%
No, not at all	4.08%	1.69%	8.33%	2.22%	5.13%	0.00%	0.00%	3.06%
No, not particularly	33.33%	16.95%	10.42%	35.56%	15.38%	14.29%	10.00%	19.42%
Yes, to a certain extent	47.82%	64.41%	54.17%	44.44%	61.54%	74.29%	60.00%	58.07%
Yes, very much	12.93%	13.56%	27.08%	17.78%	17.95%	11.43%	30.00%	18.68%
	100%	100%	100%	100%	100%	100%	100%	100%

than culture or skills teaching. Mexico, Greece and Sweden show comparatively high percentages for '100% integration of language and culture teaching' (Mexico, 17.78%, Greece, 10.26% and Sweden, 10.00%). Unfortunately, we do not know how these teachers interpreted this option. Does their answer reflect their personal conviction that a foreign language can only be used in a foreign context, and that therefore every aspect of a foreign language is related to the foreign culture? Or does it really reflect an approach to teaching in which they try to show their learners how culture is embedded in language or what sources for misunderstandings, which may be linked to linguistic and/or cultural factors, are inherent in intercultural communication?

Secondly, teachers were asked to indicate whether they would consider devoting more time to culture teaching. The results obtained (see Table 2.4) show a clear willingness to devote more teaching time to culture teaching, with 'yes, to a certain extent' being the option chosen most often. The highest percentages for 'no, not particularly' were obtained for Mexico (35.56%) and Belgium (33.33%). It should be remarked that this does not necessarily mean that teachers in these countries do not want to devote teaching time to culture. They may already be devoting time to culture teaching. It is just that they do not want to devote *more* time to it. This appears to be the case for Mexico, where 17.78% of the teachers indicate they integrate language and culture teaching 100% of their teaching time and comparatively low percentages were obtained for '80% language teaching–20% culture teaching' (40.00%) and '60% language teaching–40% culture teaching' (33.33%).

This obvious willingness to devote more time to culture teaching is not (yet) reflected in actual teaching practice, and one may wonder why this is so. In an open question, teachers were asked to mention any reasons they saw for not getting round to culture teaching more often. An analysis of these answers shows a very similar picture in all participating countries. The most frequently mentioned reason by far is 'lack of time'. Teachers refer to the overloaded curriculum, to the fact that there are not enough teaching periods to cover both the language curriculum and teach culture, and to the fact that pupils need a lot of practice time to acquire proficiency in the foreign language. The quotes below illustrate this point of view. The second quote also hints at the lack of time this teacher experiences to prepare appropriate teaching materials for teaching culture.

> I think that the main reason is that I don't have enough time to do it. You have to teach a certain number of grammatical points and there is no time to do many other things you would like to do.

> Lack of time. It would need a great deal of reflection and planning – I need time to find new materials, come up with new ideas of how to teach culture. It takes time to learn a language! Teaching culture can't be at the expense of time devoted to language proficiency. I would need to find good ways of integrating the two skills.

Curricular restrictions are also frequently mentioned. Teachers feel the curriculum has a strong focus on language teaching. Some even state that it does not contain cultural objectives. In Sweden and Poland, teachers make reference to the backwash effect they experience: one has to prepare pupils for the exams. Since the exams mainly focus on language teaching, one cannot devote much time to teaching intercultural competence. The below quotes reflect these points of view.

> The curriculum does not include culture as a separate subject.

> Exams have nothing to do with culture. They test the spelling, the grammar and the vocabulary of the language rather than cultural skills.

> You have to stick to the curriculum and with only three sessions per week you can hardly explain those cultural aspects in detail.

> The main reason in my case is that we have to follow the directions in the national curriculum, and I don't have enough time to work on the cultural aspects as much as I would like.

> The official programmes of this area give more importance to other aspects of the language (grammar, skills, etc.).

A third reason mentioned is the lack of suitable culture teaching materials. Teachers from all countries say they lack suitable materials for teaching culture. The textbooks they use do not include enough cultural information. Teachers feel textbooks do little to integrate the cultural dimension into foreign language teaching. Some teachers add that the information included in textbooks is 'cliché and stereotypical'.

> Good materials are not easily available.

> The teaching materials are out-dated. I would need to design my own teaching modules and this takes time. Much of what is shown in textbooks is cliché and stereotypical.

A small number of teachers say they are not prepared for teaching culture. They consider themselves insufficiently familiar with the foreign culture and with appropriate approaches to teaching culture. Greek teachers explicitly mention the lack of training in intercultural matters.

> No time to do it. Not very much experience in English culture. I don't like to teach culture based only on what you can read on books, cinema, etc.

> I have been prepared to teach the foreign language. We did not learn how to teach culture. For four years, I have studied linguistics and literature. Apart from literature, culture was not taught explicitly. I feel I am not sufficiently familiar with the foreign culture to be able to teach about it.

An equally small number of teachers refer to the lack of pupils' motivation and interest in culture teaching. According to these teachers, pupils consider teaching culture a waste of time. They would rather devote more time to practising the language. Relatedly, teachers state the pupils' level of proficiency in the foreign language is too low to allow for culture teaching.

> My pupils are not interested. As a teacher, I have to compete with the opportunities the media and the Internet offer. My pupils don't see the need to be taught about culture. They feel they understand everything there is to understand about the foreign culture.

Other reasons mentioned by individual teachers include: 'The cultures are so alike that it does not make sense to devote time to culture teaching' and 'Pupils do not need to be taught about the foreign culture; they are already aware of that culture'.

Chapter Summary

We have summarised this chapter's findings in Table 2.5 below. In the column 'distribution of teaching time', the percentage refers to the percentage of teachers who either ticked the option '80% language teaching–20% culture teaching' or '60% language teaching–40% culture teaching'. In both cases, teachers devote more time to language teaching than to culture teaching.

The table confirms that the results for the different countries are more similar than different. Teachers appear to define the objectives of foreign language education foremost in terms of the acquisition of the ability to use the foreign language for practical purposes and in terms of motivating pupils to learn foreign languages, with Bulgarian, Greek and Mexican teachers slightly deviating from this order of priorities. With respect to the way in which teachers define culture teaching, they are in agreement that the two most important objectives are to increase learners' familiarity

Table 2.5 Summary of the chapter's main findings

Country	*Main objective of FLT*	*Main objective of culture teaching*	*Definition of culture teaching*	*Distribution of teaching time: % = more language teaching than culture teaching*
Belgium	*Linguistically oriented.* Language for practical purposes + motivate pupils for learning languages	Acquire knowledge	Provide information on daily life	92.52%
Bulgaria	*Culturally oriented* Language for practical purposes + open mind	Acquire open mind	Acquisition of open mind	83.88%
Greece	*Culturally oriented* Motivate pupils for learning languages + promote familiarity with culture	Acquire knowledge	Acquisition of open mind + provide information on daily life	87.18%

Table 2.5 *Continued*

Mexico	*Linguistically oriented* Language for practical purposes + general learning skills	Acquire open mind	Promote reflection on cultural differences + acquisition of open mind	73.33%
Poland	*Linguistically oriented* Language for practical purposes + motivate pupils for learning languages	Acquire knowledge	Provide information on daily life + acquisition of open mind	95.92%
Spain	*Linguistically oriented* Motivate pupils for learning languages + language for practical purposes	Acquire knowledge	Provide information on daily life + acquisition of open mind	97.14%
Sweden	*Linguistically oriented* Motivate pupils for learning languages + language for practical purposes	Acquire knowledge	Acquisition of open mind	90%

with aspects of daily life and to promote openness and tolerance in pupils' attitudes. They appear to devote more time to the teaching of the language than the teaching of culture. The countries in which teachers especially support linguistic objectives, such as Spain, Poland, Sweden, and Belgium, are also the countries in which teachers define culture teaching above all in terms of providing information about daily life and routines, except in Sweden, where they appear to give more importance to the promotion of open minds and tolerant attitudes than to the passing on information regarding daily life and routines. On the other hand, those countries which are more culturally orientated, such as Bulgaria and Greece, invariably attach greatest importance to developing attitudes of openness and tolerance towards other peoples and cultures. It is interesting that these countries devote relatively more time to culture teaching than the other countries. Mexican teachers stand out somewhat too. They appear to give greatest importance to developing particular skills in their learners. They perceive the objectives of foreign language education in terms of promoting the acquisition of general learning skills, and those of culture teaching in terms of the promotion of reflection on cultural differences. Mexican teachers also devote relatively more time to culture teaching than teachers in Belgium, Poland, Sweden or Spain.

Two results deserve some additional comment. First, teachers appear to devote far more time to language teaching than to culture teaching in spite of the fact that they also express a clear willingness to devote more time to culture teaching. The impression we gained is that, to a certain extent, teachers feel frustrated that they cannot devote more time to culture teaching. They refer to overloaded curricula and curricular restraints, to the lack of appropriate teaching materials, to their pupils' preference for language learning activities or lack of interest in the foreign culture, and to their own lack of training in the area of teaching intercultural competence when asked to mention reasons for not getting round to culture teaching more often. It is remarkable that teachers in all participating countries mention the same reasons for not getting round to culture teaching more often. Though teaching circumstances differ in the different countries, they appear to be perceived by teachers in similar ways. On objective terms, the curriculum may be more overloaded in, say, Belgium than, say, Spain in view of the number of teaching periods available. Yet, teachers in Spain also perceive the curriculum as an impediment to teaching culture more often. Likewise, though teachers use different textbooks in the different countries, and often use locally produced textbooks which on objective terms sometimes differ substantially from textbooks produced for an international market, teachers in all countries state the textbooks they use constitute a reason for not devoting more time to culture teaching. Pupils, too, appear to be perceived in similar ways in terms of their demand that the larger part of teaching time be devoted to learning the language, not to culture teaching. In subsequent chapters, we will inquire into a number of these aspects in more detail, and this will sharpen our understanding of how local circumstances differ, to what extent they are perceived differently by teachers, and to what extent teachers' perceptions affect teaching practices.

The second issue concerns the fact that teachers define culture teaching more in the traditional sense of passing on information regarding the foreign culture, and in particular regarding different aspects of a culture's daily life and routines, and far less in terms of promoting the acquisition of intercultural skills or in terms of enhancing learners' ability to reflect on their own culture and identity and to relate that culture to foreign cultures. Even in those countries where relatively more importance is given to cultural objectives, teachers define culture teaching in a traditional way. Does this, perhaps, imply that teachers are not yet familiar with the enlarged objectives of foreign language education? Does this mean that more is needed than to provide teachers with teaching materials that show ways to integrate language-and-culture teaching? For, if teachers do not understand what objectives they should try to attain through their teaching, redesigning teaching materials may be of little avail to support the further interculturalisation of foreign language education. It may also be that this situation reflects the approach taken in current-day textbooks. In many classrooms, especially at beginner and intermediate levels, teachers tend to teach by the book, mainly because they want to respect the grammatical progression they believe underlies the book's structure. The cultural topics they touch upon are those that are present in the textbook. This issue will be further explored, too, when we report on the cultural topics teachers deal with most frequently in their classrooms and on the extent to which this order of topics matches that of topics in foreign language textbooks.

In following chapters we will consider the ways in which the findings here – about perception of objectives and the use of teaching time – are reflected in what teachers tell us they do in the classroom and how they think about intercultural competence.

Notes

1. All respondents can be considered as one group since the Bonferroni-multiple comparison test results (see Appendix 2) reveal that the different country

samples can be considered more similar than different in the way in which they define the objectives of foreign language education.

2. Considering the respondents as one group is allowed, since the Bonferroni-multiple comparison test results (see Appendix 2) revealed that, although significant differences exist between individual countries, the number of times a variable was scored significantly different is small enough to allow us to say that the whole sample is more similar than different when it comes to the way in which teachers define culture teaching in foreign language education.

Chapter 3

Familiarity and Contacts with Foreign Cultures

PHYLLIS RYAN and LIES SERCU

Foreign language teachers are expected to have (near-)native competence in the foreign language they teach. They need it to be able to use the foreign language in the classroom, explain it to their pupils, maintain contacts with other speakers of that language in order to enrich their teaching (for example in the context of e-mail or exchange projects), read professional literature on foreign language education, etc. This seems to be stating the obvious, and no one in the profession will dispute this requirement.

With respect to teachers' familiarity with the foreign cultures associated with the foreign language they teach, few will state that teachers need a (near-)native knowledge of these target cultures. Yet, if teachers are to pass on culture-specific and culture-general knowledge to their pupils, demonstrate to their pupils how they can relate and compare cultures, prepare their pupils for intercultural contact situations and help them to better understand their own cultural identity, they will need a thorough understanding of the target cultures as well as of their own culture, next to some understanding of foreign cultures in general.

How can teachers meet this demand? Many teacher education programmes currently emphasise the acquisition of the foreign language, foreign language teaching methodology, literature and history. For sure, literature and history teaching can promote valuable insights into the societal and historical developments, which have shaped the target cultures, as they exist today. Yet, this kind of teaching often fails to promote the knowledge, skills and attitudes in teachers which they need to teach intercultural competence. Indeed, as pointed out in the previous chapter, one of the reasons which teachers mentioned for not getting round to culture teaching more often is that they feel they are not sufficiently familiar with the cultures associated with the language they teach to be able to teach about them.

In this chapter, we explore whether this lack of familiarity, voiced by individual teachers in answer to an open question, appears to be characteristic of all participating teachers. We also look at the sources of information on the target cultures teachers use most. We believe these insights can help us to further our understanding of the reasons why some teachers appear favourably disposed towards intercultural competence teaching and others not, why some teachers are willing to devote more time to culture teaching and others not. One might indeed assume that teachers who are very familiar with the foreign culture primarily associated with the foreign language they teach will be less hesitant to interculturalise their foreign language teaching than teachers who feel they lack sufficient familiarity. The findings presented here will also shed light on the extent to which teachers are prepared for teaching intercultural competence in foreign language education, at least as far as their understanding of a particular foreign culture is concerned.

We focus on teachers' familiarity with the foreign culture *primarily* associated with the foreign language they teach only, not on their familiarity with other foreign cultures that tend to be associated with that language. The country/culture primarily associated with the English language is the UK for teachers in all participating countries, except for teachers in Sweden and Mexico, who indicate that the country primarily associated with English is the United States of America. The country/culture primarily associated with the French language is France for teachers in all participating countries, not for example Wallonia, i.e. the French-speaking part of Belgium, or Canada. German teachers in all countries primarily associate the language they teach with the Federal Republic of Germany, not with Austria or Switzerland. Teachers of Spanish link the language they teach primarily with Spain.

Teachers' Familiarity with the Culture Primarily Associated with the Foreign Language they Teach

Teachers were offered a number of cultural topics, and asked to indicate their degree of familiarity with each, observing the following instructions:

(1) You choose 'very familiar' when you feel you are so familiar with that topic that it would be very easy for you to talk about it extensively in your foreign language classroom.

(2) You pick 'sufficiently familiar' when you feel you are familiar enough with a particular topic that you could say something about it during your classes.
(3) When you choose 'not sufficiently familiar' you indicate that you yourself think that you are not well informed about a particular topic.
(4) You pick 'not familiar at all' when you feel you don't really know anything about that particular cultural aspect.

The topics offered were (a) history, geography, political system; (b) different ethnic and social groups; (c) daily life and routines, living conditions, food and drink, etc.; (d) youth culture; (e) education, professional life; (f) traditions, folklore, tourist attractions; (g) literature; (h) other cultural expressions (music, drama, art); (i) values and beliefs; (j) international relations (political, economic and cultural), with students' own country and other countries. These are mainly topics that tend to be addressed in foreign language textbooks (Sercu, 2000a). Some topics, which tend not to be included in foreign language textbooks, but are part of the minimal list of cultural topics proposed by the Council of Europe (2001: 102–103), such as 'values and beliefs' or 'international relations', have also been added. Still other topics from that list, such as body language, visiting conventions or ritual behaviour, could have been added here, but that would have made this section in the questionnaire unreasonably long. For the same reason, some cultural topics not traditionally considered together have been grouped (e.g. education and professional life; traditions, folklore and tourist attractions; daily life and routines, living conditions, food and drink).

Table 3.1 shows how familiar with the different cultural topics teachers deem themselves to be. The topics have been ranked from least familiar to most familiar on the basis of the mean scores obtained for each topic. Scores between 0.01 and 1.00 indicate that teachers consider themselves 'not familiar at all', Scores between 1.01 and 2.00 that teachers consider themselves 'not sufficiently familiar', scores between 2.01 and 3.00 that teachers consider themselves 'sufficiently familiar', and scores between 3.01 and 4.00 that they consider themselves 'very familiar'.

We see that teachers in the different countries responded very similarly.[1] Teachers in all countries say that they are most familiar with aspects of 'daily life and routines, living conditions, food and drink, etc.', and least familiar, yet still sufficiently familiar, with international relations. They consider themselves very familiar with 'daily life and routines', 'literature', 'history, geography, political system' and 'traditions, folklore, tourist attractions' and sufficiently familiar with 'education,

Table 3.1 Teacher familiarity with the country, culture and people primarily associated with the foreign language they teach

	GRE	*MEX*	*BUL*	*SPA*	*SWE*	*POL*	*BEL*	*Mean*
Index	2.98	2.97	2.97	2.94	2.91	2.90	1.97	2.95
International relations	2.70	2.76	2.53	2.43	2.91	2.90	2.49	2.65
Different ethnic and social groups	2.70	2.78	2.63	2.80	2.81	2.59	2.73	2.72
Other cultural expressions	2.79	2.93	2.76	2.63	2.70	2.55	2.72	2.73
Youth culture	2.76	3.00	2.73	3.09	2.53	2.62	2.67	2.77
Values and beliefs	2.76	3.02	2.79	2.71	2.64	2.80	2.86	2.80
Education, professional life	2.89	2.91	3.00	2.77	2.84	3.08	2.93	2.92
Traditions, folklore, tourist attractions	3.18	3.05	3.07	3.03	3.15	3.11	3.23	3.12
History, geography, political system	3.21	3.00	3.20	3.00	3.24	3.12	3.30	3.15
Literature	3.32	2.95	3.50	3.37	3.21	3.06	3.15	3.22
Daily life and routines	3.42	3.34	3.43	3.57	3.39	3.55	3.59	3.47

Scores ranging between 0.00 and 4.00:
0.01–1.00 = not familiar at all; 1.01–2.00 = not sufficiently familiar; 2.01–3.00 = sufficiently familiar; 3.01–4.00 = very familiar.

professional life', 'values and beliefs', 'different ethnic and social groups', 'youth culture', 'other cultural expressions (music, drama, art)', and 'international relations (political, economic and cultural)'.

These findings suggest that teachers feel sufficiently well equipped for culture teaching in the traditional sense of passing on knowledge about the target culture. Their knowledge is strongest in the cultural domains normally addressed in foreign language textbooks. One may therefore wonder whether the cultural contents of textbooks are a determining factor in teachers' familiarity or whether they also use other sources of information on the foreign culture, such as travel or the media.

Frequency of Travel to the Target Culture

Teachers were asked to indicate how frequently they travel to the foreign country primarily associated with the foreign language they teach. We wanted to know about different kinds of contact, because these may imply a different length of stay as well as different degrees of integration in the foreign culture. Visits to relatives or friends suggest a longer stay which guarantees an insider view of the foreign culture, whereas school trips are usually shorter in duration and more likely to promote an outsider tourist view on the foreign culture. Of course, answers are highly dependent on personal and family related circumstances. Still, we believe their answers show tendencies which offer a truthful account of the extent and kinds of contacts they mainly have.

When considering all contacts together, as in Table 3.2, we see that in none of the countries do teachers appear to travel frequently to the foreign country.

Table 3.2 Teachers' travels to the foreign countries associated with the foreign languages they teach

	BEL	*SPA*	*SWE*	*POL*	*GRE*	*MEX*	*BUL*	*Mean*
Index	1.76	1.74	1.67	1.62	1.61	1.50	1.36	1.61
Work visits, e.g. within the framework of an exchange project	1.28	1.34	1.34	1.27	1.34	1.20	1.30	1.30
School trips (one or two days)	1.95	1.31	1.26	1.50	1.21	1.11	1.13	1.35
Participation in a teacher training programme or a language course	1.50	2.09	1.77	1.53	1.82	1.49	1.80	1.71
Visits to relatives or friends	1.66	1.57	1.69	1.83	1.54	1.78	1.17	1.61
Tourist stays (lasting longer than two days) in the foreign country	2.40	2.40	2.27	1.94	2.16	1.91	1.40	2.07

0.00–1.00 = never; 1.01–2.00 = once in a while; 2.01–3.00 = often.

When comparing professional and private contacts, we see that teachers more frequently travel to the foreign country as tourists or to visit relatives and friends, than for professional reasons. The majority of teachers never take part in work visits, for example to prepare an exchange project, or in a teacher training programme abroad, though this last kind of contact is substantially more popular amongst Swedish, Greek, Spanish and Bulgarian teachers than amongst Belgian, Mexican or Polish teachers. This may be because in the former group of countries few other possibilities to travel to the foreign country exist or because this kind of in-service training is part of an officially recognised and obligatory training scheme.

About 70% of the teachers indicate they never go on a school trip to the foreign country, with the notable exception of Belgian teachers, of whom 73% indicate that their school organises school trips to the foreign country either 'often' or 'once in a while'. For Belgian schools, it is relatively easy and inexpensive to travel to France, Germany or the UK because of these countries' relative vicinity.

Though professional journeys to the foreign country tend to be limited, teachers more frequently travel to the foreign countries as tourists. A substantial part of Bulgarian (60%) and Mexican (35.56%) teachers, however, indicate they never travel to the foreign country, most probably because of the relative expense of such trips. About an equal number of the teachers indicate that they travel to relatives or friends, or do not do that.

Frequency of Contact with Foreign Cultures While at Home

Teachers were also asked to indicate how frequently they get in contact with the foreign culture while at home. The kinds of contact which they were asked to score as 'never', 'once in a while' or often were: (1) media contacts; (2) visits to cultural institutes representing the foreign country in their country; (3) contacts with people originating from the foreign country who live in their country; (4) contacts with foreign language assistants (usually natives from the foreign country) in their school; or (5) contacts with foreign teachers or pupils who visit their school.

As can be seen from Table 3.3, Bulgarian, Spanish, Mexican and Polish teachers appear to have frequent contacts with the foreign culture at home, whereas Greek, Swedish and Belgian teachers indicate they only get in contact with the foreign culture once in a while.

When we compare the mean scores obtained for contacts at home and journeys to the foreign country, teachers appear to get into contact with the foreign culture more frequently at home than through travel to the

Table 3.3 Frequency of teachers' contacts with foreign cultures at home

	BUL	*SPA*	*MEX*	*POL*	*GR*	*SW*	*BE*	*Mean*
Index	2.35	2.14	2.07	2.05	1.90	1.85	1.78	2.02
Contacts with foreign teachers or pupils who visit my school	1.80	1.86	1.53	1.71	1.24	1.63	1.46	1.60
Contacts with foreign language assistants (usually natives from the foreign country) in my school	2.07	2.17	1.67	1.53	1.34	1.34	1.15	1.61
Visits to the cultural institute representing the foreign country in my country	2.77	1.29	1.91	2.13	1.95	1.46	1.62	1.87
Contacts with people originating from the foreign country who live in my country	2.27	2.43	2.27	2.12	2.24	2.11	1.86	2.18
Media contacts (via newspapers, television, radio)	2.87	2.94	2.95	2.78	2.71	2.73	2.84	2.83

0.00–1.00 = never; 1.01–2.00 = once in a while; 2.01–3.00 = often.

foreign country. Interestingly, teachers who score low on journeys score high on contacts at home and vice versa. This is particularly obvious for Bulgaria and Belgium. Whereas Bulgarian teachers do not appear to travel much, they indicate they have frequent contacts at home. Belgian teachers, on the other hand, appear to travel most, but of all country samples have fewest contacts at home.

Teachers do not have frequent contacts with people originating from the foreign culture (teaching assistants or foreign visitors) inside the school, though Spanish and Bulgarian teachers stand out here. They make more extensive use of the possibility to interact with native speakers of the foreign language as teaching assistants than schools in the other countries.

Teachers only sporadically visit the cultural institute representing the foreign country in their country, though Polish and Bulgarian teachers say they often have such contacts. This is most probably due to the fact that the teachers who participated in the research live in or nearby a city where such a cultural institute is located. By far the most popular kind of contact with the foreign culture is media contacts, which in the majority of cases are Internet or television contacts. Television contacts may be through local television channels or internationally broadcast channels.

Summary and Comments

Table 3.4 provides a summary of this chapter's main findings. Using symbols (+, ++, +++ and ++++), we summarise the extent of teachers' familiarity with the foreign culture primarily associated with the foreign language they teach, as well as the extent of their contacts with the foreign country, culture and people. The results in the first column reflect the index of familiarity provided in Table 3.1. The symbols in the second and third column reflect the mean scores obtained with respect to the type of contact which teachers in all countries ranked first. For journeys, these are tourist stays; for contacts at home, these are media contacts. The mean scores obtained for these two contact types could yield an adequate representation of teachers' actual contacts.

Table 3.4 Summary of chapter's main findings

Country	*Familiarity with culture* (+, ++, +++, ++++)	*Direct contacts: tourist stays* (+, ++, +++)	*Contacts at home: media contacts* (+, ++, +++)
Belgium	+++	+++	+++
Bulgaria	+++	++	+++
Greece	+++	+++	+++
Mexico	+++	++	+++
Poland	+++	++	+++
Spain	+++	+++	+++
Sweden	+++	+++	+++

Symbols in column 'familiarity with culture': + = not familiar at all, ++ = not sufficiently familiar, +++ = sufficiently familiar, ++++ = very familiar; Symbols in column 'direct contacts: tourist stays' and 'contacts at home: media contacts': + = never; ++ = once in a while; +++ = often.

As the table illustrates, teachers from the seven countries indicate that they regard themselves as being sufficiently familiar with the culture of the foreign language(s) they teach. Tourist contacts in Belgium, Greece, Spain and Sweden are more frequent than in Bulgaria, Mexico and Poland. Media contacts are equally frequent in all seven countries.

In the introduction to this chapter, we stated that we wanted to investigate whether and to what extent the feeling voiced by individual teachers that they are not sufficiently familiar with the foreign culture to be able to teach about it found substantiation in our quantitative data, and whether this apparent lack of familiarity appears to be characteristic of individual teachers only, or of a larger proportion of the teachers. Our data have revealed that teachers consider themselves sufficiently familiar with the foreign culture, which means that they think they could at least say something about different aspects of the foreign culture during their lessons if they had to, without however on the whole considering themselves to be able to deal extensively with different aspects of the foreign culture. Teachers who feel they should be very knowledgeable about a particular aspect before they can teach about it will certainly share the feeling that they lack sufficient familiarity. On the other hand, teachers who are satisfied with an only partial knowledge will probably not share that feeling, although they may actually lack a sufficient degree of familiarity to be able to interculturalise their foreign language education.

We explicitly linked the extent of teachers' knowledge to language teaching, but offered more topics than those traditionally included in foreign language textbooks. Our data show that the topics with which teachers appear to be most familiar are those traditionally dealt with in foreign language textbooks, namely daily life and routines; history and geography; and folklore. In addition, teachers perceive themselves as very familiar with literature, which probably reflects the fact that in many countries, foreign language teachers receive thorough introductions to the literature of the language they are studying before or during teacher training. Other topics, of high relevance in intercultural competence teaching, however, appear less well-known, which suggests that teachers will need additional preparation if we expect them to teach intercultural competence in its full sense. In view of teachers' frequent media contacts with the foreign cultures, it is surprising that they do not feel well informed about the foreign country's international relations or, for example, the different ethnic groups living in the foreign country. Might it be that the media contacts teachers say they have are situated mainly in the entertainment sphere and less in the informational sphere? Do teachers watch movies but not foreign news programmes or pay attention to the items devoted to the foreign country's international relations in local news programmes? Or do teachers use the foreign media mainly to improve their language skills, not so much to enlarge their familiarity with different aspects of the foreign culture/Culture? A question that has to be left unanswered here is whether teachers who feel they are very familiar with daily life and routines, or very knowledgeable about a country's geography or history also actually are. It may be the case that teachers have presented a somewhat flattering image of themselves. On the other hand, 'sufficiently familiar' was defined in minimalist terms, and in picking this option teachers did not state that they considered themselves sufficiently familiar to be able to explain a particular phenomenon in detail as one might expect a lecturer in cultural studies or an anthropologist to be able to do. At any rate, it will be interesting to investigate in a later chapter to what extent teachers' familiarity finds reflection in their actual teaching practice.

As regards teachers' contacts, it is not surprising that we found that the media are an important source of information. Media are omnipresent in all countries. It may well be though, that in some countries, it is easier to gain access to Spanish or German media than in other countries. Interestingly, teachers who appear to travel little appear to compensate this lack of direct contact with more extensive contacts with the foreign culture at home, for example via visits to the cultural institute. The reverse was also found to be true. Teachers from countries that show a large extent of direct contact via travel appear less interested in visits to cultural institutes. Of course, whether or not the cultural institute lies within reasonable distance from one's home may have biased the comparison of teachers' answers. In a similar vein, not surprisingly, Belgian teachers have more frequent contacts via school trips with countries, such as France or Germany, since these countries are neighbouring countries. This does not necessarily mean that Belgian teachers are better FL&IC teachers. The reasons why school trips are organised may lie more in the general educational or linguistic domain than in the cultural domain. We will explore reasons for organising school trips and other culture experiential activities in a later chapter. Geographical factors may, again, explain the significant differences in the extent to which teachers make use of the fact that people originating from the foreign countries are living in their country. Some people happen to live in a neighbourhood where such people are living, and others not. Some countries attract more native speakers of a foreign language taught in secondary education than others. Some teachers may just not be inclined to make contacts with foreigners. The assumption generally is that foreign language teachers are by definition open to foreign cultures. It would be interesting to investigate whether or not this difference in the extent to which teachers have personal contacts with foreigners also says something about their attitude towards foreignness and foreigners in general, as well as about the extent of their familiarity with different aspects of the foreign culture. Within the confines of a self-report questionnaire, however, it is extremely difficult to gather valid data in this respect. In the next chapter, we shift our attention from the teacher to the pupil and ask this question: how open to foreigners are pupils in the eyes of their teachers?

Note

1. The Bonferroni multiple comparison test results confirms this. The number of times teachers appear to have scored each of the topics offered to them in a statistically significantly different way equals zero, which means that the different country samples can be considered alike in this respect.

Chapter 4
Pupils' Culture-and-language Learning Profile

MARÍA DEL CARMEN MÉNDEZ GARCÍA and LIES SERCU

Learner populations differ according to various parameters: whether the learners are beginners, intermediate or advanced; whether they are young children, adolescents or adult; their objectives in learning the language; the extent of their motivation to learn the language; whether their environment outside the classroom is target-language or mother-tongue; how heterogeneous or homogeneous the class is; the size of the group; and many more.

Teachers have a responsibility not only to provide opportunities for learning, but also actively to help learners to reach their full potential and make maximum progress. Foreign language teaching methodology courses usually raise teachers' awareness of the need to start from and build on their learners' current level of proficiency in the foreign language when laying out learning paths, thereby also taking account of their learners' age, interests, learning abilities, and future professional needs. In most cases, however, these courses omit to define learner-orientedness in terms of intercultural competence learning; they fail to raise teachers' awareness of the need to take account of their learners' current levels of understanding of foreign cultures or intercultural communication, their attitudes towards foreignness and foreigners or their culture learning skills. The exception is courses which prepare teachers for teaching in multicultural schools which attract a substantial number of ethnic minority community children.

This chapter prepares the ground for answering the question to what extent teachers take account of their pupils' culture learning profiles as well as their language learning profiles. We will answer this question in Chapter 9, where we consider the findings presented in Chapters 2 to 8 together, looking for relationships among different data sets. Here, we want to concentrate on teachers' perceptions of their pupils' culture-and-language learning profiles.

We asked teachers to provide information on the extent of their pupils' familiarity with the foreign cultures associated with the foreign language they are learning, their attitude toward the foreign people usually associated with that foreign language and the frequency of their contacts with the foreign country and culture. If teachers want to promote intercultural competence in their pupils, they will need to offer intercultural competence teaching which starts from their learners' current levels of familiarity with, understanding of and attitudes towards the foreign cultures and peoples usually associated with the foreign language they are learning. Teachers who perceive their pupils as 'not knowledgeable regarding the foreign culture' should devote more teaching time to enhancing their pupils' familiarity with the target culture than teachers who perceive their pupils as 'very knowledgeable'. Teachers who feel their pupils hold rather negative attitudes should work explicitly towards changing these attitudes. Similarly, teachers who understand that their pupils scarcely get in contact with the foreign country/ies or make use of a limited array of means to do so should strive to facilitate and promote different types of (direct) contact with the foreign cultural reality in the course of their lessons.

Teachers' Perceptions of Their Learners' General Disposition Towards Learning the Foreign Language and Culture

To investigate teachers' perceptions of their pupils' language-and-culture learning profile, the respondents were first asked to indicate on a ten-point scale to what extent they agreed with the following statements: 'My pupils are very motivated to learn the foreign language I teach', 'My pupils think learning the foreign language I teach is difficult', 'My pupils are very knowledgeable about the culture of the foreign language I teach' and 'My pupils have a very positive attitude towards the people associated with the foreign language I teach'. Teachers' answers to these questions have been summarised in Table 4.1 below.

As Table 4.1 reveals, teachers in all countries appear to think their pupils are reasonably to highly motivated to learn the foreign language they teach. Spanish teachers stand out, with a low mean score for pupil motivation of 4.86. In Spain, Greece and Poland, large proportions of the teachers (60.01%, 58.96% and 46.93% respectively) gave a score below 5, indicating that they consider their pupils' motivation to be on the negative side. In comparison, only 13.32% of Bulgarian teachers, 25.39% of Swedish teachers, 32.89% of Belgian teachers and 36.37% of

Table 4.1 Teachers' perceptions of their pupils' general disposition towards the foreign language they teach and towards the foreign cultures and peoples associated with that language

	BEL	*BUL*	*GRE*	*MEX*	*POL*	*SPA*	*SWE*	*Mean*
My pupils are very motivated to learn the foreign language I teach.	6.36	8.13	5.79	6.23	6.10	4.86	6.90	6.34
My pupils have a very positive attitude towards the people associated with the foreign language I teach.	6.01	7.48	5.24	5.64	7.04	4.31	7.29	6.14
My pupils think learning the foreign language I teach is very difficult.	5.76	3.77	4.54	7.04	5.80	5.97	5.63	5.50
My pupils are very knowledgeable about the culture of the foreign language I teach.	4.86	5.53	4.44	5.04	4.35	4.43	5.52	4.88

0 = complete lack of agreement; 10 = complete agreement.

Mexican teachers gave scores below 5. 46.67% of the Bulgarian teachers assigned the score '10' for pupil motivation, which is remarkably high.

As regards teachers' assumptions concerning their pupils' perceptions of the degree of difficulty involved in learning the foreign language, teachers on average assign a score between 5.00 and 6.00. Mexican and Bulgarian teachers stand out here. Whereas Mexican teachers strongly agree that their pupils find learning the language they teach very difficult (mean score = 7.04), Bulgarian teachers disagree that their pupils find it very difficult (mean score = 3.77).

Table 4.1 also shows that teachers agree that their pupils' attitudes are positive, with mean scores ranging between 5.24 (Greece) and 7.48 (Bulgaria), except, again, in Spain, where teachers disagree (mean score 4.31) and this might suggest they believe their students have negative attitudes.

Finally, Table 4.1 shows how familiar teachers believe their pupils to be with the foreign cultures associated with the language they teach. They are clearly less sure about the extent of their pupils' familiarity than in their conviction that pupils are motivated and have positive attitudes. The mean scores obtained all centre around 5, with the highest mean scores obtained for Bulgaria (5.53) and the lowest for Poland (4.35), which suggests that most teacher consider their pupils to be ignorant of the foreign country. 77.55% of Polish teachers, 71.80% of Greek teachers and 71.42% of Spanish teachers indicate that they do not deem their pupils to be knowledgeable. The lowest proportion of teachers who think that way was found in Sweden, where 'a mere' 32.79% of the teachers assigned a score between 1 and 5. Even in Bulgaria, 53.33% of teachers think their pupils are not familiar with the foreign cultures associated with the foreign language they are learning.

We have summarised these different findings in Table 4.2 below. The crosses provide indications of the extent to which teachers think the statements hold true for their pupils. The number of crosses ranges between 1 and 5. One cross matches a score between 0–2.00, two crosses between 2.01–4.00, three crosses between 4.01–6.00, four crosses between 6.01–8.00 and five crosses between 8.01–10.00.

A reasonably clear relationship appears to exist between the different dimensions of pupils' culture-and-language learning profile. Countries, in which comparatively speaking high scores are obtained for 'motivation',

Table 4.2 Summary of teachers' perceptions of their learners' general disposition towards learning the foreign language and culture

	Are highly motivated to learn the foreign language	*Have a very positive attitude towards the foreign people*	*Perceive the language as very difficult to learn*	*Are very knowledgeable regarding the foreign culture, country, people*
Belgium	++++	++++	+++	+++
Bulgaria	+++++	++++	++	+++
Greece	+++	+++	+++	+++
Mexico	++++	+++	++++	+++
Poland	++++	++++	+++	+++
Spain	+++	+++	+++	+++
Sweden	++++	++++	+++	+++

show high scores for 'attitude' and 'knowledge' and low scores for 'difficulty'. This tendency is most obvious in the Bulgarian sample. Vice versa, countries in which comparatively low scores are obtained for 'motivation' also show low scores for 'attitude' and 'knowledge' and high scores for 'difficulty'. This trend is most clearly observable in the Spanish sample. The Mexican sample stands out somewhat. There, a high score for motivation co-occurs with a high score for 'difficulty', a relatively low score for 'attitude' and a relatively high score for 'knowledge'.

What surprises us are the large differences between the country samples, especially with respect to pupils' attitudes and motivation. Whereas Bulgarian teachers perceive their pupils as very motivated and as very positively disposed towards the foreign people, Spanish teachers at the other extreme perceive their pupils as lowly motivated and as rather negatively disposed towards the foreign people associated with the foreign language they are learning. The reason for this cannot lie in the sample itself, since the different country samples have been shown to be statistically similar, except with respect to the number of teaching periods teachers teach per week and with respect to the kinds of education offered in the schools in which teachers are teaching. Also, all Spanish and Bulgarian participants are teachers of English. How come then that pupils perceive the language, culture and people in such different ways, in the eyes of their teachers? Do pupils reflect the kinds of attitudes and feelings which are present in their societies? Do Spanish pupils consider the UK in a negative light because of the situation in Gibraltar or the sometimes bad reputation of British tourists in their country? Are Bulgarian pupils attracted to the UK because that country appears to them a country of opportunities? In the second part of this chapter, we report on the specific ideas the different national pupil populations associate with the peoples and cultures associated with the foreign languages they are learning. These findings will shed some light on possible reasons for pupils' culture learning profiles, though other reasons should also be considered, such as the distance between the learners' mother tongue and the foreign language, for example, a country's general disposition towards the learning of foreign languages or the number of teaching periods reserved in the curriculum for foreign language education.

We also want to speculate here about whether a causal relationship exists between the different elements of the pupils' culture-and-language learning profile. Could it be the case that a low motivation to learn the language, also because of the language's perceived difficulty, causes pupils to be negatively disposed towards the foreign people and culture and explains their lack of interest in the foreign culture and, thus, their low degree of familiarity with it? Or can and must we dissociate between pupils' disposition towards the foreign language and their disposition towards the foreign culture and people, and can no causal link be assumed? Teachers will probably have had the experience that pupils may be motivated to learn the foreign language but that this does not necessarily also mean that they are motivated to learn about the foreign culture and people. Most probably, they can also testify that the different language- and culture-related factors in the pupil profile can reinforce each other, and that a negative stance towards the language affects the stance towards the culture and people.

This then brings us to the interesting question of how these findings could affect teachers' teaching practice. We believe they could incite teachers to teach intercultural competence, but we realise that teachers may also follow different lines of reasoning than the ones we deem desirable. Teachers could, for example, use the finding that pupils are negatively disposed towards the foreign language and culture to justify why they do not work towards intercultural competence, voicing the opinion that it will not be of any avail anyway. Likewise, teachers could take the stance that enhancing pupils' motivation to learn the foreign language and improve their language skills is what matters, and that 'the rest', namely positive attitudes and an enlarged familiarity with the culture, will follow automatically.

Pupils' Ideas Regarding the Cultures, Countries and Peoples Primarily Associated with the Foreign Language they are Learning

In this section, we report on what teachers believe their pupils think about the foreign cultures, countries and peoples primarily associated with the foreign language they are learning. We asked teachers to answer the following open question: 'How would you describe your pupils' perceptions of and ideas regarding the country/ies and people(s) usually associated with the foreign language you teach? Please use key words to describe in the area below what you think your pupils associate with the country/ies, culture(s) and people(s) that are usually associated with the foreign language you teach. Please distinguish between countries, cultures and peoples when needed'.

Because more teachers of English took part in the research project than teachers of French, German or Spanish, more data are provided with respect to English-speaking countries, cultures and people. The results are presented in four main categories, namely, (a) positive and neutral views of the foreign country; (b) negative views of the foreign country; (c) positive or neutral views of the foreign people; (d) negative views of the foreign people.

Pupils' views regarding the cultures associated with the English language

Teachers most extensively commented on the positive and negative features their pupils ascribe to the United Kingdom and the United States. Some teachers also report on their pupils' perceptions regarding Canada and Australia.

The United Kingdom: The country and its people

Teachers of English in all countries participating in our research perceive their pupils as associating positive, neutral and negative ideas with the United Kingdom and its people. These are varied and focus on diverse areas of life. As can be observed from Table 4.3 below, some of these areas are mentioned by teachers in all countries, whereas others are touched upon in one or two countries only. On the whole, Greek and Mexican teachers suggested fewer topics than their colleagues in the other participating countries. The range of cultural dimensions with respect to which pupils are said to hold negative ideas is more limited than that with respect to which they hold positive ideas. When negative personality traits are mentioned, they tend to be counterbalanced with positive ones, except in Sweden where only negative traits were mentioned.

On the whole, the UK is described on neutral or positive grounds, whereas its people seem to embody a large number of negative characteristics or faults that exceed their qualities. Bulgarian teachers noticeably believe their pupils assign Britain and its people scarcely negative and abundantly positive traits. This finding confirms the finding presented earlier with respect to teachers' impression of their pupils' overall positive attitude towards the foreign people and culture (see Table 4.1). Middle positions are taken by Greece and Mexico, which present a rather balanced image of the United Kingdom and its people, mentioning a largely similar number of positive and negative ideas. At the other end of the continuum we find Belgium, Poland, Spain and Sweden. Pupils in these countries are perceived as holding neutral to positive views of the *country*, but clearly negative opinions on the British *people*. The Swedish respondents did not even mention a single virtue of the Britons. Belgian, Polish and Spanish pupils are said to acknowledge different

Table 4.3 Teachers' perceptions of the range of topics their pupils associate with the UK, its culture and people

Ideas associated with the United Kingdom and its people							
	BEL	*BUL*	*GRE*	*MEX*	*POL*	*SPA*	*SWE*
Positive or neutral ideas associated with the country							
(1) Sports and entertainment	✓	✓			✓	✓	✓
(2) Daily life and routines, living conditions, food and drink		✓	✓		✓	✓	✓
(3) Tradition, folklore, tourist attractions	✓				✓	✓	✓
(4) Physical geography	✓				✓	✓	✓
(5) Social geography							✓
(6) History	✓	✓	✓				
(7) Institutions		✓	✓		✓	✓	✓
(8) Literature		✓			✓		✓
(9) International status and relations	✓	✓		✓			
(10) The English language				✓			
(11) Economy		✓		✓			
(12) General features	✓	✓	✓	✓	✓		
Negative ideas associated with the country							
(1) Food and drink						✓	✓
(2) Physical geography; the weather	✓	✓	✓		✓	✓	
(3) Social geography	✓		✓				
(4) International status and relations						✓	
(5) General features	✓		✓	✓	✓	✓	✓
Positive or neutral ideas associated with the people							
	✓	✓	✓	✓	✓	✓	
Negative ideas associated with the people							
	✓	✓	✓	✓	✓	✓	✓

positive traits in the British people, even though they are not as numerous as the vices or negative features ascribed to the them.

Let us now turn to the specific ideas pupils are said to associate with Great Britain and British people. We have classified pupils' positive or neutral ideas in 12 cultural categories.

- *Sports and entertainment* seems to be a rather popular field of cultural knowledge since, with the exception of Greece and Mexico, teachers in all countries comment on it. The key aspects here are the 'film' and 'music' industry together with 'sports', particularly 'football'. Some stars are also referred to ('Spice girls', 'Beatles'; 'Owen' and 'Beckham').
- In connection with *daily life and routines*, *living conditions*, and *food and drink*, teachers in five countries, namely Bulgaria, Greece, Poland, Spain and Sweden mention 'tea drinking', next to 'left-hand driving', 'horse racing', 'chats about the weather' and 'B&B' or the general word 'accommodation'.
- Teachers describe some *traditions, folklore aspects* and *tourist attractions*, underlining that their pupils have no more than tourist knowledge of the country. The specific answers given include 'bowler hat', 'quilts and bagpipes', 'pubs', 'double deckers' and 'Big Ben'.
- Teachers who speak about *physical geography*, all mention 'London'. In addition, some teachers refer to 'Liverpool', 'England' and 'Scotland'.
- *Institutions* is present as a category, too, and appears in five of the seven countries surveyed, the exceptions being Bulgaria and Mexico. Attention is paid to three issues: the monarchy ('Queen', 'Royal family', 'Diana'), politics ('Tony Blair') and the education system ('best colleges and universities', 'school system' and 'uniform').
- *British history* is said to be perceived by pupils as 'rich' in the Belgian, Bulgarian and Greek sample. The specific instances included all refer to Britain's colonial past.
- Teachers in three countries make reference to the country's *international status and international relations.* The United Kingdom is said to be considered a 'first world country' by a Mexican teacher, 'the world's number one' by a Bulgarian teacher, and an important country in the European Union by a number of Belgian respondents.
- In Bulgaria and Mexico, a limited number of teachers define pupils' perceptions of the UK's *economic situation* in terms of 'good incomes' (Mexico), 'high standards of living' and 'economically developed' (Bulgaria).

- Only Swedish teachers refer to *social geography*. They assert that their pupils associate the UK with 'class society' and 'upper class'.
- *Literature*, and in particular Shakespeare, is featured in the Bulgarian, Polish and Swedish samples. Mexican teachers depict British English as the 'pure' and 'perfect' variant of the English language.
- Finally, the *general features* which teachers ascribe to the United Kingdom, except in Spain, include 'old' or 'rich' culture, 'expensive', 'interesting', 'beautiful', 'green' and 'worth a visit'.

Apart from those neutral or positive associations with the UK, teachers also reveal clearly negative images of the country, which they think their pupils hold, even if they do so far less often.

- Only Spanish and Swedish teachers, for instance, speak about the negative side of British *food*, thought to be 'bad'. The adjective 'bad' also qualifies the *weather*, characterized by the 'rain', which makes Britain a 'dark' country. The bad weather is referred to by all teachers, except in the Mexican and Swedish sample.
- The *societal and political problems* explicitly stated include 'hooliganism', 'foot-and-mouth disease', and 'Northern Ireland', mentioned in one country only. 'Gibraltar' is mentioned by Spanish teachers as a topic perceived negatively by their pupils.
- The adjectives which teachers say their pupils use to qualify the United Kingdom include 'queer', 'old-fashioned', 'conservative', 'conventional' nature, 'expensive', 'boring', 'tasteless' and 'not very attractive to travel to'. Apart from Bulgarian teachers, all teachers contribute to these general appreciations.

British people equally provoke mixed feelings in pupils. The positive features defining the Britons are quoted by all but the Swedish teachers. In most samples, teachers say that their pupils perceive the Britons as 'polite'. This is by no means the only British virtue. Other qualities on the list include 'good-mannered', 'punctual', 'organized' and 'friendly', that is to say, the Britons are well known for their civic behaviour. One teacher, in addition, mentions that they are 'nice', 'reliable', 'clean', 'love music, their history, and their culture'. Possibly the largest number of qualities, as well as the most outstanding ones, come from Bulgarian teachers whose pupils think Britons are 'interesting', but also 'fascinating'.

Nonetheless, British people are ascribed negative features on a much more frequent basis, that is to say, these features not only outnumber the positive ones, but they seem to be part of pupils' perceptions in all countries. Except for Greek and Mexican teachers, a number of teachers in all other country samples say that their pupils consider the Britons to be 'weird', 'odd', and 'strange'. The second cluster of words named by more than two countries are 'cold' and 'distant', which gives a clue to the prevailing image of British people. The negative labels linked to the country are also associated with its people, namely, 'old-fashioned', 'snobbish' and 'boring'. The rest of the terms employed are much more heterogeneous. Spanish and Polish teachers list a large number of characteristics, such as 'self-sufficient', 'introvert', 'not easy to get along with', 'arrogant', 'noisy', 'hooligans', 'drunkards' (Spanish teachers), 'bossy', 'selfish', 'formal', 'unapproachable' and 'solitary' (Polish respondents). Polish teachers stand out since their pupils are the only ones to contemplate other groups within the United Kingdom, namely the Scots, thought to be 'mean', and the Irish, who 'drink too much alcohol' and who are categorised as 'patriotic'. Mexican teachers, on the other hand, insist on some of the personality traits already hinted at: 'impassive', 'inexpressive' and 'not very passionate'. Bulgarian, Belgian and Swedish teachers enumerate more varied features: 'verbose', 'over-polite', 'weird sense of humour' (Bulgaria), 'conservative', 'stand-offish', 'tasteless' (Belgium) and 'stiff' and 'snotty' (Sweden). To put it in a nutshell, the Britons are attributed a large amount and a wide variety of negative features and there is a clear insistence upon their strange, cold and distant character.

The United States: The country and its people

If pupils' perceptions regarding the United Kingdom are ambiguous, those concerning the United States are mostly positively biased, which does not exclude the existence of negative considerations about American society. The US is deemed to be a highly attractive and essentially positive cultural community. Mexican pupils appear to be less positively disposed towards Americans than pupils in other countries. Greek, Polish and Swedish pupils seem particularly positively disposed towards Americans, whereas pupils in Belgium, Bulgaria and Spain occupy a middle ground, associating Americans with both positive and negative features. On the whole, pupils are perceived as more knowledgeable regarding the US, its people and culture than regarding the UK. As can be observed from Table 4.4 below, some of the areas listed in connection with the country and its people are mentioned by teachers in all countries, whereas others are touched upon in one or two countries only. More positive than negative ideas tend to be associated with the country and its people, and when negative personality traits are assigned, these are counterbalanced with positive ones, except in Mexico.

Table 4.4 Teachers' perceptions of the range of topics their pupils associate with the USA, its culture and people

Ideas associated with the United States and its people							
	BEL	*BUL*	*GRE*	*MEX*	*POL*	*SPA*	*SWE*
Positive or neutral ideas associated with the country							
(1) Sports and entertainment	✓	✓	✓	✓	✓	✓	✓
(2) Daily life and routines, living conditions, food and drink	✓	✓	✓	✓	✓	✓	✓
(3) Tradition, folklore, tourist attractions	✓	✓			✓	✓	✓
(4) Social geography							✓
(5) Technology	✓	✓	✓			✓	
(6) History							✓
(7) Institutions	✓	✓			✓		✓
(8) Literature	✓						
(9) International status and relations	✓	✓	✓	✓	✓		
(10) The English language	✓				✓		
(11) Economy		✓		✓	✓		✓
(12) General features	✓	✓		✓	✓	✓	✓
Negative ideas associated with the country							
(1) Food and drink	✓						✓
(2) Social geography	✓			✓	✓	✓	✓
(3) The English language		✓				✓	
(4) General features	✓						
Positive or neutral ideas associated with the people							
	✓	✓	✓		✓	✓	✓
Negative ideas associated with the people							
	✓	✓		✓		✓	

Let us now have a look at what specific ideas the teachers in the different countries say their pupils associate with the US.

- Teachers in all countries indicate that their pupils define the United States in terms of *sports and entertainment.* Frequent reference is made to the film and music industry. The topics contemplated include 'good films', 'movies' and 'Hollywood', and 'good music', 'pop culture/music', 'hip-hop', 'rap', 'rock' and 'pop stars'. As for sports, the range of the options provided is also bigger than that in connection with the United Kingdom: 'sports', 'NBA', 'American football' or 'ice-hockey' turn out to be key words in that respect. Apart from these two, other issues within the field of entertainment are pondered, especially those related to the different mass media, either in their written ('magazines') or spoken or audiovisual form ('television' as a generic word and specific instances such as 'talk shows like Rikki Lake').
- In all countries, teachers also include aspects concerning *daily life and routines, living conditions and food and drink.* Teachers indicate their pupils generally think of American food in terms of 'fast-food', 'hot-dogs', 'hamburgers', 'McDonalds' or 'Coca-cola'. The topics featured in connection with *daily life and living conditions* are 'big towns/cities' or 'malls'. 'Big cars' are needed because students are aware of the 'big distances' between places in the American country.
- Fewer topics are mentioned in connection with *traditions and tourist attractions.* 'Halloween' and 'Valentine's Day' seem to symbolise the American traditions, whereas the tourist attractions known are restricted to 'Washington', 'California' and the two landmarks: the 'Statue of Liberty' and the 'Niagara Falls'.
- Teachers in four countries refer to *technology.* Three groups, Belgium, Bulgaria and Greece, insist on the technological development of the American nation by means of expressions such as 'the world of computers', 'the Internet', 'space travel' and 'NASA'.
- As to *American institutions* the words include 'politics', 'democracy', 'the president', '(Bill) Clinton', 'political power', and, in the educational sphere, 'high school', 'college' and 'graduation'.
- *Economy* is discussed in four countries (Bulgaria, Mexico, Poland and Sweden). 'Money' is the term most frequently used, followed by 'capitalism'. The capitalist orientation of the United States is perceived in a mainly positive light. 'Wealth', 'dollars', 'rich economy' or 'economically developed' are the keywords whereas more

explicit ideas concern the 'high standards of living', the 'good incomes', or the 'good business perspectives' the United States offers.

- *Social geography* is dealt with once by a Swedish teacher who refers to the melting pot.
- *History* does not appear to feature in pupils' minds. Only Swedish respondents refer to 'the wild west era'.
- Only in Belgium is *literature* referred to by means of the generic term 'books' and with specific writers such as 'Stephen King'. Belgian and Polish teachers say that the American language is thought of as less pure than the British variant of English, and is associated with 'slang'.
- *International status and relations* is a topic which seems to feature prominently in pupils' minds. Teachers stress the international 'power' of the big American country ('a world power', 'world's number one', 'first world country'), whose authority is acknowledged in different fields.
- Finally, teachers in all countries but Greece reveal further other positive or neutral general features. Only a few of the terms given are mentioned more than once, namely 'freedom' (four times), 'success' (three times), 'wealth', 'modern', 'luxury' and 'glamour' (twice). The bright and dazzling side of American society is also evident in other features cited: 'fashionable culture', 'trendy', 'consumption', 'the American dream', 'rich in nature' (Belgium), 'prosperity', 'personal fulfilment', 'the place to emigrate and succeed in', 'the place where dreams come true', 'green cards' (Bulgaria), 'clean' (Mexico), 'independence', 'casual lifestyle' (Poland), 'flashy', 'everything is possible', 'cool', 'large', 'great country', 'fun', 'filled with action' (Sweden). In sum, teachers underline that their pupils see the United States of America as the land of opportunities, a rich nation where freedom, success and personal advancement are possible. In the Bulgarian sample, the US is mentioned as a country one could emigrate to.

Pupils appear to associate only a few negative traits with the USA.

- *Food* is said to be 'bad', 'junk food', and the *English language* is thought to be simplified in its American variety. In a much more general way, the American culture is depicted as 'strange', 'childish' and 'poor'.
- As regards *international status and relations*, the USA is perceived as too expansionist and as imperialistic.

- No further points are added in any other field. Nonetheless, there is an area which deserves special attention, namely the social map. Pupils associate the USA with social conflicts. Apparently, 'racism' seems to be the social problem with which pupils are most familiar, followed by 'death penalty' and 'violence'. Several ideas are related to 'violence' and 'criminality', namely, 'gangs', 'shooting', 'the blacks', 'drugs', and 'guns', 'the big differences between the rich and the poor' or 'abortion'. 'Excess of fat people' also belongs here as a social problem.

Thus, even though the array of negative features ascribed to the United States is restricted and limited to a few sporadic terms, the darker side of the American society is present in the images pupils hold. Teachers in all countries contributed to this list of 'negative' aspects, except in Greece.

We now turn to teachers' perceptions of their pupils' views regarding the American people. A large number of positive qualities are mentioned, except in Mexico, where pupils appear to be more negatively disposed towards Americans. The most widely accepted quality assigned to Americans appears to be 'hard-workers (with a high degree of specialisation)'. The other positive characteristics, which practitioners believe their pupils associate with Americans, are more heterogeneous. Belgian respondents use words such as 'open-minded', 'enthusiastic', and 'progressive'. Bulgarian teachers bring up terms like 'nice sense of humour', 'pragmatic', 'lively', 'garrulous'. Greek pupils are said to view Americans as 'easy-going'. Polish pupils think of them as 'open' and 'friendly', Swedish pupils as 'free', Spanish pupils as 'appealing', 'sophisticated', 'cool' and 'influential'.

The negative characteristics associated with Americans are said to be 'naïve' (named twice), 'arrogant', 'nationalistic', 'superficial' and 'conservative', brought to light by Belgian teachers. Bulgarian teachers include 'stupid', 'negligent', 'mercantile'; Spanish respondents mention 'simple' and 'materialistic', and Mexican teachers use words such as 'gringos' and 'Yankees'. All in all, the main defects of the Americans seem to be the simplicity of their character, a somehow arrogant stance and their materialistic orientation.

Pupils' views regarding the cultures associated with the French language

Only the Belgian, Polish and Swedish samples contained teachers of French. Those teachers' answers point towards pupils' mixed feelings regarding France and its inhabitants. The nation is almost invariably depicted in the light of its bedazzling aspects (fashion, food, natural

Table 4.5 Teachers' perceptions of the range of topics their pupils associate with France, its culture and people

Ideas associated with France			
	BEL	*POL*	*SWE*
Positive and neutral ideas associated with the country			
(1) Sports	✓		✓
(2) Food and drink	✓		✓
(3) Tourist attractions	✓		✓
(4) Fashion	✓	✓	✓
(5) Culture	✓	✓	
(6) Climate	✓		
(7) The French language			✓
(8) General features			
Negative ideas associated with the country			
(1) General features	✓		
Positve and neutral ideas associated with its people			
	✓		✓
Negative ideas associated with its people			
	✓		✓

beauty or attractiveness as a tourist destination), whereas its people are felt to be a sum of both virtues and vices, with a certain negative flavour seemingly dominating pupils' impressions.

As can be seen from Table 4.5, the number of topics enumerated is largest and most varied in the Belgian sample. In that sample, both positive and negative traits of both the country and its people are mentioned. Swedish teachers comment on only positive or neutral ideas being associated with the country, and only negative traits being associated with the people. Polish teachers only mention positive ideas associated with the country.

When turning to pupils' specific associations, we found that their positive or neutral ideas relate to four areas mainly:

- France is said to be 'beautiful', which makes it a 'tempting tourist country'. It is a good choice for 'holidays' because it offers the tourist such a variety of options, from the 'seaside', 'the Riviera' and 'the Alps' to its capital city, 'Paris' with its landmark, the 'Eiffel Tower'. Moreover, the weather is thought to be always good.

- It offers excellent *food and drink.* Teachers indicate that their pupils think of France as a country with a 'rich gastronomy', which is 'famous for its good food and good wine'.
- Pupils appear to be very familiar with the world of *sports.* In particular they associate the country with an excellent soccer team, famous cyclists, and the Tour de France. As to other kinds of entertainment, only the word 'film' was cited.
- *Fashion* and *fashion designers* also appear frequently.

Belgian and Polish teachers also mention French *Culture,* France's rich cultural history and art, as topics which some pupils may think of when they think of France. In Sweden, one teacher indicates that pupils consider the *French language* itself to be beautiful.

The negative ideas which teachers think their pupils associate with France are far less numerous than the positive ones. In fact, only Belgian teachers mention them. To Flemish pupils' minds, France is an 'expensive country' where, for instance, drinks are 'expensive'. French music is 'old-fashioned'. France does not produce 'high-tech' products, its cars are 'bad', and the prevailing image is that of a 'rural country except for Paris', where 'rural' is apparently a negative trait.

The positive characteristics assigned to French people include that they are interested in, and love, culture. Apart from that, Swedish teachers refer to gastronomy and fashion, the main attributes of the French being 'gourmet', 'wine-drinkers' and 'well-dressed'. Furthermore, Belgian teachers add that their pupils think French people are 'politically conscious', 'enjoy life', and are 'friendly', 'amusing' and 'creative'.

Both Swedish and Belgian teachers mention a larger number of negative personality traits, though not the same ones, apart from 'snobbish'. Most pejorative terms come from Belgian teachers. They include: 'chauvinistic', 'arrogant', 'pretentious', 'talkative', 'aggressive drivers', 'navel-gazing', 'lazy' and 'unwilling to speak other languages'. The Swedish teachers point out not the personal, but the international and intercultural relationships French people have with other groups. They state their pupils think French people 'feel superior to other countries' and 'hate the Arabs'.

Pupils' views regarding the cultures associated with the German language

Pupils' opinions regarding Germany and its inhabitants seem to be ambiguous. The country is depicted in positive or neutral terms, even if

Table 4.6 Teachers' perceptions of the range of topics their pupils associate with Germany, its culture and people

Ideas associated with France			
	BEL	*POL*	*SWE*
Positive and neutral ideas associated with the country			
(1) Sports and entertainment	✓	✓	✓
(2) Food and drink	✓	✓	✓
(3) Traditions, folklore, tourist attractions	✓	✓	✓
(4) Physical geography	✓		
(5) Economic/technological development	✓	✓	✓
(6) International status/relations			✓
(7) The French language			✓
(8) General features	✓	✓	✓
Negative ideas associated with the country			
(1) War history	✓	✓	✓
(2) Food	✓		
(3) Media	✓		
(4) Language	✓		
(5) General features		✓	✓
Positive ideas associated with the people			
	✓	✓	✓
Negative ideas associated with the people			
	✓	✓	✓

the stormy past of the Second World War hovers over this positive image. As regards the German people, positive characteristics appear to counterbalance negative ones. As can be seen from Table 4.6, the number of different cultural aspects featured in pupils' perceptions varies per country. Polish teachers assign fewest negative attributes to German people, Belgian teachers most.

- As regards the specific positive or neutral ideas associated with Germany, German *gastronomy* occupies the first position. The key idea here is 'beer', closely followed by 'sauerkraut'. Further words included are 'sausages' (Belgium), 'potato salad', 'white bread' and 'rye bread' (Sweden).

- In the realm of *sports and entertainment*, Germany is said to be associated with 'football teams', 'football clubs' and '(good at) soccer'. In addition, Belgian teachers make reference to television series, such as 'Derrick' or 'Tatort'.
- Pupils' familiarity with *traditions, folklore* and/or *tourist attractions* appears to be limited to 'Christmas markets' and 'leather trousers' in Belgium, to 'Tirol music' or 'music bands' and 'the Alps' in Poland and Sweden. Belgian pupils also refer to the 'beautiful countryside' and 'many woods'.
- The German *economy* is thought of as 'rich', 'wealthy' and 'strong'. The country is generally characterised as 'affluent' and 'rich', even though the sole product mentioned in all three country samples is '(fast) cars'. In Sweden, this wealth is made reference to indirectly in the expression 'rich Germans buy houses in the south of Sweden'.
- Other aspects of culture are also mentioned, though they appear to occupy a more marginal role in pupils' minds. Swedish teachers make reference to Germany as a member of the European Union. They also mention that pupils think of the German language as 'similar to our language', and in terms of 'different dialects in the north and in the south'.
- The *general features* ascribed to Germany can be summarised in its 'cleanliness' (Belgium and Poland), 'rich' and interesting culture' (Sweden), 'self-sufficiency' (Belgium). Polish teachers add 'order', 'self-confidence', 'discipline', 'solidity' and a 'saving/economising' attitude.

The negative ideas associated with Germany are generally linked to its turbulent war *history.* 'Hitler' and 'concentration camps' are the terms most frequently mentioned in all three countries. Other terms include 'holocaust', 'Nazis' and 'slave labour' (Poland). In Sweden, reference is made to the 'divided country'. Belgian teachers also widely acknowledge that their pupils perceive the *German language* as 'difficult' and 'ugly', *German media* as 'backward', and *German food* as 'bad'.

As regards German people, pupils appear to perceive them as 'diligent', 'hard-working', 'industrious', 'systematic at work', 'with a gift for organisation' and 'with precision'. The Germans are likewise admired for their 'friendliness', 'hospitality' and 'reliability'. In Sweden, they are perceived as 'war conscious' and 'with canoes, boats and bikes on their cars when travelling to Sweden for a holiday'. Apart from the professional and personal attributes of the Germans, their more relaxed side is also commented on, although exclusively by Swedish respondents who say that their pupils believe Germans to be 'not very different from us'.

Though Germans tend to be seen in a positive light, some of these positive characteristics are viewed more negatively when they become excessive. Germans are then depicted as 'careerist', 'materialistic', 'too perfectionist', 'noisy' or 'loud'.

Additional negative labels attached to the Germans include 'distant', 'dominant', 'pretentious', 'aggressive', 'non humorous', 'harsh discipline', 'strict rules' and 'unpleasant tourists'. Swedish pupils are said to associate Germans with unpleasant tourists, who steal 'road signs with elks on them', are 'loud and noisy' and 'dominate the places they come to'.

Pupils' views regarding the cultures associated with the Spanish language

Only the Belgian and Swedish samples contain teachers of Spanish. The country principally associated with the Spanish language is Spain. In both countries, Spain is perceived as a place for 'holidays', and is further characterised by means of words such as 'leisure' and 'sunshine', 'beaches', 'hot weather' and 'shopping'. The tourist attractions, mentioned only by Belgian teachers, include 'historical cities' ('Toledo', 'Granada') and its 'rich cultural heritage' ('Gaudí', 'Dalí', 'Picasso') (see Table 4.7).

Table 4.7 Teachers' perceptions of the range of topics their pupils associate with Spain, its culture and people

Ideas associated with Spain, its people and culture		
	BEL	*SWE*
Positive and neuteral ideas associated with the country		
(1) Tourist attractions	✓	✓
(2) Culture/history	✓	

Comparison of English, French, German and Spanish teachers' perceptions of their pupils' views compared

When comparing the pictures of the cultures, countries and people associated with the English, French, German and Spanish language, we see, first, that pupils are perceived as most knowledgeable about the countries associated with the English language. With respect to the UK and the USA, a larger number of different cultural aspects are said to feature in pupils' minds than with respect to France, Germany or Spain. Spain appears to be the country about which pupils hold least diversified ideas.

Secondly, there is a remarkable degree of similarity in the pictures of the different countries. All pupils hold positive ideas regarding the USA; all pupils think of France in terms of 'good food' and 'fashion designers'; all pupils associate 'sausages and beer' with the German lifestyle and think of the country as a well-organised and hard-working nation. The 'old' stereotypes thus appear to prevail. On the other hand, pupils in different countries hold very specific ideas regarding particular cultures. Bulgarian pupils, for example, think of the USA as a country they might emigrate to; Swedish pupils label the Germans as 'rich people who come to buy houses in the south of Sweden' or 'tourists who steal road signs with elks on them'.

Obviously, the perception data presented in this chapter are limited. The teachers will no doubt have tried to provide an adequate description of what they believe their pupils think of the foreign culture. On the other hand, we have to admit that they may not have mentioned everything they could have, in view of the fact that they were in the middle of answering a questionnaire and had more questions ahead of them. The data can also not be characterised as a complete data set because not all teachers answered the question, some answers were far more elaborate than others, and the number of English teachers by far exceeds that of teachers of the other languages. We have tried to take into account these limitations when analysing and presenting our data. One question that fascinates us and which we cannot answer, is whether the positive disposition which teachers may have towards the foreign culture associated with the foreign language they teach has affected their reports on their pupils' perceptions. Could it for example be the case that the positive ideas that teachers hold of German people have affected their report on their pupils' perceptions of German people? Though we have no data to substantiate our answer, we believe teachers have been successful in providing truthful accounts of their pupils' perceptions. It appears to us that their reports are adequate, for the pictures they sketch coincide with those provided in earlier research which directly inquired into pupils' views (e.g. Byram *et al.*, 1991; Cain & Briane, 1994; Sercu, 2000a).

This then again brings us to the interesting question of how these findings might be related to teachers' teaching practice. Cultural knowledge is an essential part of intercultural competence. What becomes known becomes less frightening. What one can relate to the cultural background, in which it is meaningful, becomes better understood. When teaching intercultural competence, teachers could and ought to start from the ideas which exist amongst their pupils. They should try to enlarge upon ideas which bear a close resemblance to reality, rectify wrong or stereotypical ones, and promote familiarity with important unknown aspects of the foreign culture. Teachers have an obligation to help pupils realise that 'different' does not mean 'wrong' or 'inhuman', and to show them that their own cultural behaviour may appear strange, inhuman or distasteful in the eyes of others. Teachers who know what their pupils believe and feel can select cultural contents and culture learning tasks which can promote the acquisition of intercultural competence. Again, we are aware that teachers may not take the desired stance here and can take the position that trying to alter pupils' perceptions is no use; that nothing can be done; that in comparison with the effect the media have on pupils, their influence is minor and cannot alter pupils' ideas. And perhaps with respect to this last point, they are right to a certain extent, for the ideas pupils hold appear to be images prevailing in contemporary media.

Pupils' Contacts with the Target Country/ies

In this section, we inquire into what teachers believe to be their pupils' principal sources of information regarding foreign countries, cultures and people. The respondents were asked to indicate with respect to five different sources whether they thought their pupils used them 'often', 'once in a while' or 'never'. Table 4.8 provides an overview of the results obtained.

We see that Bulgarian, Polish and Swedish teachers believe their pupils have frequent contacts with the foreign culture, whereas Mexican, Greek, Belgian and Spanish pupils are reported to have contact with the foreign culture once in a while. Spanish pupils appear to get into contact with the foreign countries least often, Bulgarian pupils most often.

The table also shows that teachers believe that their pupils' main sources regarding foreign cultures are television and the Internet. In Poland, Sweden, Mexico and Belgium television is thought to be more important than the Internet. In Bulgaria, Greece and Spain, the reverse is true. It is remarkable that 33.33% of Greek teachers and 31.43% of Spanish teachers think that their pupils never use television as a source of information on the foreign culture.

Table 4.8 Teachers' perceptions of their pupils' contacts with the country primarily associated with the foreign language

	BUL	*POL*	*SWE*	*MEX*	*GRE*	*BEL*	*SPA*	*Mean*
Index	2.34	2.11	2.03	2.00	1.89	1.85	1.81	2.00
Use the Internet to learn more about the foreign country	2.77	2.31	2.22	2.31	2.28	2.02	1.91	2.26
Watch one of the country's television channels	2.70	2.49	2.27	2.53	2.05	2.03	1.86	2.28
Read literature written by authors living in the foreign country or originating from the foreign country	2.55	1.91	1.95	1.78	1.79	1.74	2.23	1.99
Travel to the foreign country (holiday with family)	1.73	1.94	1.97	1.42	1.56	2.04	1.54	1.74
Read one of the country's newspapers or magazines	1.93	1.92	1.74	1.96	1.76	1.41	1.51	1.75

Mean scores 0.00–1.00 = never; 1.01–2.00 = once in a while; 2.01–3.00 = often.

Teachers in all countries agree that their pupils will only read foreign newspapers or magazines once in a while.

With respect to travel, Belgian teachers stand out. It is only in Belgium that pupils are assumed to travel to the foreign countries often. In all other countries, the mean scores obtained for travel fall below 2.00. 62.22% of Mexican teachers, 48.57% of Spanish teachers and 43.59% of Greek teachers think their pupils never travel to the foreign country.

As regards the reading of literature, Spanish and Bulgarian teachers affirm that their pupils frequently read literature written by authors living in the main target country, whereas teachers in other countries assert that their pupils only read literature once in a while. It is remarkable that 31.43% of Spanish teachers and no less than 58.62% of Bulgarian teachers indicated their pupils read literature frequently.

The fact that pupils primarily draw on television and the Internet should not surprise. Television and the Internet are all prevailing and pupils make widespread use of them in the Western world. It is more surprising that teachers in some countries, notably Bulgaria and Spain, think their pupils also draw on literature as an important source of information. Could it be the case that teachers are confusing their own sources of information with those of their pupils, or is it indeed the case that Spanish and Bulgarian pupils read more books than pupils in other countries? The fact that only Belgian pupils are said to travel frequently to the countries associated with the foreign languages they are learning has to be interpreted in the light of the fact that both Germany and France are neighbouring countries to Belgium, and that travelling abroad is relatively easy. As regards the other countries, the high proportions of teachers who state that their pupils never travel abroad is worrying. The fact that large numbers of pupils cannot travel abroad means that they have to rely on secondary sources of information regarding foreign cultures. This is not to say that we think direct travel is by definition a better kind of contact than other kinds of contact: people may come back from such travels with reinforced stereotypes. It is to say, however, that large numbers of pupils obviously lack the chance to go and see 'with their own eyes' what the foreign country and culture look like, and experience what the foreign people are like when they are at home.

Again, we want to speculate about how these findings could and should affect teaching practice. Teachers who take intercultural competence teaching seriously could design learning environments that help pupils to reflect on which ideas they gain from which sources and on the degree of truth in these different ideas. But, again, we realise that not all teachers will be willing or able to grasp the chances inherent in working with pupils' sources of information to sharpen their culture learning skills or their ability to interpret cultural information in a critical way.

To conclude this chapter, we want to point out an interesting tendency that becomes apparent when linking the three kinds of findings presented in this chapter. The tendency is most visible when comparing the results obtained for the Bulgarian and the Spanish samples. Bulgarian pupils excel over pupils in other countries in all four dimensions distinguished. In the view of their teachers, they are more motivated, have a more positive attitude towards the foreign people, perceive the language as less difficult to learn and are more knowledgeable about the foreign culture, country and people than pupils in other countries, except with respect to Swedish pupils who appear to be as knowledgeable as Bulgarian pupils. These data correlate with the contact data, for these data too reveal that, of all pupils, Bulgarian pupils are in contact with the foreign culture most frequently. By contrast, Spanish pupils who are in contact with the foreign culture least frequently are also the pupils perceived to be least motivated, least positively disposed towards the foreign people and amongst the pupils who are least knowledgeable about the foreign culture. An implication of this is that teachers who feel their pupils run the risk of getting into a downward spiral, accumulating negative feelings regarding learning the language and developing strong feelings of dislike or even hostility towards the foreign culture, should take active measures to prevent the situation from getting to the point of no return.

In the next chapter, we will look at what teachers actually do in their classrooms in the intercultural realm. It will be interesting to compare the Spanish and the Bulgarian sample again and see whether Spanish teachers appear to be making special efforts to entice their pupils into culture-and-language learning.

Chapter 5

Culture Teaching Practices

EWA BANDURA and LIES SERCU

In Chapter 1, we pointed out that research into teachers' beliefs has revealed that teachers' perceptions directly affect the way in which they shape their teaching practice. Teachers' personal, often implicit, theories of learning can be seen in practice in their day-to-day teaching. A language teacher who believes in the value of direct correction of oral mistakes will not wait until after a pupil has finished speaking to remark on any mistakes the pupil has made. A teacher who does not believe in the value of group work will prefer pair work, individual work or whole class work to group work. Teachers rely upon a mixture of intuitive theories of how different pupils learn, their recollections of their own language learning, and formal theories expounded to them during professional training. These theories will have been mainly linguistic and literary theories since most teachers have been formed in the mould of linguistics and literary studies and criticism. Their intuitions regarding language learning are acquired partly through experience, partly through discussion with others in the profession and partly through the more or less implicit guidance of textbooks and other pedagogically structured materials. Through trial and error, teachers acquire beliefs regarding which teaching principles and techniques work and which do not. Once acquired, these beliefs are difficult to change (see Counts, 1999; Pajares, 1992; Prosser & Trigwell, 1997; van Driel *et al.*, 1997; Woods, 1996).

What is true for language teaching-and-learning theories is true for culture teaching-and-learning theories. In the previous chapters, we have outlined some dimensions of teachers' language-and-culture learning theories. We have shown that teachers define the objectives of foreign language education mainly in linguistic terms and those of culture teaching mainly in terms of the passing on of information, and that they consider themselves sufficiently familiar with the foreign culture to be able to teach about it in the foreign language classroom. If a direct link exists between teachers' beliefs and their teaching practice, these findings suggest that quite a gap will exist between actual culture-teaching practice and the kind of teaching practice envisaged by intercultural competence teaching theorists. We can expect that teachers will not teach intercultural competence with the same rigour as they teach language competence, and that culture teaching will most probably be defined mainly in terms of the passing on of knowledge.

It is the purpose of this chapter to examine whether these expectations are indeed reflected in teachers' reports of their culture teaching practice. We asked the teachers to indicate which cultural contents they touch upon in their foreign language classrooms and with what frequency they do so, and which culture teaching activities they practise. A third topic we addressed was the preparatory and follow-up work teachers do in their classrooms in connection with school trips to one of the target countries or international exchange projects.

In a previous chapter, we have already shown that teachers devote far more time to language teaching than to culture teaching. In later chapters, still other aspects of teachers' culture teaching practices will be addressed: on the one hand, teachers' views regarding the quality of the cultural dimension of the foreign language teaching materials they use, and on the other, their views regarding the effect of school trips and exchange programmes on pupils' perceptions and attitudes towards foreign cultures. This last topic then shifts the focus from teachers' culture teaching practices in the classroom to activities outside the classroom that may also contribute to promoting learners' acquisition of intercultural competence.

Kinds and Frequency of Culture Teaching Activities Practised

To find out about teachers' culture teaching activities, we asked them to indicate for a number of possible culture teaching activities how often they practise them: regularly, once in a while or never. Apart from inquiring into how often teachers include culture learning activities in their teaching, we also wanted to find out which culture teaching approaches they appear to prefer. First, we wanted to explore whether and to what extent they prefer a teacher-centred approach to a pupil-centred one. In the former case, it is the teacher who decides on the cultural topics dealt with in the classroom. In the latter case, the pupils themselves can choose what topics they want to explore. Secondly, we were curious to find out whether teachers practise only teaching activities that target cognitive objectives, or whether they also use activities that address the attitudinal or skills dimensions of intercultural competence. Do they appear to identify intercultural competence teaching with passing on information, or do they also aim to enhance their learners' ability to explore cultures independently, compare cultures or explain aspects of their own culture?

In the list of culture teaching activities below, we have indicated between brackets which activities we consider representative of which approach. Some activities have been termed both teacher-centred and pupil-centred, since depending on how a teacher uses them they can indeed be both. Nevertheless, some will be more typical of a teacher-centred than of a pupil-centred approach. Similarly, though some activities mainly address the cognitive dimension of intercultural competence learning, they may at the same time also address attitudinal or skills learning aspects. An analysis of the list reveals that activities which we classified as mainly pupil-centred are also the activities which are most clearly directed towards the acquisition of culture learning skills. The activities have been listed in the order of frequency with which they appear to be practised. The score between brackets is the mean score obtained for the whole sample.[1]

(1) I tell my pupils what I heard (or read) about the foreign country or culture. (2.67) (cognitive, teacher-centred).
(2) I tell my pupils why I find something fascinating or strange about the foreign culture(s). (2.60) (cognitive, attitudinal, teacher-centred).
(3) I ask my pupils to compare an aspect of their own culture with that aspect in the foreign culture. (2.50) (skills, teacher-centred or pupil-centred).
(4) I talk with my pupils about stereotypes regarding particular cultures and countries or regarding the inhabitants of particular countries. (2.40) (cognitive, attitudinal, teacher-centred or pupil-centred).
(5) I talk to my pupils about my own experiences in the foreign country. (2.34) (cognitive, attitudinal, teacher-centred).
(6) I comment on the way in which the foreign culture is represented in the foreign language materials I am using in a particular class. (2.29) (cognitive, teacher-centred).
(7) I ask my pupils about their experiences in the foreign country. (2.28) (cognitive, attitudinal, pupil-centred).
(8) I ask my pupils to describe an aspect of their own culture in the foreign language. (2.22) (cognitive, skills, pupil-centred or teacher-centred).

(9) I use videos, CD-ROMs or the Internet to illustrate an aspect of the foreign culture. (2.09) (cognitive, teacher-centred).
(10) I ask my pupils to think about the image which the media promote of the foreign country. (2.09) (cognitive, skills, teacher-centred or pupil-centred).
(11) I ask my pupils to think about what it would be like to live in the foreign culture. (2.08) (cognitive, attitudinal, skills, pupil-centred).
(12) I decorate my classroom with posters illustrating particular aspects of the foreign culture. (2.05) (cognitive, attitudinal, teacher-centred).
(13) I bring objects originating from the foreign culture to my classroom. (2.01) (cognitive, attitudinal, teacher-centred).
(14) I ask my pupils to independently explore an aspect of the foreign culture. (2.00) (skills, pupil-centred or teacher-centred).
(15) I ask my pupils to participate in role-play situations in which people from different cultures meet. (1.88) (attitudinal, skills, teacher-centred or pupil-centred).
(16) I touch upon an aspect of the foreign culture regarding which I feel negatively disposed. (1.83) (attitudinal, teacher-centred).
(17) I invite a person originating from the foreign country to my classroom. (1.46) (cognitive, attitudinal, teacher-centred).

From the list, it can, first, be seen that teachers most frequently employ teacher-centred activities, where *they* define the cultural contents, over pupil-centred activities, where *pupils* can decide on the cultural contents, mainly represented by the activities ranked 7th, 8th, 11th and 14th. The first activity that is unambiguously pupil-centred is the seventh activity where the teacher asks his/her pupils about their experiences in the foreign country. Though some of the activities ranked higher could in some cases also be interpreted as pupil-centred activities, they are really activities in which the teacher takes the initiative; that is, it is the teacher who talks about what interests him or her. In the seventh activity, by contrast, it is the pupils who can talk about what interests them.

Secondly, teachers appear to use teaching activities that foremost address the cognitive and attitudinal dimensions of intercultural competence – the acquisition of knowledge and positive attitudes. The intercultural skill, which teachers say they practise quite frequently, is 'comparison of cultures' (activity ranked third). Other intercultural skills, such as 'reflect critically on one's sources' – this is also cognitive – (ranked 10th), 'empathise with someone living in the foreign culture (ranked 11th)', 'explore an aspect of the foreign culture' (ranked 14th) or 'practise skills useful in intercultural contact situations' (ranked 15th) appear relatively low in the list.

Thirdly, teachers in all countries indicate they practise particular activities often (scores $\geq$2.01). We need to be careful here not to interpret this finding as an indication of extensive culture teaching in almost every lesson. In the light of what we found earlier regarding the balance between time devoted to language teaching and time devoted to culture teaching, we can merely interpret this finding as a sign of teachers practising some culture teaching-and-learning activities relatively more often than other culture teaching-and-learning activities.

With respect to the activities ranked 7th, and 9th to 15th, the picture is such that teachers in some countries practise them often and those in other countries no more than once in a while (see Table 5.1 below). With respect to 'I bring objects originating from the foreign culture to my classroom', for example, Mexican, Swedish and Belgian teachers indicate they practise this activity once in a while, whereas teachers in other countries appear to prefer that activity relatively more often over the other activities in the list. The same is true for 'I ask my pupils to participate in role-play situations in which people from different cultures meet', where only Bulgarian and Spanish teachers appear to practise this activity frequently.

When looking at the proportions of the different country samples that appear to practise particular activities frequently, an even more differentiated picture arises. The two countries that stand out are Mexico and Bulgaria, for in these countries large proportions of teachers have scored teaching activities differently from their colleagues in other samples. Mexican, and especially Bulgarian, teachers appear to practise particular teaching activities relatively speaking more often. This is obviously the case with respect to 'I ask my pupils to think about the image which the media promote of the foreign country'; 'I ask my pupils to independently explore an aspect of the foreign culture'; 'I comment on the way in which the foreign culture is represented in the foreign language materials I am using in a particular class'; 'I ask my pupils to compare an aspect of their own culture with that aspect in the foreign culture' and 'I ask my pupils to describe an aspect of their own culture in the foreign language' (only in Bulgaria). These are the activities that have been labelled 'intercultural skills activities'. Mexico and Bulgaria also stand out with respect to 'I talk to my pupils about my own experiences in the foreign country', but this time in the sense that larger proportions of teachers in those countries than in other countries indicate that they never practise this activity.

Table 5.1 Frequency of culture teaching activities practised

	BUL	*SPA*	*GRE*	*MEX*	*SWE*	*POL*	*BEL*	*Mean*
Index	2.31	2.21	2.19	2.14	2.13	2.10	2.06	2.16
I invite a person originating from the foreign country to my classroom	1.66	1.46	1.23	1.33	1.77	1.38	1.39	1.46
I touch upon an aspect of the foreign culture regarding which I feel negatively disposed	1.90	1.60	1.90	1.84	1.87	1.88	1.79	1.83
I ask my pupils to participate in role-play situations in which people from different cultures meet	2.00	2.20	1.93	1.93	1.58	1.90	1.65	1.88
I ask my pupils to independently explore an aspect of the foreign culture	2.28	1.83	1.90	2.20	2.07	1.80	1.95	2.00
I bring objects originating from the foreign culture to my classroom	2.27	2.03	2.13	1.93	1.80	2.08	1.86	2.01
I decorate my classroom with posters illustrating particular aspects of the foreign culture	2.20	2.09	2.10	1.62	2.13	2.14	2.08	2.05
I ask my pupils to think about what it would be like to live in the foreign culture	2.40	2.20	2.35	2.05	1.89	1.90	1.80	2.08
I ask my pupils to think about the image, which the media promote of the foreign country	2.30	2.00	2.13	2.34	2.02	1.88	1.99	2.09

(*continued*)

Table 5.1 *Continued*

	BUL	*SPA*	*GRE*	*MEX*	*SWE*	*POL*	*BEL*	*Mean*
I use videos, CD-ROMs or the internet to illustrate an aspect of the foreign culture	2.07	2.31	1.95	2.00	2.42	1.80	2.09	2.09
I ask my pupils to describe an aspect of their own culture in the foreign language	2.66	2.17	2.15	2.11	2.13	2.18	2.11	2.22
I ask my pupils about their experiences in the foreign country	2.43	2.34	2.33	1.91	2.34	2.32	2.31	2.28
I comment on the way in which the foreign culture is represented in the foreign language materials I am using in a particular class	2.50	2.46	2.28	2.44	2.16	2.20	2.00	2.29
I talk with my pupils about stereotypes regarding particular cultures and countries or regarding the inhabitants of particular countries	2.57	2.31	2.43	2.42	2.32	2.42	2.31	2.40
I talk to my pupils about my own experiences in the foreign country	2.03	2.69	2.58	2.09	2.38	2.32	2.33	2.34
I ask my pupils to compare an aspect of their own culture with that aspect in the foreign culture	2.77	2.60	2.60	2.73	2.31	2.38	2.09	2.50

(*continued*)

Table 5.1 *Continued*

	BUL	*SPA*	*GRE*	*MEX*	*SWE*	*POL*	*BEL*	*Mean*
I tell my pupils why I find something fascinating or strange about the foreign culture(s)	2.63	2.54	2.60	2.69	2.50	2.56	2.66	2.60
I tell my pupils what I heard (or read) about the foreign country or culture	2.70	2.69	2.70	2.71	2.60	2.58	2.68	2.67

Mean scores per country. Mean score 0.00–1.00 = never; mean score 1.01–2.00 = once in a while; mean score 2.01–3.00 = often.

Table 5.2 Additional culture teaching activities mentioned

Familiarise pupils with the foreign culture through a variety of media 'Use authentic materials: read and discuss newspaper or magazine articles'; 'tell and interpret foreign jokes'; 'discuss songs, films, TV programmes'; 'focus on cultural differences while reading literature'; 'discuss dossiers concerning certain cultural aspects, surveys on certain topics'
Motivate and involve pupils in culture learning 'Try to get the students more involved in culture learning through the element of entertainment through drama activities, recitation of poems or recording the students imitating foreign commercials'; 'quizzes and competitions'
Promote culture learning skills 'Compile a portfolio about current affairs'; 'interview tourists'

Finally, we want to point out here that teachers were also asked in an open question to give examples of still other culture teaching activities they practise. We have classified their answers in three categories. A first set of activities aims to familiarise pupils with the foreign culture through a variety of media. A second set tries to motivate and involve pupils in culture learning. A final set groups activities which are pupil-centred in the sense that they promote learner autonomy and, to a large extent, allow the pupils to determine the cultural topics addressed (see Table 5.2).

Our findings confirm our expectations based on the picture of teachers' beliefs regarding the objectives of foreign language education and culture teaching presented in the previous chapters. Quite a gap appears to exist between actual culture teaching practice and the kind of teaching practice envisaged by intercultural competence teaching. Traditional teacher-centred approaches, addressing foremost the acquisition of knowledge and positive attitudes, dominate in culture teaching in all countries and techniques involving the students' initiative and autonomy are less popular. Teachers more often tell students about their knowledge and views rather than encourage them to search for information in different sources, analyse it independently and present their findings in order to discuss them with others. Activities aiming to develop learners' intercultural skills feature less prominently in teachers' descriptions of their teaching practice than activities addressing cognitive and affective aspects of intercultural competence. Though 'comparison of cultures' appears to be an activity frequently practised, other activities aiming at the acquisition of intercultural skills, such as 'reflect critically on one's sources of information', 'explore an aspect of the foreign culture' or 'practise skills useful in intercultural contact situations' are not.

It strikes us that the picture in the different countries is similar. We can only speculate about possible reasons for this high degree of similarity. The fact that teacher-centred approaches are still more common than pupil-centred ones can be seen in the light of the fact that social-constructivist approaches to teaching and learning and learner autonomy approaches have only recently been introduced on a larger scale in many European schools. Schools are presently struggling to find a balance between teacher-centred approaches and more pupil-centred autonomy fostering approaches to learning. The fact that the only intercultural skill practised on a regular basis in foreign language classrooms is 'comparison of cultures' can be seen in this light, too. The other activities addressing the intercultural skills dimension of intercultural competence are also activities that can be said to be more typical of learner autonomy approaches than of teacher-centred approaches to education.

The fact that Mexico and Bulgaria stand out, in the sense that teachers from these countries appear to favour autonomy and culture learning skills more often than teachers in other countries may mean that these teachers indeed devote a larger amount of their teaching time to culture teaching. The reasons why Mexico and Bulgaria stand out need not be the same, though. As for the Bulgarian teachers, the fact that they appear to devote more attention to the promotion of intercultural competence in foreign language education may be the result of the fact that the British Council has supported several initiatives aimed at helping Bulgarian teachers to introduce an intercultural aspect in foreign language teaching. For instance, as many as sixty secondary school teachers were involved in writing materials resulting in *Branching Out: A Cultural Studies Syllabus* (Davcheva & Docheva, 1998), which was followed by *Intercultural Studies for Language Teachers* (British Council and Teacher Training Institute Sofia, 2001), a distance learning course. One can hardly avoid connecting these teacher training projects with the answers given by the Bulgarian teachers, especially in view of the fact that the teaching materials included in these courses repeatedly demonstrate the activities which Bulgarian teachers practise relatively more often than their colleagues in other countries. As for the Mexican teachers, we remark a parallel between their definitions of the objectives of foreign language education and culture teaching on the one hand and, on the other, the kinds of culture teaching activities they practise. Mexican teachers generally emphasise the acquisition of general learning skills more than teachers in other countries. The activities they practise in their foreign language classroom reflect this, emphasising the acquisition of intercultural skills more than in most other countries. The reasons for this may lie in Mexican curricular guidelines, the kinds of teaching materials available, teacher education, or, doubtless, in a combination of these and perhaps other factors. Here too, our assumptions have to remain speculative. A comparison of these different aspects and how they interrelate in the different countries involved in our study fell outside the scope of our study, and would have to be the subject of a separate study.

Amount of Time Devoted to Different Cultural Topics During Teaching Time

The amount of time teachers devote to different aspects of the foreign culture in their classrooms can also provide insights in the way in which teachers actually shape the teaching of culture and intercultural competence. We asked teachers to indicate whether they deal with each of these aspects extensively, merely mention them briefly or never touch upon them. The cultural aspects we addressed are the same as those where we asked teachers to indicate how familiar they were with them.

The order in which teachers ranked the various cultural topics dealt with in class is as follows:[2]

We can see that teachers in all countries deal most extensively with 'daily life and routines', 'traditions and folklore', 'youth culture' and 'education and professional life'. The sole topic more than 50% of teachers in each country say they deal with extensively is 'daily life and routines' (Table 5.3). The majority of teachers deal with all other topics,

Table 5.3 Teachers' perceptions of the extent to which they dealt with upon a number of cultural aspects in the foreign language classroom

	MEX	*BUL*	*SWE*	*GRE*	*SPA*	*BEL*	*POL*	*Mean*
Index	2.27	2.24	2.12	2.12	2.11	2.06	2.05	2.14
International relations (political, economic and cultural) with students' own country and other countries	2.04	1.79	1.87	1.78	1.51	1.72	1.64	1.77
Different ethnic and social groups	2.11	2.03	2.02	1.85	1.71	1.84	1.70	1.89
Other cultural expressions (music, drama, art)	2.27	2.17	2.03	2.03	2.00	1.97	1.86	2.05
Values and beliefs	2.41	2.25	2.04	2.03	1.80	1.92	1.94	2.05
Literature	1.91	2.20	2.15	1.93	2.26	2.03	1.94	2.06
History, geography, political system	2.04	2.13	2.15	2.03	2.03	2.17	2.16	2.10
Education, professional life	2.29	2.33	2.07	2.15	2.09	2.07	2.16	2.17
Youth culture	2.51	2.20	2.17	2.28	2.43	2.07	2.04	2.24
Traditions, folklore, tourist attractions	2.51	2.52	2.18	2.48	2.40	2.23	2.36	2.38
Daily life and routines, living conditions, food and drink, etc.	2.57	2.73	2.50	2.69	2.86	2.57	2.70	2.66

Mean scores 0.00–1.00 = never; mean scores 1.01–2.00 = once in a while; 2.01–3.00 = extensively.

except international relations, once in a while. Large proportions of teachers say they never deal with 'international relations', except in Mexico, where teachers appear to devote a substantial amount of time to clarifying the international position of the USA vis-à-vis other countries. Likewise, a larger proportion of Mexican teachers deal more extensively with 'different ethnic and social groups' than in other countries. The same can be said with respect to 'literature' for Bulgarian and Spanish teachers.

The agreement amongst teachers as to which cultural topics should be dealt with extensively and which topics can be left aside is striking. Interestingly, the topics that teachers say they deal with most extensively are also the topics which textbook analyses have shown to be the topics dealt with most extensively (Méndez García, 2003; Sercu, 2000a). Teachers teach by the textbook and the topics dealt with are the ones dealt with in class. The topics not or not extensively dealt with in textbooks, such as international relations, different ethnic and social groups or values and beliefs, do not feature extensively in classrooms. In the next chapter, we explore teachers' perceptions of the quality of the cultural dimension of the foreign language textbooks they use. Teachers' answers may corroborate our claim that they teach by the book, or they may point in a different direction.

In Chapter 9 we also investigate whether and to what extent the findings regarding teachers' familiarity with particular aspects of the foreign culture coincide with the ones presented in this chapter. Does it appear to be the case that the topics teachers indicate they are most familiar with are also the topics dealt with most extensively in the foreign language classroom? In Chapter 9 we likewise explore to what extent teachers take account of their pupils' familiarity and contacts with the foreign culture. Do they mainly address topics with respect to which they believe their pupils are not familiar? Do they prefer topics of which they think they will help their pupils to find their way around when they travel to the foreign country as tourists, or when they take part in an exchange project? Or do they mainly address topics with which they consider their pupils somewhat familiar, and with respect to which they assume their pupils will want to find out more? For now, we want to conclude that teachers on the whole do not offer a representative picture of the foreign society, touching more or less extensively upon a limited number of cultural topics only.

School Trips and Exchanges: Preparatory and Follow-Up Work in the Foreign Language Classroom

Finally, we look at the amount of time teachers spend on preparing and following-up on school trips and international exchange projects in their classrooms. By school trips we mean short trips to the foreign country, which may last one day or longer. Exchange programmes involve a longer stay in the foreign country and additionally, involve receiving the inhabitants from the other country in one's own country. We assumed that teachers who attach importance to the promotion of intercultural competence in their learners would spend class time on preparatory or follow-up work.

School trips

Of all teachers, 50.33% say their school organises school trips to foreign countries, but percentages differ substantially between countries,[3] with 94% of Belgian teachers but a mere 20.5% of Greek teachers indicating they do so. Of the teachers who indicate their school organises school trips, a great majority of all teachers (65.92%) – and in Bulgaria and Spain even more than 80% – say they do not consider it part of their teaching role to prepare a school trip during foreign language classes. Similar proportions say they do not consider it part of their teaching role to follow-up on a school trip during foreign language classes, either. Only in Belgium did more than half of the teachers answer both questions positively.

As regards the amount of time spent on preparatory or follow-up work where it exists, the number of hours varies between several hours just before the trip and a number of weeks over the whole year, on the understanding that with 'week' teachers mean 'all the teaching periods available for foreign language teaching during one week'. Teachers appear to do four kinds of things. They provide information about the places that will be visited, prepare the programme of the trip with their pupils as well as the assignments which pupils have to complete while in the foreign country, or do some language work in preparation for the trip. They may select reading materials, slides or videos. The pupils themselves may collect information, write letters to tourist offices, read travel guides or brochures, do Internet searches, and present the results of their group work to the class in the foreign language (e.g. information on the history and the cultural heritage of the places they are going to visit, or regarding the map of the city, the food they can buy, the currency, the transportation, etc.). Sometimes pupils organise the trip themselves, make the reservations, and decide on the itinerary. Travelling and accommodation arrangements are discussed in class (Mexico, Greece). Pupils may also practise particular dialogues that will help them to find their way around or buy something while they are in the foreign country.

Teachers may devote several teaching periods to follow-up activities. The kinds of activities practised include evaluating the trip, looking at the photographs taken during the trip and dealing with the assignments which pupils had to complete during the trip. Pupils are asked to report on their general impressions, cultural differences, or whether they experienced what they had expected to experience. Some teachers ask their pupils to fill in a questionnaire and provide suggestions for future trips. Evaluation sometimes takes the form of a writing task or even a test. Pupils may also be asked to prepare and publish the results of a project.

Exchange projects

Of all teachers, 45.92% says their school takes part in exchange projects. Of these teachers, about two-thirds do not consider it part of their teaching job to prepare such a project in the foreign language classroom, but in Greece, slightly more than half of the teachers do. Teachers' answers about follow-up work yield a similar picture. This time, more than half of the Greek, but also the Swedish and Polish teachers, do consider it their job to follow-up on exchange projects.

The amount of time spent on preparing or following-up on exchange projects as well as the kinds of teaching activities mirror the situation for school trips, though cooperative work, mutual contacts and intercultural skills receive greater attention now. Students are invited to discuss cultural differences, culturally determined expectations or mutual stereotypes.

The overall impression gained is that teachers focus more on preparing the students to survive in a foreign country as tourists rather than observe and reflect as ethnographers, though that element is present in some teachers' comments regarding exchange projects. This again suggests that teachers teach culture mainly in a traditional rather than an interultural vein.

The unfortunate finding that teachers do not generally consider it part of their teaching role to prepare or follow-up on school trips or international exchange projects deserves some comment. The most likely reason for this is probably lack of time. We have already pointed out that the main reason which teachers mention for not getting round to culture teaching more often is lack of time, due to an overloaded curriculum and a limited number of teaching periods. It should not surprise therefore that they have no time available for preparatory or follow-up work in connection with school trips or exchange projects, unless they find ways to integrate language-and-culture teaching in such work. In Chapter 9 we look at the extent to which teachers believe school trips and exchange projects have a positive effect on pupils' perceptions and attitudes towards foreign countries, cultures and peoples. If teachers think school trips and exchange projects have a positive effect anyhow, they may think it superfluous to actually prepare pupils for such trips, or to follow-up on them. It may also be the case that teachers believe intercultural competence is the responsibility of all subjects, not just foreign language teaching, and therefore do not consider it their role to try and promote the acquisition of intercultural competence in their learners when they take part in school trips or exchange projects. We will comment further on this issue when we discuss the conditions under which teachers would be willing to interculturalise foreign language education. For now, we will continue to focus on teaching practice. The next topic we explore is teachers' perceptions of the quality of the intercultural dimension of their language textbooks and other teaching materials.

Notes

1. Since the results of the Bonferroni-multiple comparisons test (Appendix 2) reveal that the different country samples are more similar than different with respect to the frequency with which particular culture teaching activities are practised, we first present the results obtained for the whole sample.
2. The results of the Bonferroni multiple comparisons test (Appendix 2) reveal that with respect to the extent to which teachers say they touch upon the different cultural topics offered to them the different country samples are more similar than different. Because of this high degree of similarity, we first present the findings for the whole group of teachers.
3. The Bonferroni multiple comparisons test results (Appendix 2) reveal that the country samples differ significantly with respect to the percentage of teachers who indicated their school organises school trips.

Chapter 6

Culture in Foreign Language Teaching Materials

LEAH DAVCHEVA and LIES SERCU

More than anything else, textbooks continue to constitute the guiding principle of many foreign language courses throughout the world. Certainly at the beginners' level textbooks provide guidance with respect to grammatical and lexical progression. They translate the objectives specified in the curricula into structured units, offering data materials, task sheets, reference, practice and sometimes also test materials. To a large extent textbooks determine the selection of texts, the choice of classroom work forms and audio-visual materials.

Despite their convenience, textbooks have often been criticised for being too rigid, not being able to cater for the needs of all pupils, not being good at presenting multiple sides of any issue or at addressing timely and topical issues, imposing particular teaching styles onto teachers and learning styles onto learners, allowing insufficient space for teacher or learner creativity, presenting a highly fragmented picture of the foreign culture and stereotypical tourist views on the target people. Other criticisms are typically levelled at the unmotivating selection of texts, the number and types of exercises on offer, the degree of variation in text types and exercise types, the overall visual presentation (Sercu, 2000b).

Yet, textbooks continue to have a presence in foreign language classrooms. In their article 'What Textbooks Can – and Cannot – Do' Christenbury and Kelly (1994) discuss other reasons, apart from linguistic progression, which teachers may have to use textbooks in their classes, with time, money, convenience, reassurance and school's desire to control teachers being the major reasons addressed.

Whereas some teachers pride themselves on rarely using textbooks and, if so, only as a resource for developing their own innovative plans, and some others may be found who insecurely clutch to the text and faithfully follow its sequence, questions and testing programmes, probably the majority of teachers use textbooks, supplementing them with materials of their own choice, adapted to their particular teaching circumstances and learning groups.

In this chapter, we examine and compare the views and practices of foreign language teachers with regard to the cultural dimension of the teaching materials they use in class. Given the integral part that textbooks and learning materials play in the process of foreign language education it is essential that we understand how teachers perceive the potential of textbooks and teaching materials for promoting intercultural learning. We aim to shed light on the potential of textbooks as pedagogic tools in the hands of the teachers when they are involved in teaching towards intercultural competence. Via collecting information on how widely spread the use of textbooks is, finding out which textbooks tend to be most often used across the countries investigated, looking at the criteria teachers apply when they have the freedom of choice and, very importantly, investigating how teachers evaluate and interact with the cultural contents of the materials available, we tried to find out whether and to what extent teachers in the different countries appear to differ in their textbook using practices, and whether and to what extent teachers consider the quality of the cultural dimension of textbooks when deciding on which textbook to adopt.

Use of Textbooks

Our data show that the large majority of teachers from all the responding countries do use textbooks in their teaching (see Table 6.1). None of the respondents from Spain and Bulgaria indicate that they do not use textbooks. Two percent of Greek teachers and 4% of Polish teachers say they do not use textbooks. Slightly more teachers in Belgium (8%) and Sweden (15%) use exclusively other materials than textbooks. The highest percentage of teachers who do not use textbooks at all is in Mexico – 24%. Teachers either use one textbook or materials from different textbooks. Of the respondents from Greece, 84.62% indicate that they mainly use one textbook. This proportion is higher than in the other countries, where larger proportions use different textbooks. The lowest percentages of teachers who use only one textbook come from Bulgaria – 36.67% and Mexico – 33.33%.

Teachers also tend to use additional materials like audio and video tapes; media materials – newspapers, magazines, advertisements; the

Table 6.1 Teachers' use of textbooks and other teaching materials

	BEL	*SWE*	*POL*	*MEX*	*GRE*	*SPA*	*BUL*	*Mean*
I don't use textbooks. I use other materials	8.05%	14.75%	4.08%	24.44%	2.56%	0.00%	0.00%	7.70%
I do use textbooks. I use materials from different textbooks	33.56%	40.98%	55.10%	42.22%	12.82%	57.14%	63.33%	43.59%
I do use textbooks. I use mainly one book per class	58.39%	44.26%	40.82%	33.33%	84.62%	42.86%	36.67%	48.71%

Internet; song lyrics; graded readers; tourist brochures, leaflets and maps; photographs and paintings. In a later section, we comment on the reasons teachers give for using additional materials.

Titles of Books and Place of Origin

The results presented above leave no doubt that teachers across the countries investigated use textbooks extensively. It is therefore important to know what books teachers use, where they come from and who publishes them. When it would appear that teachers in different countries use the same textbooks, we could say that pupils in Europe and Mexico are presented with the same view on the foreign culture. Investigating whether teachers use textbooks written by local authors is also relevant. When teachers of, say, English prefer to work with textbooks produced by UK or US authors, this implies that they present their pupils with an image of the foreign culture as natives of these countries see it. It may also imply that teachers are influenced by and apply the approaches to the teaching of culture adopted by UK or US writing teams. When teachers use books produced by local authors this implies that pupils may view the foreign culture through the eyes of non-natives of the countries, cultures and people associated with the foreign language they are learning.

Thus, we asked teachers to list the title(s) of the textbook(s) they use and the country where each book is published. The results obtained in terms of titles and places of origin produce a picture which is quite varied. It varies from country to country and it also varies depending on the language taught. The information is most ample with regard to teachers of English, and not at all sufficient regarding other foreign languages.

Teachers of English

Teachers of English from nearly all countries (Sweden makes an exception) use both locally produced books and books produced in the United Kingdom. Less often teachers make use of textbooks produced in the United States. It is only in Sweden that teachers exclusively use textbooks published in Sweden. While in Spain and Poland most of the English textbooks are published in the UK, in Bulgaria the main course book is locally written and published. UK produced books are used as additional material. In Mexico the books used are produced both in the UK and in the US.

With respect to textbooks that are being used by more than one country the data reveal the following: *Headway* (OUP, UK) (Soars & Soars, 1997) is used in Belgium, Bulgaria, Mexico and Poland; *Blueprint* (Longman, UK) (Abbs & Freebairn, 1989) in Belgium, Bulgaria, Greece and Poland; *Hotline* (OUP, UK) (Hutchinson, 1992) in Belgium, Bulgaria and Greece; *Streetwise* (OUP, UK) (Nolasco, 1992) in Bulgaria and Greece; *Reward* (Longman, UK) (Greenall, 1995), *Snapshot* (Longman, UK) (Abbs *et al.*, 2000) and *Grammarway* (Express Publishing, UK) (Evans & Dooley, 1994) in Bulgaria, Greece and Poland; *Look Ahead* (Longman, UK) (Hopkins *et al.*, 1995) in Belgium and Greece; *Enterprise* (Express Publishing, UK) (Evans & Dooley, 2000) in Greece and Poland; *Grapevine* (OUP, UK) (Viney & Viney, 1992) in Belgium, Mexico and Poland; and *Matters* (Longman, UK) (Bell & Gower, 1995) in Belgium and Poland.

Teachers of German, French and Spanish

Teachers of German in Sweden, Belgium and Poland use textbooks published locally. Both Flemish and Swedish teachers of French mostly use locally published textbooks. Belgian teachers of Spanish predominantly use textbooks published in Spain while Swedish teachers use textbooks produced in their own country.

These factual data confirm the supposition that the use of textbooks in school education is massive. They also start shaping a picture of the types of textbooks used in the countries which took part in the survey. In addition, these answers give us a sense of the culture teaching agendas and orientaions each of the countries follows. The results also allow us to see whether there are textbooks for teaching English that are being used in Europe and beyond, thus revealing a picture of learners being presented with similar information and approaches to cultural learning. We shall now turn to the presentation of data which refers to the possibility for teachers to choose textbooks and the approaches they adopt when making their choice. In particular, we will explore whether teaching for intercultural competence ranks high on the perceptual and practical agenda of teachers.

Choice of Textbooks and the Criteria Teachers Apply

Possibility of choice

The results in Table 6.2 indicate that teachers in most countries can indeed choose their own textbooks. Bulgaria is the only country where only 53% of the respondents say that teachers can make their own choice of textbooks. For the rest of the countries the percentage is above 85%. We can trace a certain degree of dependence here between this result and the highest percentage of teachers from Bulgaria who tend to use materials from different textbooks, thus making up for the relative lack of freedom when choosing the main textbook. In Greece, teachers can indeed choose their own books but they can only select from a list provided by the Greek Ministry of Education.

Table 6.2 Textbook selection: Freedom of choice

	SPA	*POL*	*GRE*	*BEL*	*MEX*	*SWE*	*BUL*	*Mean*
No	2.86%	6.12%	7.89%	10.49%	13.51%	14.55%	46.67%	14.58%
Yes	97.14%	93.88%	92.11%	89.51%	86.49%	85.45%	53.33%	85.42%

Selection criteria

We also asked about the criteria teachers observe when selecting a textbook. From a list of 11, the respondents were asked to tick the six textbook characteristics which appear most important to them and may affect their choice in favour of a particular textbook. The criteria were: (1) the fact that additional materials come with the book (workbook, listening materials, tests, video, etc); (2) the layout; (3) the price; (4) the quality of the teacher's manual; (5) the degree to which the textbook meets the curricular requirements; (6) the degree to which the book is attuned to the level and the age of my pupils; (7) the pace of the book, the speed with which the book progresses; (8) the amount of cultural information the book offers; (9) the degree to which the book can motivate my pupils; (10) the textbook author's nationality; (11) the degree of matching between the amount of materials offered and the number of teaching periods assigned to my subject.

We found that selection criteria vary across countries but not considerably. There is a fair degree of similarity with regard to the five most important criteria for the choice of textbooks.[1] These criteria are (1) the degree to which the book is attuned to the level and age of the pupils; (2) the degree to which the book can motivate the pupils; (3) the fact that additional materials come with the book; (4) the degree to which the textbook meets the curricular requirements; (5) the amount of cultural information the book offers.

Last in the group of the five most important criteria is the amount of cultural information that the book offers. The only country which deviates from the mean result here is Bulgaria. For the Bulgarian teachers the amount of cultural information in the book ranks third, only preceded by the degree to which the book suits the age and the level of the pupils, and the availability of additional materials in the textbook pack. There is some variation among countries here: teachers from Sweden rank this criterion fourth, from Belgium, Poland and Mexico fifth, from Spain and Greece sixth.

The rest of the suggested characteristics – the price, the pace of the book and the speed with which it progresses, the degree of matching between the amount of materials offered and the number of teaching periods assigned to the study of the foreign language, the layout, the quality of the teacher's manual and the nationality of the textbook author – all these rate consistently lower. A teacher of German from Belgium makes a reference to the fact that the book has to be written by Dutch speaking authors as Dutch and German are similar languages and the books can progress at a speedier pace; books written for the international market progress too slowly.

When asked, in an open question, to indicate any additional criteria they apply when deciding on whether or not to use a particular book, teachers either elaborate on the categories suggested in the first part of the question or mention other criteria. Both types of answers relate to the contents of the textbooks, the methodology they employ and the acceptability of the books by different stakeholders. *Content-wise,* teachers prefer textbooks which deal with environmental issues (Greece), international and cross-cultural themes and expressions (Poland, Mexico), moral issues (Greece), the contemporary way of life (Bulgaria) and a variety of topics in general (Belgium). Swedish teachers find it important that textbooks offer a good coverage of the English speaking countries and different periods of history. The textbook characters should be true to life (Poland, Mexico,

Greece), speaking with different accents and type of pronunciation (Bulgaria). Good textbooks should contain samples from novels, poems, authentic press articles (Belgium), information about art (Poland) and should provide encyclopaedic knowledge and terminology (Greece). As regards *methodology,* teachers approve of books which are well structured and systematic (Belgium) and offer good and balanced skills presentation and development (Spain, Poland, Bulgaria, Greece, Belgium). Teachers from Poland, Mexico and Greece express their preference for adaptable exercises which promote reasoning. Problem solving activities at reasonable levels of difficulty are also valued (Poland, Mexico). Teachers from Belgium explicitly disapprove of approaches which are childish and predictable. The list also includes enough and well-balanced vocabulary (Belgium, Greece); fun and games (Belgium), coherence between reading, listening and video texts on the one hand and theory on the other (Spain), attractive visual presentation and layout (Poland, Mexico, Bulgaria); and a good proportion of authentic texts (Sweden) which should not be too long (Belgium). Communication oriented activities (Bulgaria) and activities for which the pupils need to use the internet (Belgium) are also mentioned as positive features. Greek teachers would like textbooks to make reference to Greece and to take account of local educational requirements. A teacher from Belgium points out that s/he prefers textbook series that offer a volume for each level. This allows teachers to build on what the pupils have acquired during the previous year. Finally, teachers from Mexico and Bulgaria state that they would go for textbooks which the majority of their colleagues use, thus expressing a concern that the textbooks they use be *acceptable to different kinds of stakeholders.* In Poland it is important that the Ministry of Education and the exam boards approve of the book. Less often teachers mention the availability of the textbooks on the market as a criterion they consider (Mexico, Poland, Bulgaria).

Teachers' Satisfaction with the Cultural Materials in the Textbooks they Use

In this section we explore to what extent teachers are satisfied with the cultural materials in textbooks. A second, related area is concerned with the textbook characteristics which make teachers positively or negatively disposed to the books they use. We assume that when teachers appreciate the cultural contents of textbooks, this will influence them favourably and motivate them to adopt the approach employed by the books, and conversely, if teachers disapprove of what they find in the teaching materials available, they will develop strategies which they perceive to be more in tune with their understanding of culture teaching.

Degree of satisfaction

The first set of results, presented in Table 6.3 below, reveals that most teachers are satisfied at least to a certain extent with the cultural materials in their textbooks. The variation between countries is not significant. While the mean score for complete satisfaction is not very high, 16.42%, the mean for a positive degree of satisfaction is quite higher up – 80.18% (63.76% for 'yes, up to a certain extent' + 16.42% for 'yes, very much so'). The two countries where teachers state they are very satisfied with the cultural contents of textbooks are Sweden (20.37%) and Bulgaria (20.00%). This result is not consistent with the finding that these exactly are the two countries where the percentage of teachers who use additional materials is highest – 96.67% for Bulgaria and 96.30% for Sweden.

About 20% of the teachers say they are not satisfied with the cultural contents of their textbooks. The countries with the strongest negative orientation regarding the cultural contents of textbooks are Spain (23.53%) and Belgium (22.54%). This result is consistent with the inclination of the teachers from these two countries to use additional materials. The proportion of teachers in these countries who indicate they use additional materials is high: for Spain the percentage is 91.18% and for Belgium 94.37%.

Table 6.3 Teachers' degree of satisfaction with the cultural contents of the foreign language textbooks they use

	BEL	*BUL*	*GRE*	*MEX*	*POL*	*SPA*	*SWE*	*Mean*
No, not at all	4.23%	3.33%	0.00%	0.00%	0.00%	5.88%	3.70%	2.45%
No, not really	18.31%	16.67%	17.95%	15.79%	20.41%	17.65%	14.81%	17.37%
Yes, up to a certain extent	62.68%	60.00%	64.10%	68.42%	65.31%	64.71%	61.11%	63.76%
Yes, very much so	14.79%	20.00%	17.95%	15.79%	14.29%	11.76%	20.37%	16.42%

Reasons for positive or negative orientation

The overriding tendency seems to be that of satisfaction, though a fair amount of dissatisfaction is also noticeable. Generally teachers feel more inclined to elaborate on their dissatisfaction with the cultural contents of textbooks and to offer criticism. In this section we explore what features make teachers express favourable opinions on the textbooks they use. In the next section we will explore what makes teachers feel negatively disposed towards them. Some of the opinions voiced in the second section mirror ideas voiced in this section. The absence of a certain feature may be criticised, its presence valued.

For the sake of clarity of presentation, we have classified the positive features teachers mention spontaneously in answer to an open question in several categories, namely amount of cultural information provided, type of cultural information selected, presentation of information, and approaches to the teaching of culture. The negative features pertain to the amount and short life of cultural information contained in the textbooks; the selection of cultural information and its thematisation; the presentation of cultural material; and, finally, the methodology of culture teaching.

Amount of cultural information

While some teachers think that the amount of cultural information provided by the textbooks they use is plenty (Spain, Belgium), others state that they could do with more (Sweden). Teachers from Belgium and Spain find it useful when the amount of cultural information matches the level of their pupils' language proficiency and can be dealt with within the limited number of teaching periods. They also appreciate the fact that each chapter of their textbook offers cultural information, usually at the end of the chapter. One teacher favourably reports that alongside every dialogue in the textbook s/he uses, there is a page containing information regarding various socio-cultural aspects of the foreign country(ies).

A certain number of respondents from Bulgaria express their approval of textbooks produced in the UK because they claim that UK made books are the ones which offer cultural information (e.g. *Headway* (OUP, UK) (Soars and Soars, 1997), *Blueprint* (Longman, UK) (Abbs & Freebairn, 1989), *English Together* (Longman, UK) (Webster & Worrall, 1997) while locally produced books do not. Teachers from Sweden also point to the fact that internationally produced textbooks in comparison with locally produced ones provide 'something extra'. They claim that international books give the teacher different perspectives and new starting points for discussion.

Type of cultural information selected for presentation

Respondents from all the participating countries claim to be satisfied with the textbooks they use when the cultural information presented matches the interests of their students. Materials about teenagers and their different life situations as well as travelling are regarded as having a potential to motivate and stimulate the learners.

Teachers value a selection of cultural materials that is up-to-date and deals with the diversity of life in the countries associated with the foreign language(s) (Sweden, Belgium, Mexico). Textbooks should also touch upon the countries which are traditionally less directly associated with the language taught, such as Jamaica, Zambia, Ireland or New Zealand for English (Sweden) or the Latino cultures for Spanish (Belgium). Teachers from Sweden, Bulgaria and Mexico find textbooks useful when they offer a choice of texts which present a variety of customs and traditions, aspects of history, geography, civics, religion and make reference to the cultural heritage of the country. Teachers appreciate it when the textbook presents people from every level in society, rather than the standard textbook population of stereotypical characters. Teachers also mention that textbooks should make an effort to alter students' stereotypical perceptions regarding the countries associated with the foreign language they teach (teachers of English and French from Belgium).

Presentation of cultural information and approaches to the teaching of culture

Teachers' comments on this issue are generally scarce. With respect to the way cultural information is presented they value textbooks which offer a humorous, colourful and attractive presentation (Belgium). A textbook is regarded positively when cultural background is presented both verbally and visually (Mexico) and the materials are pleasant to read (Belgium). Similarly teachers prefer textbooks which offer different types of materials, both fictional and factual (Bulgaria, Belgium).

In terms of the methodology of culture teaching, teachers approve of textbooks which present cultural information through dialogues and when cultural awareness is achieved through work on various projects (Greece). Teachers also approve of texts which are suitable for comparison between the foreign and the pupils' own culture and provide a good basis for further culture learning activities. The teachers from Poland mention the variety of tasks as a positive feature.

Insufficient amount and short life of cultural information

Not surprisingly, a major reason for dissatisfaction is the scarcity of cultural information that textbooks provide (Greece, Mexico, Belgium, Bulgaria). Teachers state they often need to supplement the book with additional materials, e.g. media texts, texts from the internet, video and audio materials, etc. They think that social and cultural topics could and should be treated in more detail. Commenting on the inadequacy of the cultural contents, teachers from Sweden and Bulgaria acknowledge the fact that culture cannot be taught from textbook materials exclusively and that no single book can cover everything needed. The role of textbooks is only to initiate the work. The rest must be looked for and found elsewhere.

Some of the Bulgarian respondents complain that books which are locally produced do not provide cultural information at all. A Belgian teacher, on the other hand, states that the book s/he uses contains too much information. According to this teacher a large number of pages provide cultural information, in black and white, and these appear to be too difficult for the students. S/he thinks that textbooks should not play the role of reference books, but should remain genuine foreign language courses.

Nearly all the teachers comment negatively on the fact that cultural information in textbooks becomes outdated quickly. As one teacher from Bulgaria puts it, 'textbooks wear off the minute they are published and other sources of information need to be found'. Bulgarian teachers also think that textbooks produced in Bulgaria, compared to those published in the UK, are dated.

Narrow selection of cultural information and themes

A considerable number of the responding teachers comment on the one-sidedness of the information selected and on the lack of representativeness (Belgium, Sweden, Poland). In the first place they claim that the selection of countries represented is fairly narrow. It often happens that textbooks of English focus on the UK only, rather than on the wider English-speaking world (Sweden, Belgium). Similarly but with attention to own culture, a teacher from Greece complains that the books they use in Greece have no references to Greece and Greek culture. A comment from Spain concerns the fact that textbooks fail to discuss the presence and reception of the foreign culture in Spanish culture. Secondly, the textbooks mainly tend to present tourist attractions, cities and urban culture rather than a variety of places (Belgium). And thirdly, as teachers from Sweden note, textbooks mostly deal with middle class culture at the expense of social diversity. They abound in 'specialised peculiarities' while important cultural themes and essential features can be found missing, e.g. beliefs, folklore, music, cultural stereotypes. Textbook situations do not deal with typicalities, but with topics of superficial and general interest only (Bulgaria, Spain, Sweden, Belgium).

Another source of dissatisfaction is that textbooks restrict their cultural contents to factual information about the history and geography of specific countries (Sweden). And yet, for some of the teachers from Mexico, historical background information is largely absent from textbooks, as is information about a country's cultural heritage, values and beliefs. Teachers sometimes note the predominantly international character of course books and indicate that they disapprove of the topics chosen (Belgium, Mexico).

Some of the teachers also find that sometimes textbooks are too heavily tied to the tastes of young people. However, other teachers (Sweden, Belgium, Poland) complain that the cultural contents are boring and positioned too far from the students' daily lives and interests.

A number of teachers, e.g. from Belgium and Bulgaria, complain that literary texts are increasingly omitted from textbooks and replaced by what one teacher from Belgium refers to as 'hamburgarised nonsense'. A teacher from Poland voices the same complaint by noting that the textbooks focus too much on subjects connected with the media and mass culture or as s/he calls it 'plastic culture'. Rather than devote more time and space to 'the true aspects of culture' – understood as art, music, films, literature, and history – books put all the emphasis on daily life, food and drink. When literary texts do appear in textbooks, they are often abbreviated or simplified. This complaint links in with the high degree of the respondents' familiarity with the literary aspect of the foreign cultures they teach and is an example of how the textbooks in use fall out of harmony with teachers' competences.

Lastly, teachers complain about the lack of authentic materials. They say that certain types of texts are completely missing from textbooks, e.g. authentic dialogue (Greece).

Inadequate presentation of material

Respondents disapprove of the fact that the cultural content of textbooks is often presented in a way which appears superficial, shallow, chaotic and simplified and in some cases impersonal or neutral (Poland, Sweden, Bulgaria, Spain). It often gives the impression of being artificially constructed, thus failing to motivate the students to relate the culture presented to reality. This is true especially when youth culture finds its way onto the pages of a textbook (Belgium).

Some of the teachers state that textbooks offer stereotypical representations of cultures. By avoiding authentic, 'true to life' representation they reinforce stereotypes (Spain). It is often the case that problematic areas, e.g. immigration problems in France, are not presented (Sweden).

Several teachers from Bulgaria comment that the cultural issues contained in the textbooks they use are not stated in a straightforward manner and they have to be 'specially dug up'. According to another Bulgarian teacher, texts are not well organised and systematised, unconnected and chosen at random. As a result students cannot form consistent ideas about specific cultural traits and norms of behaviour. They fail to develop a more complex perception of certain cultural trends.

Faulty approaches to culture teaching

The fourth major reason for dissatisfaction is that the teachers perceive methodology of culture teaching as missing from the textbooks altogether. They are information based and do not provide enough activities or variety of tasks (Spain, Bulgaria, Belgium). Individual teachers from Belgium point out that they would prefer a less boring approach to culture teaching while teachers from Spain would like to see a 'deeper treatment' of culture, one that facilitates reflection.

Teachers from Belgium point out that culture files are often set apart from the rest of the lessons; all that pupils have to do is read the information and at best answer some comprehension questions. It would be better if language and culture could be dealt with in an integrated, systematic manner and if language and culture learning could be interwoven. Another teacher from Belgium also suggests that culture should be dealt with in a contrastive way.

Yet another criticism concerns the texts on which culture teaching is based. The cultural information contained in them remains largely implicit. Teachers would prefer an approach where pupils process the information in an autonomous manner (Belgium). There is no progress and no building onto previously acquired knowledge (Belgium, Bulgaria). Texts deal with but do not really develop cultural learning and if a teacher wants to go into the full depth of issues and develop understanding s/he needs to look for additional materials. Teachers are especially negative about how literary texts are used. These are included only because they can be linked to the topic which is being dealt with and not for their intrinsic literary worth (Belgium). Tasks are set which do not aim to foreground the literary qualities of the text.

Teachers find it wrong when textbook authors readily assume previous cultural knowledge on the part of the students, e.g. a French textbook in Belgium, written by French authors. The burden of explaining and filling in the gaps falls on the teacher.

From the presentation of the findings above it can be concluded that the teachers who provided an answer to the open question inquiring into the reasons for their satisfaction or dissatisfaction with their textbooks adopt a fairly critical attitude to the textbooks they use. Although the specific reasons for dissatisfaction may differ slightly from country to country, teachers generally share the inclination to widen the range of teaching materials and culture learning tasks for the classroom. We will now proceed with the presentation of data regarding the reasons that teachers give for using additional materials. This will enable us to gain yet another insight into the teachers' understanding of what it means to teach for intercultural competence and how in practice they overcome the inadequacies of the textbooks.

Reasons for Using Additional Materials

As can be seen from Table 6.4 below, the survey established that nearly all the respondents from all the participating countries use additional materials (mean score 91.66%). The countries with the highest mean score of teachers using additional materials are Bulgaria (96.67%) and Sweden (96.30%) and those with the lowest Poland (81.63%) and Greece (87.18%).

In the case of Bulgaria the widespread use of additional materials can perhaps be attributed to the relatively limited freedom teachers have in selecting the textbooks for their classrooms (53.33% compared to 97.14% for Spain or 93.88% for Poland, etc.). In the case of Sweden the reason is possibly linked to the dominant use of locally published course books.

Some of the reasons that teachers give in an open question for using additional materials are related to the teaching of the foreign language, e.g. providing additional grammar practice and/or reinforcing the

Table 6.4 Teachers' use of additional materials

	BUL	*SWE*	*BEL*	*MEX*	*SPA*	*GRE*	*POL*	*Mean*
Yes	96.67%	96.30%	94.37%	94.29%	91.18%	87.18%	81.63%	91.66%
No	3.33%	3.70%	5.63%	5.71%	8.82%	12.82%	18.37%	8.34%

teaching of vocabulary. Other reasons refer to the development of the four skills, e.g. speaking practice, and to filling in the perceived gaps in the existing textbooks. A teacher from Belgium gives her/his own reason which is related to the ownership of materials and ideas. S/he finds that using materials that s/he has identified and found appropriate is much more acceptable.

However, the respondents also list reasons which are closely connected with the cultural dimension of teaching and learning. We will focus on those now. They are more or less the same for the seven countries and can be provisionally presented in four categories: bringing variety to lessons, increasing students' motivation, enabling students to learn with up-to-date materials, and working with authentic materials.

Variety

For the teachers from Belgium, Sweden and Poland variety is the main reason for using additional materials. They help break the monotony and boredom in the classroom thus making the class more dynamic and memorable. For the teachers from Mexico using additional materials means 'enriching their classes'. In addition to supplementing the textbook, additional materials provide more information, a broader and more diverse picture of the target country. As the teachers from Bulgaria note, additional materials also provide opportunities for more cultural activities, more practice and a variety of perspectives, comparison and contrast. As opposed to textbooks which often present the target culture stereotypically, additional materials offer a more varied and spiced up picture (Bulgaria). They enable the students to consider a variety of perspectives rather than reinforce the idea that knowledge comes from one source, be it the textbook or the teacher (Sweden, Bulgaria).

Motivation

Another reason for bringing in additional materials, closely linked to variety, is enhancing the motivation of the students. Teachers from Greece, Bulgaria, Mexico and Spain consider motivating students to be the main driving force for introducing additional materials into the classroom. Motivation is perceived as a complex construct and teachers break it down into components like creating expectations, giving students additional practice and enabling autonomous learning. Teachers find that extra practice with extra materials is necessary as there are cases when the students themselves ask for it and their interests stretch beyond the material covered in the textbook (Bulgaria, Mexico).

Another aspect of motivation, as understood by the teachers, is the effect culture teaching has on students and the way they are affected by the process. A teacher from Sweden says that 'culture cannot only be read, it has to be seen, heard and experienced'. It is good to surprise the students, to stir up their curiosity (Bulgaria). Additional texts are far more interesting and real, compared to those in the book and they provide the students with a dynamic starting point for reflection, discussions, drama work, writing or even painting (Sweden, Spain).

Updating

A third reason for using additional teaching resources is the desire on the part of the teachers to update the materials, thus compensating for the fast dating of the textbooks. Complaining that the texts in their textbooks are too old, a teacher from Sweden jokingly remarks that 'apartheid was not abolished in the South Africa text yet'. Additional materials allow teachers to be flexible and respond quickly to the latest information and news on hot issues, e.g. foot and mouth disease in the UK (Bulgaria). Putting the learners in touch with the latest news and novelties will enable them to relate the foreign culture to their own lives. Current events are more likely to initiate and stimulate good discussions (Sweden).

Authenticity and reality

Yet another reason for seeking additional materials concerns the teachers' desire to respond to their students' perceived need for authenticity (Greece). They feel closer to the target country when learning from authentic materials (Poland). The idea of reality and different facets of it is also strongly present in the teachers' responses (Bulgaria, Belgium, Sweden). They use expressions like 'real language', 'real people', 'real perspective' when listing the advantages of introducing additional materials in the classroom (Spain, Sweden, Belgium). Video- and audiotapes help the teachers visualise the cultural topics presented. These provide truly realistic examples of the foreign country, language and people in real situations (Mexico, Bulgaria, Belgium).

Conclusion

The significance of the textbook in foreign language education in all the countries is indisputable. Teachers who do not use textbooks at all are very much in the minority. Teachers, independent of their country of origin, were found to use textbooks extensively, thus confirming our expectation that textbooks present an important constituent of the teaching/learning process. We can therefore rightly assume that textbooks can significantly impact on the way culture is taught in the foreign language classroom. The reasons for this wide use can probably be found in the fact that textbooks are a means to reduce preparation time, and guarantee that the teacher can approach the teaching of the foreign language in a systematic way, teaching particular syntactic structures before others.

The variety of textbooks used is huge. Teachers teach with both locally published books and books published in the UK or the USA, thus offering their students a fairly diverse diet of culture teaching agendas. Expectations are that from the locally published course books learners get a starting point of cultural encounters which is closer to their own worldview and understandings, while from the UK/US published books they access an agenda which in terms of contents and presentation can be defined as international, and adopts a look at the target culture from the inside. Our data do not allow us to say that teachers have a clear preference for either locally or internationally produced textbooks. Some teachers point out that the topics addressed in internationally produced textbooks are not relevant to their pupils and that the books lack references to the pupils' own culture. Other teachers complain about the limited selection of topics in their locally produced textbooks. Of course, these opinions largely depend on the actual textbook(s) a teacher is using, and do not allow us to draw general conclusions.

As pointed out, teachers to a large extent teach by the textbook. Yet, our survey also obtained enough evidence to prove that teachers have ways and means to counterbalance excessive dependence on textbooks. Firstly, it was observed that teachers exercise a considerable amount of freedom in selecting the teaching materials for their classroom. Secondly, they unquestionably turn to additional teaching materials when textbooks do not meet their expectations. Thirdly, our survey findings also point to the conclusion that teachers adopt a strongly critical attitude to textbooks with regard to the cultural dimension of foreign language teaching.

At first glance it is difficult to draw a meaningful correlation between the teachers' willingness to resort to the use of additional materials and the stated satisfaction with the textbooks they have either chosen or have been asked to teach with. However, the two practices reflect the complex nature of the teaching and learning process. Seemingly incompatible, they usefully complement each other, thus on the one hand confirming the important role that textbooks play in foreign language education and on the other accounting for the drive and creativity that teachers have to explore new territories and sources of learning.

If we compare the features of textbooks which make teachers feel unhappy about them and the reason they point to for using additional materials it can be easily noted that use of additional materials aims to make up for the gaps and weaknesses that their textbooks present teachers with. Obviously the abundance and freshness of additional materials counterbalance the scarcity and short-life of the cultural information present in textbooks. The variety of perspectives and the motivational potential make up for the limited selection of themes, texts and cultural aspects. While teachers disapprove of the simplified and sometimes impersonal presentation of culture in textbooks they can turn to the 'real' and 'true-to-life' quality of outside materials.

We can therefore affirm that there is a conflict between what teachers want to achieve with regard to culture teaching and their textbook practices. On the one hand, teachers perceive textbooks as not enormously helpful in approaching the cultural dimension of teaching, and on the other they massively use them in their classrooms. Can we then, on the basis of what was found in the survey, conclude that textbooks fall short of the teachers' aspirations and present a potential barrier to the promoting of intercultural competence? Perhaps this is partially the case but the barrier does not seem impossible to lift as it became clearly evident that teachers do interrogate the worth of textbooks and supplement them extensively.

There also appears to be a conflict between teachers' actual teaching practice, as described in previous chapters in terms of the cultural topics they deal with most extensively and the culture teaching activities they practise most often, and the comments they make on their textbooks. The conflict is: although teachers see the limitations of their textbooks, in actual teaching practice they do not appear to make up for them. Teachers, for example, demand that textbooks present a representative picture of the different social groups in the foreign society, but do not usually touch upon the social composition of the foreign society in their teaching. Similarly, teachers complain about the narrow selection of cultural information and themes, but do not make up for that through dealing extensively with topics not included in the foreign language textbook, such as international relations, environmental issues, or values and beliefs.

A final example concerns teachers' complaints about what we have termed 'faulty approaches to culture teaching' in textbooks, but they do not appear to teach by a different approach. Yet, this could be done relatively easily, starting from the materials that are in the textbook but approaching them in more pupil-centred learner autonomy fostering ways. We may wonder why teachers complain but omit to choose a different route to culture teaching than that they condemn in textbooks. Is it because of lack of preparation time? Changing the culture teaching approach of a complete textbook indeed requires a good deal of effort and time and teachers who are willing and able to do so are thin on the ground. It may also be that the teachers who answered the open question inquiring into their reasons for a negative or positive appreciation of their textbook, are also the teachers who do practise less traditional culture teaching approaches in their classrooms, and go beyond the passing on of information. Our findings regarding teaching practice have shown that a minority of teachers indeed invite their pupils to reflect on the images of the foreign country presented in the textbook or in the media, or to independently explore particular aspects of the foreign culture. An implication of this is that the other teachers, namely those who employ traditional approaches to culture teaching and constitute the majority, may not perceive the weaknesses in the culture teaching approaches in their textbooks as easily as their more critical colleagues, or they may see other areas of their teaching which are in more urgent need for change and not get excited so easily about shortcomings concerning a textbook's culture teaching approach. Because not all teachers answered the open question on which part of this chapter is based, we cannot easily link the information regarding textbook opinions to culture teaching practices. Therefore, the above suggestions have to remain speculative.

Finally, we perceive a third conflict, namely that between the obvious importance teachers attach to the cultural dimension when asked to point out strengths and weaknesses of their textbooks' cultural dimension on the one hand and the fact that considerations regarding the cultural dimension of foreign language textbooks do not feature a central role in the teachers' minds when it comes to choosing a particular textbook. When looking at the selection criteria more closely though, it can be seen that the criteria ranked above the criterion 'quality of cultural dimension of textbook materials' can all be seen as also paying attention to the intercultural dimension, albeit very indirectly. The criterion which teachers considered most important is *the degree to which the textbook is attuned to the age and level of the pupils.* Though not obviously and readily linked with the cultural dimension of textbooks, the fact that a textbook is attuned to the age and the level of the pupils who use it is central to enhancing the textbooks' potential for promoting intercultural learning. When foreign language textbooks take into account the cognitive resources of the learners they are more likely to encourage active information processing and involvement with the learning process. If the textbook chosen falls below the affective and cognitive threshold level of the learners or stretches beyond their conceivable limits, it may fail to become an agent that influences the learning of culture.

The same holds true for the second criterion regarding *the degree to which the textbook can motivate the pupils.* When motivation is high, i.e. when pupils find the information presented novel and interesting and the learning tasks acceptably challenging, then they are more inclined to reconsider preconceptions and existing attitudes. This factor is specifically emphasised by the data obtained in Spain. *Rating the availability of additional materials in textbooks,* third, reflects the massive tendency across all countries investigated for teachers to seek to supplement the main course books with additional materials, that can make up for the lack of cultural information in the textbook. The additional materials often come in the form of video films, maps, slides, etc. on the foreign cultures and countries associated with the foreign language taught. The fourth criterion concerns *the degree to which the textbooks meet the curricular requirements* in the countries participating in the survey. These curricular requirements will concern the acquisition of the language in the first place, and to a lesser extent the acquisition of cultural knowledge and intercultural competence. When teachers say they want textbooks that abide by the curriculum, they also indirectly point towards the fact that they want textbooks that meet the curricular guidelines in the cultural dimension.

In the next chapter, we shift our attention to out-of-classroom work in the area of intercultural competence teaching, and investigate teachers' views regarding the effect which school trips and exchange projects may have on pupils' perceptions of the foreign cultures, countries and people associated with the foreign language they are learning.

Note

1. The Bonferroni multiple comparisons test results confirm this finding.

Chapter 7

Experiential Culture Learning Activities: School Trips and Exchange Projects

CHRYSSA LASKARIDOU and LIES SERCU

Teaching a foreign language differs from teaching a second language in that teaching takes place in a classroom which is geographically removed from a country in which people speak the language taught, either as their mother tongue or as an official language of their country. Though foreign language teachers make efforts to bring the foreign language to life through using authentic materials, documentaries, films and the like, the pupils may still experience the foreign society as distant and unfamiliar. What is more, outside the classroom pupils have next to no opportunity to use the foreign language they are learning in real communication.

To make up for this, curricular guidelines have long advised schools to organise trips to a foreign country in which the language the pupil is learning is (one of) the national language(s). More recently, European funding has made it possible for schools in Europe to take part in exchange projects. The purposes are diverse and many of them are not specific to language and culture teaching. Schools expect their pupils to become more independent persons, to gain confidence, to co-operate or to get to know each other in a different context. Nevertheless, offering pupils opportunities to use the foreign language they are learning and chance to broaden their horizons motivates the schools to take part in an exchange project.

In Byram (1989: 136–148), a model for language and culture teaching is presented which apart from a language learning, language awareness and culture learning component, also comprises a cultural experience component. Experiential learning in intercultural situations offers opportunities which ordinary classroom teaching cannot provide. Pupils can really experience the relationship between language and culture and engage in the foreign culture in a way they cannot when remaining physically inside the classroom. In most cases, experiential learning activities are viewed as taking place abroad, in the foreign country. This is not to say that they cannot be organised in the pupils' home country. It is just that chances that experiential learning takes place are potentially larger in the foreign environment. The way in which school trips and exchange projects are conceived, however, determines to a large extent how effective in terms of intercultural competence acquisition these activities can be. School trips tend to be short in duration and very often place the pupils in the role of tourists. Their potential for promoting intercultural skills and an intercultural identity may be limited (but need not be, as shown in Snow & Byram, 1997). That offered by exchange projects, which are, generally speaking, longer in duration and involve home stays and real contacts with peers and other insiders of the foreign culture is potentially larger, on the condition that pupils have received adequate preparation.

Exchange projects tend to involve teachers of other subjects as well as foreign languages teachers. However, school trips remain the responsibility of foreign language teachers, sometimes in co-operation with history, geography or arts teachers. In this chapter we explore what reasons foreign language teachers see for organising school trips or taking part in exchange projects. Do they situate these initiatives in an intercultural perspective, or do they focus above all on linguistic or general educational reasons? Do they distinguish between school trips and exchange projects as far as their potential for the promotion of intercultural competence in pupils is concerned? Do they believe that these kinds of direct contacts can raise pupils' cultural awareness and reduce stereotypes? Or are they of the opinion that pupils come back with more stereotypical rather than more nuanced views of the foreign people and culture? Before inquiring into all this, we present some factual data regarding the number of schools that organise school trips or take part in exchange projects and the preferred destinations. We focus on school trips first.

School Trips

Frequency and destinations

As Table 7.1 shows, the proportions of teachers who indicate their school organises school trips vary considerably between countries.[1]

Schools in Spain, Mexico and Greece appear to organise fewer school trips. Belgium stands out with an exceptionally high score (94.04%),

Table 7.1 Percentages of schools that organised school trips

	BEL	*POL*	*BUL*	*SWE*	*SPA*	*MEX*	*GRE*	*Mean*
Yes	94.04%	70.00%	53.33%	50.00%	37.14%	27.27%	20.51%	50.33%
No	5.96%	30.00%	46.67%	50.00%	62.86%	72.73%	79.49%	49.67%

which indicates that nearly all Flemish teachers work in schools which organise school trips abroad.

Reasons for organising school trips

We asked teachers to rank five possible reasons for organising school trips in decreasing order of importance (Table 7.2), and to name any additional reasons they see.

Teachers clearly consider the first four reasons more important than the last one.[2] All countries ranked *foster pupils' independence* last. We can also see that teachers deem linguistic reasons (*create an opportunity for pupils to practise their foreign language skills* and *enhance pupils motivation*

Table 7.2 Reasons for organising school trips

	BEL	*BUL*	*GRE*	*MEX*	*POL*	*SPA*	*SWE*	*Mean*
Foster pupils' independence	1.95	2.11	2.41	2.02	1.98	1.61	1.93	2.00
Increase pupils' familiarity with the foreign culture	3.09	3.24	2.84	2.68	2.48	3.24	3.20	2.97
Increase pupils' interest in the foreign culture	3.38	3.17	2.82	3.27	3.07	3.27	3.52	3.21
Enhance pupils' motivation to learn the foreign language	3.26	2.86	3.62	3.73	3.76	3.70	3.53	3.49
Create an opportunity for pupils to practise their foreign language skills	3.36	3.34	3.76	3.77	3.48	3.51	3.83	3.58

Scores ranging between 1.00 and 5.00.

to learn the foreign language) more important than cultural reasons (*increase pupils' interest in the foreign culture* and *increase pupils' familiarity with the foreign culture*), except in Belgium and Bulgaria where linguistic and cultural reasons are considered of more or less equal importance. This pattern, then, mirrors the pattern found with respect to teachers' perceptions of the objectives of foreign language education. Generally speaking, linguistic objectives are placed before cultural or general educational objectives.

Only a small percentage of teachers mention additional reasons, which makes it difficult to draw general conclusions. We have grouped them in three categories: cultural, linguistic and other reasons.

Cultural

New experiences, first hand experience helps to foster understanding of foreign country and culture; meet students from different countries; broaden horizons; learn more about themselves; challenge perceptions of their own values and cultures; become more open-minded; increase tolerance of other cultures and people, break down stereotypes; promote cultural awareness; inform others about own country; to learn a foreign language also means learning about its culture and people; direct contact with foreign culture, experience and deal with cultural diversity.

Linguistic

Practice of the foreign language; part of the curriculum; understand usefulness of what they learn.

Other

Fun; motivation; group spirit; tradition; establish friendships, make friends; foster pupils' independence.

The largest variety of answers can be found in the category 'cultural reasons'. Apart from general phrases, such as 'broaden one's horizons' or 'gain new experiences', teachers demonstrate an awareness of specific opportunities for learning intercultural competence which school trips offer, making reference to the possibility of meeting students from other countries, the chance to inform others about one's own country or learn more about one's own culture, or the expectation that tolerance towards other cultures will increase and stereotypes will be broken down. To our mind, it is more likely that these kinds of opportunities will arise in the course of an exchange project than on the occasion of a school trip. School trips are usually short and, including visits to a number of cultural heritage sites, tend to offer pupils a tourist view of the foreign culture rather than an insider view, based on direct contacts with peers or other inhabitants. Yet, our data suggest that teachers believe school trips have a role to play in the promotion of intercultural competence: on average 97% of the teachers believe school trips have a positive effect on pupils. By contrast, a small number of teachers report on the negative effects school trips may have, stating that students may have negative experiences which would reinforce negative perceptions; that school trips can only have a temporary effect and that short trips, especially, may increase prejudice.

Exchange Projects

Frequency and destinations

In general, slightly fewer teachers (45.92%) take part themselves in exchange projects compared to the number of teachers (50.33%) who indicate their school takes part in exchanges.[3]

As can be seen from Table 7.3, Bulgarian and Greek schools lag behind Polish, Swedish, Mexican, Belgian and Spanish schools as far as the frequency of participation in exchange projects is concerned.

Table 7.3 Percentages of schools that participate in exchange projects

	GRE	*BUL*	*SPA*	*BEL*	*MEX*	*SWE*	*POL*	*Mean*
No	74.36%	72.41%	54.29%	53.59%	47.73%	44.26%	31.91%	54.08%
Yes	25.64%	27.59%	45.71%	46.41%	52.27%	55.74%	68.09%	45.92%

Reasons

Table 7.4 shows how teachers ranked the five reasons we suggested for organising exchange projects suggested to them.

The order in which teachers ranked the given reasons is exactly the same as that obtained for school trips with only slight differences in mean scores.[4] The linguistic reasons are again considered more important than the cultural ones and *Fostering pupils' independence* is once more ranked last. However, in the case of Bulgaria, *Enhance pupils' motivation to learn the foreign language* is positioned fourth, after the cultural reasons.

The additional reasons mentioned for taking part in exchange projects to a large extent match those mentioned in connection with school trips.

Cultural

Broadens horizons; breaks down stereotypes; increases tolerance of other cultures and people; takes away prejudices; creates better understanding of differences resulting in changes in the perception of the foreign culture; exchange ideas and understand foreigners; pupils

Table 7.4 Reasons for taking part in exchange projects

	BEL	*BUL*	*GRE*	*MEX*	*POL*	*SPA*	*SWE*	*Mean*
Foster pupils' independence	1.95	2.00	2.55	1.91	1.93	1.53	1.86	1.96
Increase pupils' familiarity with the foreign culture	2.95	3.27	3.00	2.53	2.83	3.00	3.12	2.96
Increase pupils' interest in the foreign culture	3.39	3.54	2.82	3.12	2.98	3.15	3.45	3.21
Enhance pupils' motivation to learn the foreign language	3.07	2.88	3.32	3.74	3.54	3.76	3.71	3.43
Create an opportunity for pupils to practise their foreign language skills	3.74	3.42	4.00	3.95	3.56	3.85	4.02	3.79

feel closer to foreign language and native speakers; pupils work with peers from different cultural backgrounds; enhances interest in foreign culture; enhances awareness of own culture; learn about own culture; promote own culture; comparison with own culture leads to reflection of own values; pupils learn skills required to cope for when coming into contact with other cultures; help towards international understanding (Sweden); learn to think globally (Belgium); learn to think of themselves as European citizens (Belgium).

Linguistic

Practise foreign language skills; help understand more about language.

Other

Boost teachers' professional confidence and add to qualifications; School becomes more attractive; improve computer skills through e-mail; make friends.

Interestingly, in connection with exchange projects, teachers also make reference to 'European citizenship' and 'international understanding' as well as to the skills dimension of intercultural competence. This then suggests that teachers do indeed distinguish to a certain extent when considering the effect of exchanges on pupils. As was the case with school trips, large proportions of teachers (96.31% of the total for all countries) in each country believe exchange projects do have an effect on pupils. Whilst most teachers see positive effects, some Bulgarian teachers voiced reservations. Five teachers state that they do not believe the time and effort spent on the exchange project is worth the effort. They doubt that their pupils' language skills will improve and they question whether the students come back with fewer prejudices and real knowledge of the foreign culture. Two teachers fear that pupils' motivation to learn the foreign language may actually decrease as a result of negative experiences in the foreign country. Both a Flemish teacher and some Polish teachers who fear that small misunderstandings may reinforce stereotypes also express this concern.

Conclusion

In the previous chapter, we pointed out that teachers do not normally consider it part of their teaching duty to prepare pupils for school trips or exchange projects during classroom teaching. In this chapter, we have explored teachers' perceptions regarding two kinds of experiential learning activities, namely school trips and exchange projects, somewhat further. Our data reveal that only about half of the teachers questioned state their school organises school trips or takes part in exchange projects, that teachers see mainly linguistic reasons for these initiatives, but also demonstrate an awareness of the potential for intercultural learning inherent in direct contacts with the foreign culture and country. They see mainly positive effects on pupils, but some teachers also point towards the negative implications of such contacts: they reinforce stereotypes and decrease, rather than increase, pupils' motivation to learn the foreign language.

Some interesting differences between countries have become apparent with respect to the frequency of school trips and exchanges. Greek and Spanish schools tend to organise fewer trips or are less frequently involved in exchange projects than schools in other countries. In Bulgaria, about half the schools organise school trips, whereas only about a quarter are involved in exchange projects. In Belgium, almost all schools organise school trips, but less than half of the schools are involved in exchange projects. The fact that almost all Belgian schools appear to organise school trips is perhaps not surprising. Belgium is a small country. Travelling to neighbouring countries, such as France or Germany, is relatively inexpensive, and does not take much time. The high frequency of travel may also reflect the importance attached to foreign language learning in Belgian schools. Though other countries may also think it is of crucial importance that pupils travel to other countries while at school, financial reasons and the sometimes large distances that have to be covered may prevent schools from travelling to foreign countries more often. The fact that fewer schools are involved in exchange projects than in school trips may again be due to financial reasons. It may also be due to the fact that exchange projects are far more demanding in terms of preparation time. Some teachers, especially in Belgium and Bulgaria, indeed express doubts regarding exchange projects. They wonder whether it is all worth the effort. The case of Greece and Spain is interesting too. In an earlier chapter, we pointed out that teachers in these countries perceive their pupils as less motivated to learn the foreign language than in other countries. We wonder whether we can now link this finding to the fact that Greek and Spanish pupils take part in school trips and exchanges less frequently than their peers in other countries. Is it because they are less motivated that no school trips are organised for them? Or is their lack of motivation due to the fact that they do not have the prospect of actually going to the foreign country and using the language they are learning?

As regards teachers' reasons for organising trips and exchanges, they seem to be related primarily, but not exclusively, to language learning. Teachers also see general educational reasons and reasons related to intercultural learning. This pattern confirms the pattern we found earlier with respect to the way in which teachers perceive the objectives of foreign language education. We found a clear preference for linguistic objectives in all countries and a stronger emphasis on (language) learning skills than on culture learning. The fact that in answer to an open question, teachers provided a variety of culture learning reasons for organising school trips and exchanges does not mean that they attach great importance to them. General educational reasons, such as 'enhance the group spirit' or 'put pupils in a situation where they are on their own and have to get by on their own' appear to be at least as important as cultural reasons.

It was also interesting to find out that teachers, to a certain extent at least, distinguish between school trips and exchange projects when commenting on their potential for intercultural learning. Teachers believe exchange projects have a role to play in the development of European citizenship and international or even global understanding. When the European Union started to subsidize exchanges between schools, it was certainly with a view towards the development of a European citizenship. The European Union wants to promote a sense of belonging in the different European member states, much like in the United States of America, where citizens feel they are American citizens, and not just citizens of Missouri or California. Through their comments, some teachers at least indicate that they support this idea of European citizenship and want to contribute to its realisation.

Finally, as far as teachers' views regarding the effect of school trips and exchange projects on pupils' perceptions and attitudes towards foreign cultures, countries and people are concerned, it appears that teachers mainly believe such experiential activities have a positive effect, though some remarks regarding the negative effect and the reinforcement of stereotypes could also be found, both in connection with school trips and exchange projects. Though the negative opinions were few in number, they should not be disregarded, as they reflect possible dangers involved in school trips and exchange projects. We have already pointed out that only a minority of the teachers considers it part of their teaching role to prepare or follow-up on school trips and exchange projects. The fact that pupils embark on such contacts without adequate preparation can explain the negative effects teachers see. A more adequate preparation of pupils and a more thorough debriefing after having come home may contribute to diminishing the danger that pupils adhere to or reinforce existing stereotypes. Even when preparing pupils adequately, it is doubtful whether a one-time exchange project can help pupils shift their viewpoints to such an extent that they can look upon the foreign culture and peoples as insider inhabitants rather than outsider visitors. In that sense, we believe teachers are right in being sceptical about overambitious claims regarding the potential for intercultural learning inherent in exchanges. Modest expectations will prevent teachers from discarding exchanges and school trips from the school curriculum altogether.

From Chapter 5, we know that the majority of teachers do not devote teaching time to preparing or following-up on school trips or exchange projects and when they do, this work is directly related to the trip or the project. From Chapter 2, we know that only a very slight minority of teachers integrate language teaching and culture teaching 100% of teaching time and even then we are not sure whether this 100% integration results from an approach to teaching which promotes intercultural communicative competence. We would have liked to find more teachers who stated that an important part of their language course, or even their whole course, is directed towards preparing their learners for intercultural contact situations and experiential learning activities. The general impression we have gained now is that teachers isolate school trips or exchange projects from the rest of their teaching, and that little positive backwash effect on day-to-day teaching originates from the fact that a school undertakes experiential activities of the kinds considered in this chapter. Such a backwash effect could for example result in a teaching programme that systematically devotes attention to the facets of the foreign culture that may be particularly relevant in intercultural contact situations or to culture learning skills. These facets include for example cultural differences in body language or speaking conventions (taking turns, pausing, taboo subjects), or differences in the associations attached to daily life topics (e.g. breakfast; be on time; appropriate present; appropriate expression of respect; appropriate behaviour in public; privacy). We fear some teachers may take the following stance: 'there is a school trip in May. Pupils can only truly learn something about cultural differences when they travel abroad. Therefore, I will not devote teaching time to teaching culture or intercultural competence. Intercultural skills cannot be acquired at school anyway'. In the next chapter, we explore teachers' opinions regarding different facets of intercultural competence teaching. One of these facets is the extent to which teachers are convinced that intercultural skills can be acquired at school, another that the teaching of intercultural competence should be undertaken in a cross-curricular mode. If we were to find that the majority of teachers in the different countries indeed hold these convictions, this would mean the profession is a long way away from putting intercultural competence teaching into practice.

Notes

1. The Bonferroni multiple comparisons test results (Appendix 2) confirm that some countries differ significantly from others with respect to the organisation of school trips.
2. The Bonferroni multiple comparisons test results (Appendix 2) indicate that the different country samples can be considered similar in this respect.
3. The Bonferroni multiple comparisons test results (Appendix 2) indicate that the results with respect to the seven participating countries are more similar that different.
4. The Bonferroni multiple comparisons test results, again, confirm that the different country samples do not differ significantly in the way in which teachers perceive reasons for organising school trips.

Chapter 8

Opinions Regarding Different Facets of Intercultural Competence Teaching

LIES SERCU

Until now, we have been concerned with the present, with what teachers are currently doing in their classrooms and with how they perceive the pupils they are teaching. We have had to conclude that, at present, intercultural competence teaching is largely confined to promoting pupils' familiarity with those aspects of the foreign culture that are dealt with in foreign language textbooks, leaving aside less visible aspects, such as norms, values or attitudes. We have found few teachers who define culture learning also in terms of the acquisition of intercultural skills, such as the independent exploration of cultures or the ability to mediate successfully in intercultural situations. When teachers compare cultures, they do so to familiarise their pupils with the foreign culture, not to help their pupils reflect on their own cultural identity and deeper insights in their own culture.

In this chapter, we want to look at the future, at how teachers envisage intercultural competence teaching, at their general disposition towards it. Innovation is inherently threatening and can only succeed when teachers support it and when the method of implementation takes account of what they are currently doing and how they conceive the called for innovation. Information regarding teachers' views of the future is particularly relevant for teacher educators preparing in-service or pre-service programmes centring on bridging the gap between communicative competence teaching with a cultural add-on and the integrated teaching of language-and-culture towards intercultural competence. Knowing how teachers are currently teaching and how they perceive the called for innovation will certainly help teacher trainers to select the right kind of approaches and materials. Showing teachers ways to depart from and build on their current teaching is the line to take, rather than provide the impression that intercultural competence teaching requires them to jettison the teaching principles they have believed in and know work well.

We explored teachers' opinions through asking them to score a number of opinion statements on a 'agree completely–disagree completely' scale. Whereas in the previous chapters, we had to speculate about possible reasons underlying teacher decisions regarding teaching practice, the findings in this chapter are based on research data that directly reflect teachers' opinions. First, we explored to what extent teachers are positively disposed towards intercultural competence teaching. We asked them whether they want to teach intercultural competence at all. In view of the fact that in a number of countries, intercultural education is primarily linked with the education of ethnic minority community children we also inquired into whether teachers want to teach intercultural competence in all classes without exception or only in classes with ethnic minority community children. Furthermore, we asked whether they think intercultural competence can and should be taught at school and whether they believe intercultural competence teaching will affect their pupils positively. If teachers, for example, feel that not they, but other caretakers, such as parents or youth movements, should promote intercultural competence, or that no effect is to be expected from intercultural competence teaching at school, there is little hope that they will actually change their approach to teaching a foreign language. Finally, we inquired into how they envisage intercultural competence teaching in practice. Do they prefer to teach it cross-curricularly or within the confines of their own subject? Do they want to start teaching intercultural competence right from the beginning of a language course or do they prefer to wait till their pupils have acquired a level of competence in the foreign language that will allow them to react in the foreign language to intercultural issues? Relatedly, do they think the mother tongue can be used in a foreign language classroom to deal with intercultural matters? Would they prefer to teach language and culture separately or rather opt for an integrated approach? Does traditional culture teaching suffice or do they perceive skills education as part of their teaching duty? Are they prepared to assist their pupils to reflect on their own culture or do they think it sufficient to promote their learners' familiarity with the foreign culture? Finally, do they aim to present an attractive picture of the foreign culture or do they consider it an essential part of intercultural competence education that pupils are presented with a realistic image of the foreign culture and thus also become acquainted with the less positive sides of the foreign societies?

More Similarities than Differences Between Countries

Each of the above topics was addressed by means of two statements which the teachers had to score on a five-point agree–disagree scale. A first salient finding concerns the fact that teachers in the different countries do not appear to differ significantly in their opinions and convictions regarding the different facets of intercultural competence teaching addressed in the final part of the questionnaire.[1] This similarity can very clearly be observed from Table 8.1 below. The table contains the mean scores obtained for each subtopic. The meaning of the scores, ranging between 0.00 and 5.00, is explained at the bottom of the table. When taking a vertical perspective, it can be seen that the order in which the 12 expressions have been ranked applies to all countries. Thus, teachers in all countries disagree to a certain extent that it is only when there are ethnic minority community children in one's class that one should try to promote the acquisition of intercultural competence or that language and culture cannot be taught in an integrated way. Teachers in all countries, except in Spain, are not convinced that intercultural education has no effect on pupils' attitudes (third topic). Teachers in Spain are more convinced than teachers in other countries that intercultural education has no effect on pupils' attitudes. As the mean scores obtained for statements 4 and 5 reveal, teachers are undecided as to whether or not intercultural skills can be acquired at school and a sufficiently high level of language proficiency is needed before one can start teaching culture. They also look upon the importance of culture teaching vis-à-vis language teaching in the same way in different countries: they agree to a certain extent that culture teaching is as important as language teaching. Finally, teachers in all countries completely agree that the teaching of intercultural competence should be undertaken in a cross-curricular mode; that foreign language teaching should not only deal with foreign cultures, but also help pupils deepen their understanding of their own culture; that more knowledge and a larger familiarity with the foreign culture will lead to a more tolerant attitude; and that foreign language teachers should present a realistic image of the foreign culture. The score obtained for 'willingness to teach intercultural competence' (tenth statement) points to a clear willingness on the teachers' side to teach intercultural competence through foreign language education. The highest mean was obtained for 'conviction that all pupils

Table 8.1 Teachers' opinions regarding different facets of intercultural competence teaching

	BEL	*BUL*	*GRE*	*MEX*	*POL*	*SPA*	*SWE*	*Mean*
Conviction that it is only when there are ethnic minority community children in one's class that one should try to promote the acquisition of intercultural competence	1.50	1.57	2.00	1.91	1.65	1.77	1.27	1.67
Conviction that language and culture cannot be taught in an integrated way	1.70	1.31	2.12	1.51	1.72	1.90	1.55	1.69
Conviction that intercultural education has no effect on pupils' attitudes	1.90	1.93	2.00	2.16	1.88	2.33	1.62	1.97
Conviction that intercultural skills cannot be acquired at school	2.30	1.78	2.65	2.32	2.23	2.19	2.18	2.24
Conviction that a sufficiently high level of language proficiency is needed before one can start teaching culture	2.65	2.56	2.47	2.82	2.60	2.53	2.47	2.59
Conviction that culture teaching is important, but has to give way to language teaching when one only has a limited number of teaching periods available	3.78	3.39	3.62	3.49	3.45	3.46	3.47	3.52
Conviction that the teaching of intercultural competence should be undertaken cross-curricularly	4.02	4.45	3.98	4.17	4.00	3.96	4.31	4.13

(*continued*)

Table 8.1 *Continued*

	BEL	*BUL*	*GRE*	*MEX*	*POL*	*SPA*	*SWE*	*Mean*
Conviction that foreign language teaching should not only deal with foreign cultures, but also help pupils to deepen their understanding of their own culture	3.89	4.80	4.29	4.70	4.15	4.36	4.43	4.37
Conviction that more knowledge and a larger familiarity with the foreign culture will lead to a more tolerant attitude	4.18	4.63	4.29	4.57	4.37	4.46	4.31	4.40
Willingness to teach intercultural competence	4.26	4.88	4.30	4.64	4.40	4.47	4.67	4.52
Conviction that a foreign language teacher should present a realistic image of the foreign culture	4.71	4.74	4.49	4.68	4.55	4.23	4.77	4.60
Conviction that all pupil should acquire intercultural competence, not only pupils in classrooms with ethnic minority children	4.73	5	4.46	4.58	4.41	4.54	4.87	4.66

Mean scores, ranging between 0.00 and 5.00. 0.00–1.00 = disagree completely; 1.01–2.00 = disagree to a certain extent; 2.01–3.00 = undecided; 3.01–4.00 = agree to a certain extent; 4.01–5.00 = agree completely.

should acquire intercultural competence, not only pupils in classrooms with ethnic minority children.

Intranational Disagreement

A final parallel which we want to point out and which sheds additional light on the similarities pointed out earlier concerns the fact that pronounced intranational disagreement appears to exist with respect to two topics, and with respect to these two topics only. The topics are 'conviction that a sufficiently high level of language proficiency is needed before one can start teaching culture' (Table 8.2), and 'conviction that intercultural skills cannot be taught at school' (Table 8.3). Whereas with respect to other topics the data show a clear tendency towards either agreement or disagreement, with respect to these two topics the data reveal that large percentages of teachers of one country are either in agreement or in disagreement with the statement. This tendency is most outspoken with respect to Belgian and Mexican teachers, but it is also observable in other countries. Whereas 42.5% of Belgian teachers disagree that pupils have to possess a sufficiently high level of proficiency in the foreign language before one can teach culture or do anything about the intercultural dimension of foreign language teaching, 49.67% agree with it. As regards the statement 'intercultural skills cannot be acquired at school', Mexican teachers appear to be in largest disagreement, with 25.58% of teachers disagreeing completely, 39.53% disagreeing to a certain extent, 11.63% being undecided, 16.25% agreeing to a certain extent and 6.95% agreeing completely.

Clear Willingness

That teachers in all participating countries as a group are clearly in favour of teaching intercultural competence, deserves some further comment here. As can be seen from Table 8.4, teachers in Bulgaria and Sweden appear the strongest proponents. On the whole, in all countries at least 79.48% of all teachers either agree to a certain extent or agree completely with the statement 'I would like to teach intercultural competence through my foreign language teaching'. The largest percentages of teachers who are undecided can be found in Greece (20.51%) and Poland (16.67%). In Belgium, only about two-thirds of teachers are clearly in favour of teaching intercultural competence.

The fact that teachers in all countries are clearly willing to interculturalise foreign language education is encouraging. In the next chapter, we will investigate whether this willingness is unconditional for all teachers,

Table 8.2 Teachers' degree of conviction that a sufficiently high level of language proficiency is needed before one can start teaching culture

		BEL	*GRE*	*MEX*	*POL*	*BUL*	*SPA*	*SWE*	*Mean*
Disagree completely	1	17.65%	23.08%	20.93%	35.42%	19.35%	25.71%	39.34%	25.93%
Disagree to a certain extent	2	24.84%	33.33%	44.19%	27.08%	45.16%	54.29%	34.43%	37.62%
Undecided	3	7.84%	0.00%	0.00%	8.33%	6.45%	2.86%	4.92%	4.34%
Agree to a certain extent	4	35.29%	38.46%	25.58%	12.50%	25.81%	5.71%	18.03%	23.05%
Agree completely	5	14.38%	5.13%	9.30%	16.67%	3.23%	11.43%	3.28%	9.06%
	Mean	3.04	2.69	2.58	2.48	2.48	2.23	2.11	2.52

Table 8.3 Teachers' degree of conviction that intercultural skills cannot be taught at school

		GRE	*MEX*	*BEL*	*SWE*	*POL*	*SPA*	*BUL*	*Mean*
Disagree completely	1	26.32%	25.58%	35.53%	40.98%	51.02%	31.43%	63.33%	39.17%
Disagree to a certain extent	2	28.95%	39.53%	39.47%	37.70%	22.45%	48.57%	20.00%	33.81%
Undecided	3	13.16%	11.63%	11.18%	3.28%	8.16%	20.00%	13.33%	11.53%
Agree to a certain extent	4	28.95%	16.28%	11.84%	18.03%	14.29%	0.00%	3.33%	13.25%
Agree completely	5	2.63%	6.98%	1.97%	0.00%	4.08%	0.00%	0.00%	2.24%
	Mean	2.53	2.40	2.05	1.98	1.98	1.89	1.57	2.06

Table 8.4 Teachers' degree of willingness to interculturalise foreign language education

		BUL	*SWE*	*MEX*	*SPA*	*GRE*	*POL*	*BEL*	*Mean*
Disagree completely	1	0.00%	0.00%	0.00%	0.00%	0.00%	2.08%	0.65%	0.39%
Disagree to a certain extent	2	0.00%	0.00%	0.00%	0.00%	0.00%	0.00%	0.65%	0.09%
Undecided	3	0.00%	1.69%	6.82%	8.57%	20.51%	16.67%	11.76%	9.43%
Agree to a certain extent	4	10.34%	23.73%	20.45%	28.57%	20.51%	22.92%	42.48%	24.14%
Agree completely	5	89.66%	74.58%	72.73%	62.86%	58.97%	58.33%	44.44%	65.94%
	Mean	4.90	4.73	4.66	4.54	4.38	4.35	4.29	4.55

or whether teachers' degree of willingness is dependent on particular factors, through looking for statistical relations between teachers' willingness on the one hand and, other opinion factors and factors relating to teaching practice on the other. It might for example be the case that teachers who are less positively disposed towards the integration of intercultural competence teaching in foreign language education also believe that only classes with ethnic minority community children should be taught for intercultural competence, or that pupils should first have acquired a high degree of proficiency in the foreign language before one can start teaching for intercultural competence. By contrast, teachers who are clearly willing to interculturalise foreign language education might also be the teachers who think it is possible to integrate language-and-culture teaching.

As a group, teachers appear to be in doubt regarding at least three facets of intercultural competence teaching. They are not convinced of the effect intercultural competence teaching can have on pupils. They wonder whether intercultural competence can be acquired at school, and are undecided as to whether or not one should postpone the teaching of intercultural competence until learners have acquired a sufficiently high level of competence in the foreign language. This last issue especially reaches to the heart of foreign language education, and forces teachers to really take a stand as to how important they deem the teaching of culture and intercultural competence. Their hesitation to take a clear stand is confirmed by the fact that the respondents did not take extreme positions when asked whether they thought language and culture could be taught in an integrated way. When trying to convince foreign language teachers of the need to interculturalise foreign language education, it will be important to acknowledge these doubts, to provide proof of the effect intercultural competence teaching at school has on pupils, and to show ways as to how to integrate the teaching of language and culture.

As a group, teachers appear to perceive intercultural foreign language education in similar ways. They agree that intercultural competence teaching is best undertaken in a cross-curricular mode, that enlarging pupils' familiarity with the foreign culture will enhance their tolerance towards foreignness, and that intercultural competence teaching should include the pupils' own culture. These findings suggest that teachers envisage an approach that builds on, but also moves on from the traditional foreign cultural approach, which focuses on enlarging pupils' knowledge regarding the foreign culture. Teaching across the curriculum may be a relatively new development in some countries, but teachers tend to agree that intercultural competence teaching is best undertaken in this way. This may mean that teachers do not know how to integrate intercultural competence teaching in their own foreign language teaching. It may, however, also mean that teachers are really convinced that cross-curricular teaching constitutes the way forward. It will be interesting to compare how teachers' perceptions of future 'foreign language and intercultural competence teaching' relate to their current teaching practice, as will be done in the next chapter.

Finally, we want to point out that it is remarkable that teachers who mainly teach with textbooks that present, sometimes unrealistically, positive images of the foreign cultures and with which the majority of teachers are satisfied at least to a certain extent completely agree with the statement that a *realistic* image of the foreign culture should be presented. Because we found that teachers are largely satisfied with the way in which textbooks approach culture teaching, one may wonder whether the fact that they were asked to reflect on this issue in the questionnaire made them realise that indeed a realistic, not an overly positive image of the foreign culture should be presented, or whether they were already convinced of this before being offered the statement. In any event, the positive outcome of this is that at least those who participated in the research will have realised that there is more value in presenting a realistic image of a foreign culture than in trying to motivate pupils to learn the foreign language through presenting an overly attractive image of it.

Note

1. Though the different teacher groups do appear to behave differently with respect to some aspects regarding which they were asked to voice their opinion, the Bonferroni multiple comparisons test results (Appendix 2) reveal that the groups are more similar than different with respect to each facet investigated.

Chapter 9

The Foreign Language and Intercultural Competence Teacher

LIES SERCU

In the previous chapters, we have addressed different aspects of foreign language teachers' professional self-concepts with a specific focus on the teaching of culture and intercultural competence. We have shown how they define the objectives of foreign language education, what culture teaching activities they practise and what cultural topics they deal with in the foreign language classroom, how satisfied they are with the cultural dimension of the teaching materials they use, how they view their pupils' knowledge and attitude regarding the foreign cultures, to what extent they think school trips and exchange projects affect their pupils' intercultural competence, and how their general disposition towards the teaching of intercultural competence in foreign language education can be characterised. For reasons of surveyability and researchability, we have viewed these different facets in relative isolation. This jigsaw image may, however, not adequately reflect how teachers look upon their teaching job. It is probable that they perceive themselves in a holistic way, as making decisions regarding teaching on the basis of a largely coherent set of convictions. This is not to say that teachers are at all times consciously aware of their applying these personal teaching guidelines. Depending on the number of years of teaching experience, their teaching principles will have become more or less internalised, implicit, unconscious and automatised.

In this chapter, we want to view the different components of teachers' perceptions in relation. We will consider to what extent the different facets appear to build a coherent teacher profile. This approach will shed light on the degree of centrality or periphery of particular subsets of teachers' beliefs. Using statistical techniques, we will make patterns in teachers' beliefs visible which would otherwise remain hidden. We aim to investigate these possible patterns from three different angles. First, we will consider which factors affect a teacher's willingness to teach intercultural competence in foreign language education. In the previous chapter, we have shown that teachers are clearly willing to teach intercultural competence. Do particular convictions make teachers hesitant or unwilling to change their actual instructional behaviour and teaching practice? Do they believe particular conditions have to be met first before they are willing to reconsider familiar teaching approaches? Does the way in which they envisage intercultural competence teaching affect the extent of their willingness? Secondly, we will examine to what extent actual culture teaching appears consistent. A high degree of coherence would testify to some kind of system underlying teaching. Teachers would then not just respond to events as they present themselves in a one-off way. They would then operate from some kind of mental map or checklist of the kinds of teaching activities they need to plan for, the selection of cultural topics they can choose from, the sorts of intercultural contact situations they are likely to need to deal with and need to prepare their learners for, etc. The specific questions we will ask include: is it the case that teachers who say they deal with particular cultural topics frequently, also report frequently practising culture teaching activities and devoting a considerable part of their teaching time to culture teaching? In that section, we will also examine to what extent teachers take account of their pupils' current level of understanding of and familiarity with the foreign culture when shaping their teaching practice. Finally, we draw the two previous components together and consider to what extent teachers' obvious willingness to teach intercultural competence is reflected in their reports of their current teaching. A clear reflection would allow the conclusion that teachers are already now doing more than paying lip-service to intercultural competence teaching. Thus, in the final part of the chapter, we will reflect on the extent to which teachers' actual teaching profile reflects the envisaged profile of the intercultural competence teacher, as we have described it in the introductory chapter to this book.

The Favourably and the Unfavourably Disposed Teacher

In the literature regarding teachers' beliefs, a relatively direct relationship is assumed between teachers' motivation and willingness to do something and their actual teaching practices. In the previous chapter we saw that teachers in all countries appear to be very willing to interculturalise foreign language education. Here, we will attempt to draw teachers' mental map. We will first consider which variables – opinion variables and others – appear to co-variate with teachers' degree of willingness to interculturalise foreign language education. Our data will reveal that we can speak of two distinct teacher profiles: the favourably disposed teacher who is willing to teach intercultural competence and the unfavourably disposed teacher who takes a much more hesitant and even rejecting stance. Both groups have their own distinct, but clearly clustered, opinions regarding the preconditions that need to be met before one can start teaching intercultural competence and the way in which intercultural competence should be taught.

Willingness and opinion variables

We will first concentrate on the relationships that exist between teachers' willingness on the one hand and the opinion variables we included in our study. Table 9.1 summarises the independent opinion variables (from 1 to 12) that were found to co-variate with the dependent variable 'willingness' (in the top left of the table) (Pearson correlations). The relationship is significant (Sig. two-tailed) either at the 5% (*) or at the 1% (**) level. We have only listed the parameters which appeared to be significantly related to the dependent variable for more than half of the country samples. We have listed them in descending order of the number of country samples for which a significant relation was found. The test results allow defining the strength of the relationships that exist between teachers' willingness and other variables. A positive relationship indicates that the larger the extent of a teacher's support of a particular view, the more willing s/he appears. Vice versa, the less a teacher appears to support a particular view, the less willing s/he will be to interculturalise foreign language education.

The higher the degree of significance of the relationship, the higher the r-value is. r-Values, i.e. the figures next to 'Pearson correlation', can vary between $+1$ and -1. $r = +1$ indicates there is a perfect positive relationship; $r = -1$ indicates that there is a perfect negative relationship. $N =$ the number of respondents per country for which a value was obtained with respect to a particular independent variable. BUL = Bulgaria, GRE = Greece, MEX = Mexico, POL = Poland, SPA = Spain, SWE = Sweden and BEL = Belgium.

From Table 9.1, a number of observations can be made. First, the first variable, namely 'I would like to teach intercultural competence through my foreign language teaching' is, not surprisingly, significantly, strongly and positively related to teachers' degree of willingness.

Secondly, we can see that five facets of teachers' beliefs, sometimes represented by two variables, appear to be positively related ($r =$ a positive

Table 9.1 Factors affecting teachers' willingness to interculturalise foreign language education

Willingness		*BEL*	*BUL*	*GRE*	*MEX*	*POL*	*SPA*	*SWE*
(1) I would like to teach intercultural competence through my foreign language teaching	Pearson	0.853(**)	0.854(**)	0.763(**)	0.758(**)	0.899(**)	0.932(**)	0.639(**)
	Sig.	0.000	0.000	0.000	0.000	0.000	0.000	0.000
	N	151	28	39	44	47	35	57
(2) Intercultural education is best undertaken cross-curricularly	Pearson	0.502(**)	−0.272	0.746(**)	0.477(**)	0.303*	0.495(**)	0.579(**)
	Sig.	0.000	0.146	0.000	0.001	0.036	0.003	0.000
	N	151	30	39	44	48	35	58
(3) The more pupils know about the foreign culture, the more tolerant they are	Pearson	0.345(**)	−0.268	0.547(**)	0.355(*)	0.429(**)	0.480(**)	0.591(**)
	Sig.	0.000	0.153	0.000	0.018	0.002	0.004	0.000
	N	151	30	39	44	48	35	59
(4) All pupils should acquire intercultural competence, not only pupils in classrooms with ethnic minority community children	Pearson	0.364(**)	0.235	0.579(**)	0.301(*)	0.374(**)	0.501(**)	0.413(**)
	Sig.	0.000	0.137	0.000	0.049	0.009	0.002	0.001
	N	150	30	39	43	48	35	59
(5) It is impossible to teach the foreign language and foreign culture in an integrated way	Pearson	−0.186(*)	0.003	−0.318(*)	−0.327(*)	−0.509(**)	−0.514(**)	−0.054
	Sig.	0.022	0.986	0.049	0.030	0.000	0.002	0.682
	N	151	30	39	44	48	35	59
(6) In a foreign language classroom, teaching culture is as important as teaching the foreign language	Pearson	0.320(**)	0.130	0.591(**)	0.475(**)	0.022	0.502(**)	0.372(**)
	Sig.	0.000	0.494	0.000	0.001	0.884	0.002	0.004
	N	151	30	39	43	48	35	58

(*continued*)

Table 9.1 *Continued*

Willingness		*BEL*	*BUL*	*GRE*	*MEX*	*POL*	*SPA*	*SWE*
(7) Every subject, not just foreign language teaching, should promote the acquisition of intercultural skills	Pearson	0.353(**)	−0.179	0.617(**)	0.283	0.300(*)	0.475(**)	0.362(**)
	Sig.	0.000	0.353	0.000	0.066	0.038	0.004	0.006
	N	151	29	38	43	48	35	57
(8) Only when there are ethnic minority community pupils in your classes do you have to teach intercultural competence	Pearson	−0.214(**)	0.103	−0.411(**)	−0.104	−0.511(**)	−0.380(*)	−0.308(*)
	Sig.	0.008	0.595	0.009	0.502	0.000	0.024	0.019
	N	151	29	39	44	48	35	58
(9) Providing additional cultural information makes pupils more tolerant towards other cultures and peoples	Pearson	0.367(**)	−0.203	0.368(*)	−0.005	0.402(**)	0.548(**)	0.392(**)
	Sig.	0.000	0.282	0.021	0.972	0.005	0.001	0.003
	N	149	30	39	44	48	35	57
(10) A foreign language teacher should present a positive image of the foreign culture	Pearson	0.137	−0.397(*)	0.340(*)	0.621(**)	0.265	0.177	0.460(**)
	Sig.	0.094	0.030	0.034	0.000	0.069	0.309	0.000
	N	151	30	39	44	48	35	59
(11) Intercultural education has no effect whatsoever on pupils' attitudes	Pearson	−0.384(**)	−0.068	−0.155	−0.366(*)	−0.323*	−0.514(**)	−0.210
	Sig.	0.000	0.719	0.346	0.016	0.025	0.002	0.113
	N	150	30	39	43	48	35	58
(12) Language and culture cannot be taught in an integrated way. You have to separate the two	Pearson	−0.229(**)	0.022	−0.285	−0.247	−0.528(**)	−0.496(**)	−0.269*
	Sig.	0.005	0.910	0.079	0.106	0.000	0.002	0.041
	N	151	29	39	44	48	35	58

Pearson's correlations test results. N = number of respondents. Pearson correlation = r. Sig. = level of significance (1%(**) or 5%(*)).

value for the country samples for which a significant relation was obtained) to 'degree of willingness' for teachers from at least four countries. These facets are:

- conviction that intercultural education is best undertaken cross-curricularly (variable 2);
- conviction that providing pupils with more knowledge regarding the foreign cultures associated with the foreign language pupils are learning makes them more tolerant towards other cultures and people (variables 3 and 9);
- conviction that all pupils should acquire intercultural competence, not only pupils in classrooms with ethnic minority community children (variable 4);
- conviction that teaching culture and teaching the foreign language are as important in the foreign language classroom (variable 6);
- conviction that every subject, not just foreign language teaching, should promote the acquisition of intercultural skills (variable 7).

Three other facets of teachers' beliefs appear negatively related ($r =$ a negative value for the country samples for which a significant relation was obtained) to 'degree of willingness' for teachers from at least four countries. They are:

- conviction that it is impossible to teach the foreign language and foreign culture in an integrated way (variables 5 and 12);
- conviction that only when there are ethnic minority community pupils in one's classes one has to teach intercultural competence (variable 8);
- conviction that intercultural education has no effect whatsoever on pupils' attitudes (variable 11).

From the previous chapter, it will be remembered that Bulgarian teachers are the teachers most clearly in favour of interculturalising foreign language education. Before returning to the general picture, we want to comment here on the specific Bulgarian situation in some more detail. It is interesting to note that few of the variables that appear to be significantly related to teachers' degree of willingness to interculturalise foreign language education are also significantly related to Bulgarian teachers' degree of willingness. It is even the case that on some occasions, the r-value obtained is negative where the r-value obtained for the other country samples is positive. This is the case with respect to variables 2, 3, 7, 9, 10. The reverse is true for variables 8 and 12, though the r-value is close to 0, which means that the degree of relationship between these variables and the dependent variable 'willingness' is weak. This then appears to indicate that Bulgarian teachers hold different views from teachers in other samples, though the difference tends to be too small to be significant. Applying this to the related variables 2 and 7, for example, this would mean that Bulgarian teachers believe foreign language teachers should teach intercultural competence, whereas teachers in other countries are more inclined to think that promoting the acquisition of intercultural competence amongst pupils is not the (sole) responsibility of foreign language teachers, and intercultural competence is best taught across the curriculum. Likewise, Bulgarian teachers appear to define their role as promoters of intercultural competence less in terms of enhancing their pupils' familiarity with the foreign culture than teachers in other countries (variables 3 and 9). They may realise that the traditional approach to culture teaching, which consists in the passing on of information regarding the foreign culture mainly, does not suffice to promote intercultural competence in learners. The Bulgarian sample is special in that it contains quite a number of teachers who participated in a British Council project focusing specifically on the acquisition of intercultural competence through foreign language education. Participation in this project will have helped the teachers realise that intercultural skills are an essential part of intercultural competence and that a teacher who merely promotes a greater familiarity with a foreign culture does not serve learners too well. Finally, the variable 'a foreign language teacher should present a positive image of the foreign culture' stands out too. It is positively related to 'willingness' in Greece, Mexico and Sweden, but negatively related to it in Bulgaria. In other words, teachers in Bulgaria who do not support the view that one should present a positive image of the foreign culture are more willing to interculturalise foreign language education than their colleagues. It is interesting to note in this respect that the statement 'a foreign language teachers should present a realistic image of a foreign culture, and therefore should also touch upon negative sides of the foreign culture and society' did appear to be significantly related (at the 5% level) to 'willingness' in one country only, namely Mexico. From this observation, it can be derived that Bulgarian teachers who are willing to interculturalise foreign language education support the view that one should present a realistic image of the foreign culture, not a merely positive one, but that they do not necessarily also support the view that one should also touch upon negative aspects of the foreign culture.

Let us now return to the general picture. Other opinion variables included in Table 9.1 were found to be either positively or negatively significantly related to 'willingness' in one, two or three country samples only. They include: 'the extent to which teachers support the view that one should include the learners' own culture when teaching intercultural competence'; 'the extent to which teachers believe intercultural misunderstandings arise equally often from linguistic as from cultural differences'; and 'the extent to which teachers believe learners can only acquire additional knowledge in the foreign language classroom, not intercultural skills'. The opinion variables that were found not to co-variate significantly with the 'willingness index' in any of the country samples are 'the extent to which teachers believe that their pupils should have acquired a sufficiently high level of proficiency in the foreign language before one can start to do anything in the area of intercultural competence' and, relatedly 'the extent to which teachers support the view that one should discuss cultural topics in the mother tongue as long as the pupils have not reached a sufficiently high level of significance to do so in the foreign language'.

Considering these different observations together, we can say that our findings clearly point towards the existence of two teacher profiles: the teacher who is favourably disposed towards the integration of intercultural competence in foreign language education and the teacher who is unfavourably disposed towards its integration. Teachers who are not in favour of the integration of intercultural competence teaching in foreign language education believe that it is impossible to integrate language and culture teaching. They also believe that intercultural skills cannot be acquired at school, let alone in the foreign language classroom. On the whole, these teachers do not believe in the positive effect of intercultural competence teaching on pupils' attitudes and perceptions. The only effect they see is a negative one: intercultural competence teaching reinforces pupils' already existing stereotypes. In addition, these teachers believe that it is only when there are ethnic minority community children in one's classes that one should teach intercultural competence. By contrast, teachers who are favourably disposed share a number of convictions too. They believe that teaching culture is as important as teaching the foreign language, and that it is possible to integrate the two. To their minds, intercultural competence teaching makes pupils more tolerant. These teachers prefer an approach that is cross-curricular and are convinced that teachers of every subject should teach intercultural competence, not only foreign language teachers. In addition, they do not think intercultural competence should only be taught in schools with ethnic minority community children; it should be taught to all pupils. In addition, teachers who are in favour of interculturalising foreign language education do not necessarily believe learners should have acquired a high degree of proficiency in the foreign language before one can start teaching intercultural competence. They also do not necessarily support the view that one cannot use the learners' mother tongue to promote the acquisition of intercultural competence. In some countries, teachers in favour of intercultural competence teaching are also convinced that one should include the learners' own culture in one's teaching, or that one can promote the acquisition of intercultural skills in the foreign language classroom, next to enhancing learners' familiarity with foreign cultures.

That teachers in favour of intercultural competence teaching in foreign language education want all children to benefit from intercultural competence teaching is not surprising. This finding most probably testifies to the fact that teachers realise that all learners need intercultural skills in the world in which they are growing up. That teachers favour an approach that is at the same time cross-curricular and supported by work in every subject does not surprise either. In many schools, cross-curricular initiatives already arise from the different subjects, and, vice-versa, subject teachers contribute to cross-curricular projects. Though foreign language education might be considered the ideal subject for teaching intercultural competence in view of the fact that learning a foreign language by definition involves contact with other cultures, these teachers are convinced they cannot be the sole teachers responsible, and that other subject teachers too should contribute to enhancing learners' intercultural competence. In teachers' minds, there may also be a certain feeling of uneasiness, or unhappiness, about the fact that intercultural competence teaching might entail a reduction of the teaching time that can be devoted to improving the learners' language skills. This assumption appears to be supported by the fact that teachers in favour of interculturalising foreign language education are not in favour of using the mother tongue in situations where the learners' language skills are too limited to deal with cultural issues in the foreign language, and also by the fact that teachers advocate an approach in which the teaching of language and culture are integrated.

Willingness and other variables

So far, we have only commented on relationships between teachers' willingness to interculturalise foreign language education and their opinions regarding different aspects of how one might conceptualise intercultural competence teaching. Here we want to consider other variables and comment on which of these variables appear to co-variate or not co-variate significantly with the willingness index.

Interestingly, we found a significant relationship between teachers' willingness to interculturalise foreign language education and the frequency with which culture-teaching activities are practised or particular cultural topics are addressed in the foreign language classroom, but in a minority of the countries only (see Tables 9.2 and 9.3). In the Belgian and Greek sample, willingness is significantly related to both indicators of teaching practice. In the Swedish sample, it is only significantly related to the frequency with which culture-teaching activities are practised in the foreign language classroom, and in the Spanish sample, only with the frequency with which cultural topics dealt with in the foreign language classroom.

Thus, we can conclude that, despite teachers' obvious willingness to support the integration of an intercultural competence dimension in foreign language education in all countries, this willingness does not necessarily imply more extensive culture teaching. In only three out of seven countries do teachers who are favourably disposed appear to teach culture more extensively than their colleagues who are less favourably disposed.

This finding is confirmed when looking at the relationship between willingness and the conviction that enhancing pupils' familiarity with the foreign culture will lead to a more tolerant attitude towards foreign cultures. As can be seen from Tables 9.4 and 9.5, a significant relationship exists between willingness and the 'more culture more tolerance' variable in the same country samples as the ones mentioned above, namely the Belgian, Greek, Swedish and Spanish samples. This finding allows the conclusion that in three out of seven countries, teachers who belief that providing pupils with more cultural knowledge will enhance their tolerance towards foreign cultures do not necessarily deal with cultural topics more frequently or use culture teaching activities more extensively than their colleagues who do not believe so.

The other variables that were found not to co-variate significantly with the 'willingness index' in any of the country samples include: 'the extent to which teachers believe their pupils are knowledgeable about the foreign culture'; 'the frequency of teachers' contacts with the foreign culture'; 'the percentage of immigrants in the teacher's school' and the reasons teachers mention for organising school trips or exchange project. The way in which teachers define the objectives of foreign language education and culture teaching in foreign language education were also not found to co-variate with the willingness variable.

The lack of relationship between 'willingness' and the extent of pupils' knowledge regarding foreign cultures is somewhat unfortunate. One would have liked to find that teachers who perceive their pupils as not

Table 9.2 Teachers' beliefs and their teaching practice. Relationship between 'willingness' and 'frequency of culture teaching activities'

Teachers' willingness to interculturalise foreign language education		***BEL***	***BUL***	***GRE***	***MEX***	***POL***	***SPA***	***SWE***
Frequency of culture teaching activities	Pearson	0.413(**)	−0.012	0.506(**)	0.244	−0.154	0.248	0.335(**)
	Sig.	0.000	0.949	0.001	0.110	0.295	0.151	0.009
	N	149	30	39	44	48	35	59

*p < 0.05, **p < 0.01.

Table 9.3 Teachers' beliefs and their teaching practice. Relationship between 'willingness' and 'frequency with which cultural topics are touched upon in the foreign language classroom'

Teachers' willingness to interculturalise foreign language education		***BEL***	***BUL***	***GRE***	***MEX***	***POL***	***SPA***	***SWE***
Frequency with which cultural topics are touched upon in the foreign language classroom	Pearson	0.366(**)	−0.177	0.361(*)	0.214	−0.085	0.449 (**)	0.155
	Sig.	0.000	0.349	0.024	0.163	0.568	0.007	0.242
	N	149	30	39	44	48	35	59

*p < 0.05, **p < 0.01.

Table 9.4 Teachers' beliefs and teaching practice. Relationships between variable 'frequency of culture teaching activities' and 'belief that more cultural information leads to more tolerance'

Frequency with which culture teaching activities are practised in the foreign language classroom		***ALL***	***BEL***	***BUL***	***GRE***	***MEX***	***POL***	***SPA***	***SWE***
Conviction that more cultural knowledge leads to more tolerance	Pearson	0.165(**)	0.205(*)	−0.244	0.412(**)	0.024	−0.193	0.145	0.222(*)
	Sig.	0.001	0.012	0.194	0.009	0.879	0.188	0.406	0.091
	N	404	149	30	39	44	48	35	59

$^{*}p < 0.05$, $^{**}p < 0.01$.

Table 9.5 Teachers' beliefs and teaching practice. Relationships between variable 'frequency with which cultural topics are touched upon in the foreign language classroom' and 'belief that more cultural information leads to more tolerance'

Frequency with which cultural topics are dealt with in the foreign language classroom		***ALL***	***BEL***	***BUL***	***GRE***	***MEX***	***POL***	***SPA***	***SWE***
Conviction that more cultural knowledge leads to more tolerance	Pearson	0.200(**)	0.179(*)	−0.053	0.398(*)	−0.047	0.024	0.491(**)	0.160
	Sig.	0.000	0.029	0.780	0.012	0.763	0.872	0.003	0.226
	N	404	149	30	39	44	48	35	59

$^{*}p < 0.05$, $^{**}p < 0.01$.

knowledgeable would be more willing to teach culture than teachers who perceive them as very knowledgeable, assuming that these pupils do not need extra culture teaching. This finding appears to suggest that teachers are still conceptualising teaching more in a teacher-centred than in a pupil-centred way. That the frequency of teachers' own contacts with the foreign culture does not affect their degree of willingness is a fortunate finding. This lack of relationship implies that pupils taught by teachers living in countries where it is more difficult to get into direct contact with the target cultures have equal chances of meeting teachers who are favourably disposed as pupils who live in countries where direct contacts are more frequent. The lack of relationship between a teacher's degree of willingness to teach intercultural competence and the percentage of immigrant pupils in the school where that teacher is teaching confirms the finding that teachers want all pupils to be taught intercultural competence, irrespective of whether there are ethnic minority community children in the school or not.

As far as the lack of relationship between willingness and reasons for organising school trips and exchange projects are concerned, we know from Chapter 5 that only a minority of the teachers working in schools that organise school trips or take part in exchange programmes consider it their duty to do preparatory or follow-up work in connection with these experiential learning activities. This kind of work is considered peripheral to their day-to-day teaching practice. Therefore, it should not surprise that no significant relationships appear to exist between teachers' willingness to teach intercultural competence and the reasons for organising school trips that inquired into aspects relating specifically to culture learning, namely 'increase pupils' interest in the foreign culture' and 'increase pupils' familiarity with the foreign culture'. Despite positive expectations towards the effect of school trips and exchange programmes, as voiced by some teachers in answer to an open question, it is clear that school trips and exchange projects do not play a prominent role in teachers' overall conception of culture and language teaching.

Finally, the fact that no significant positive or negative relationship was found between willingness to teach intercultural competence and the way in which they defined the objectives of foreign language education and 'culture teaching in foreign language education' on the other is encouraging. Even teachers who believe that foreign language education should be mainly geared towards the acquisition of linguistic competence in the foreign language are not necessarily unwilling to teach intercultural competence in foreign language education. Teachers who believe the main objective of foreign language education is the acquisition of communicative competence in the foreign language may still believe it is possible to teach language and culture in an integrated way.

Consistency in Teaching: A Reflection of Teachers' Familiarity and Contacts with the Foreign Culture

In this section, we look at teachers' reports of their teaching practice more closely and investigate the extent of its consistency. We examine to what extent the different indicators of teaching practice as identified in the study appear to be related. A strong positive relationship will mean that teachers do not just respond to events as they present themselves in a one-off way, but apply a goal-directed culture teaching strategy. We will also examine to what extent the pupils' degree of familiarity with the foreign culture and their attitude towards it relates to the way in which teachers shape their teaching practice. Do teachers take account of their pupils' current levels of cultural understanding and intercultural competence, or do other factors, such as the teacher's own familiarity with the foreign culture play a more decisive role in determining the teacher's culture teaching strategy?

Consistency in teaching

The different components distinguished as indicators of a teacher's teaching practice were the frequency with which teachers deal with particular cultural topics during classroom teaching, the frequency with which they practise particular kinds of culture teaching activities, the way in which they distribute their teaching time over language teaching and culture teaching, and finally, the extent to which cultural aspects are considered when selecting teaching materials.

Our findings show that very clear relationships exist between three important indicators of culture teaching practice, namely the way in which teachers divide their teaching time over language teaching and culture teaching, the frequency with which they practise culture teaching activities and the frequency with which they deal with cultural topics. As Table 9.6 reveals, a significant positive correlation exists between the frequency with which teachers practise particular culture teaching activities and the frequency with which they touch upon particular cultural topics in all countries. Similarly, a significant positive correlation exists between 'distribution of teaching time' on the one hand and, on the other, the frequency with which teachers practise particular culture teaching activities and the frequency with which they deal with particular cultural topics. As can be seen from Table 9.7, which provides the data for the second

Table 9.6 Consistency of teaching practice. Relationship between 'frequency with which cultural topics are touched upon in the foreign language classroom' and 'frequency with which culture teaching activities are practised'

Frequency with which cultural topics are touched upon in the foreign language classroom		*ALL*	*BEL*	*BUL*	*GRE*	*MEX*	*POL*	*SPA*	*SWE*
Frequency with which culture teaching activities are practised in the foreign language classroom	Pearson	0.557$^{(**)}$	0.558$^{(**)}$	0.587$^{(**)}$	0.548$^{(**)}$	0.554$^{(**)}$	0.598$^{(**)}$	0.547$^{(**)}$	0.507$^{(**)}$
	Sig.	0.000	0.000	0.001	0.000	0.000	0.000	0.001	0.000
	N	407	149	30	39	45	49	35	60

$^{*}p < 0.05$, $^{**}p < 0.01$.

Table 9.7 Consistency of teaching practice. Relationship between 'distribution of teaching time over language teaching and culture teaching' and 'frequency with which cultural topics are touched upon in the foreign language classroom'

Distribution of teaching time over 'language teaching' and 'culture teaching'		*ALL*	*BEL*	*BUL*	*GRE*	*MEX*	*POL*	*SPA*	*SWE*
Frequency with which cultural topics are touched upon in the foreign language classroom	Pearson	0.352$^{(**)}$	0.316$^{(**)}$	0.302	0.178	0.445$^{(**)}$	0.463$^{(**)}$	0.479$^{(**)}$	0.319$^{(*)}$
	Sig.	0.000	0.000	0.105	0.277	0.002	0.001	0.004	0.014
	N	404	147	30	39	45	49	35	59

$^{*}p < 0.05$, $^{**}p < 0.01$.

variable, this relationship exists in the majority of the countries included in the research, but not in all.

These findings allow the conclusion that teachers have been consistent in the way in which they answered the different questions about how they shape their language and culture teaching practice. From Chapter 5, we know that traditional teacher-centred approaches appear to dominate culture teaching whereas techniques involving the students' initiative and autonomy are less popular. Consistency does not necessarily also imply that teachers deem culture teaching of prime importance. The findings presented in Chapter 2 have shown that they devote substantially more teaching time to language than to culture teaching. The criteria which they use to select textbooks and teaching materials confirm that culture teaching is second in importance, after teaching communicative competence. The main reasons teachers have given include lack of time, lack of training and lack of appropriate teaching materials.

Teacher Familiarity as Reflected in Teaching Practice

In the remainder of this section, we consider to what extent teachers' culture teaching practice appears to be affected by, on the one hand, their own familiarity with the foreign culture, and on the other, their perceptions of their pupils' familiarity and attitudes regarding the foreign cultures.

As Table 9.8 reveals, clear positive significant relationships exist between the frequency with which teachers address cultural topics and their degree of familiarity with the foreign culture, and the extent of their contacts with it. The first variable is significantly and positively related to 'teacher familiarity' in all countries, and to 'frequency of contacts at home' in all but one country. The second variable (Table 9.9) is significantly and positively related to 'teacher familiarity' in five countries, to 'frequency of contacts at home' in six countries and to 'frequency of travel to the foreign country' in four countries. The variable 'distribution of teaching time over language teaching and culture teaching' (Table 9.10) is clearly linked to 'teacher familiarity' in five countries, but not to teachers' degree of contact with the foreign culture.

These findings then allow the conclusion that the more familiar a teacher is with a particular culture, the more time will be devoted to culture teaching, the more frequently cultural topics are dealt with and the more often culture teaching activities are practised.

Table 9.8 Teacher familiarity and teaching practice. Relationship between 'frequency with which cultural topics are touched upon in the foreign language classroom' and 'degree of teacher familiarity', 'frequency of teacher travel to the foreign country' and 'frequency of teacher contacts with the foreign culture at home'

Frequency with which cultural topics are dealt with in the foreign language classroom		*ALL*	*BEL*	*BUL*	*GRE*	*MEX*	*POL*	*SPA*	*SWE*
Extent of teacher familiarity	Pearson	0.425(**)	0.451(**)	0.397(*)	0.319	0.450(**)	0.497(**)	0.434(**)	0.443(**)
	Sig.	0.000	0.000	0.030	0.051	0.002	0.000	0.009	0.000
	N	406	149	30	38	45	49	35	60
Frequency of teacher travel	Pearson	0.142(**)	0.190(*)	0.349	0.141	0.384(**)	0.227	−0.037	0.204
	Sig.	0.004	0.02	0.059	0.398	0.009	0.116	0.834	0.118
	N	406	149	30	38	45	49	35	60
Extent of teacher contact at home	Pearson	0.337(**)	0.276(**)	0.442(*)	0.102	0.374(*)	0.382(**)	0.320	0.279(*)
	Sig.	0.000	0.001	0.014	0.542	0.011	0.007	0.061	0.031
	N	406	149	30	38	45	49	35	60

$^{*}p < 0.05$, $^{**}p < 0.01$.

Table 9.9 Teacher familiarity and teaching practice. Relationship between 'frequency with which culture teaching activities are practised in the foreign language classroom' and 'degree of teacher familiarity', 'frequency of teacher travel to the foreign country' and 'frequency of teacher contacts with the foreign culture at home'

Frequency with which culture teaching activities are practised in the foreign language classroom		*ALL*	*BEL*	*BUL*	*GRE*	*MEX*	*POL*	*SPA*	*SWE*
Extent of teacher familiarity	Pearson	0.382$^{(**)}$	0.387$^{(**)}$	0.0910	0.463$^{(**)}$	0.511$^{(**)}$	0.217	0.362$^{(*)}$	0.551$^{(**)}$
	Sig.	0.000	0.000	0.631	0.003	0.000	0.135	0.032	0.000
	N	406	149	30	38	45	49	35	60
Frequency of teacher travel	Pearson	0.270$^{(**)}$	0.345$^{(**)}$	0.297	0.402$^{(*)}$	0.515$^{(**)}$	0.080	0.011	0.504$^{(**)}$
	Sig.	0.000	0.000	0.111	0.012	0.000	0.586	0.950	0.000
	N	406	149	30	38	45	49	35	60
Extent of teacher contact at home	Pearson	0.460$^{(**)}$	0.504$^{(**)}$	0.430$^{(*)}$	0.440$^{(**)}$	0.440$^{(**)}$	0.417$^{(**)}$	0.210	0.391$^{(**)}$
	Sig.	0.000	0.000	0.018	0.006	0.003	0.003	0.226	0.002
	N	406	149	30	38	45	49	35	60

$^{*}p < 0.05$, $^{**}p < 0.01$.

Table 9.10 Teacher familiarity and teaching practice. Relationship between 'distribution of teaching time over language teaching and culture teaching' and 'degree of teacher familiarity', 'frequency of teacher travel to the foreign country' and 'frequency of teacher contacts with the foreign culture at home'

Distribution of teaching time over 'language teaching' and 'culture teaching'		*ALL*	*BEL*	*BUL*	*GRE*	*MEX*	*POL*	*SPA*	*SWE*
Extent of teacher familiarity	Pearson	0.237(**)	0.239(**)	0.305	0.0310	0.374(*)	0.334(*)	0.339(*)	0.219
	Sig.	0.000	0.004	0.101	0.851	0.011	0.019	0.046	0.095
	N	403	147	30	38	45	49	35	59
Frequency of teacher travel	Pearson	0.076	0.106	0.234	0.056	0.274	0.173	0.076	−0.020
	Sig.	0.129	0.203	0.213	0.738	0.069	0.236	0.663	0.879
	N	403	147	30	38	45	49	35	59
Extent of teacher contact at home	Pearson	0.119(*)	0.174(*)	0.060	−0.0310	0.372(*)	0.103	0.296	−0.0520
	Sig.	0.017	0.035	0.753	0.851	0.012	0.483	0.084	0.693
	N	403	147	30	38	45	49	35	59

$^*p < 0.05$, $^{**}p < 0.01$.

These results lead to the striking finding that the extent of teachers' familiarity with a particular cultural topic is next to perfectly mirrored in the extent to which teachers deal with those different cultural topics in the classroom. As can be seen from Table 9.11, the relationship is significant for all topics in the larger samples (Belgium and 'all countries considered together') and for many topics in the smaller samples. Accepting a significance level of 0.10 for the smaller samples, would lead to an even more striking picture.

The burning question that remains is whether teachers' perceptions of their pupils' familiarity with and attitude towards the foreign culture also affect their teaching practice. We found that the relationship between teachers' familiarity with the foreign culture and their culture teaching practice is far more marked than that between teachers' perceptions of their pupils' familiarity and their teaching practice. In other words, the way in which teachers shape their teaching tends not to take account of the extent of pupils' familiarity with or attitudes regarding the foreign cultures associated with the foreign language they are learning. This is not to say that no positive significant relationships were obtained between the extent to which culture is dealt with in the foreign language classroom and the extent of pupils' knowledge. As can be seen from Table 9.12, in four countries a positive significant relationship was obtained. This finding then suggests that teachers who perceive of their pupils as already somewhat knowledgeable will be more inclined to teach culture than teachers who perceive of them as not knowledgeable. As pointed out in Chapter 4, teachers generally perceive their pupils to be rather unfamiliar with foreign cultures.

As regards pupils' attitudes, the results presented in Chapter 4 have shown that teachers' perceptions tend to vary between countries, with Bulgarian, Polish and Swedish teachers perceiving their pupils as positively disposed towards the foreign peoples associated with the language they are learning, Spanish, Mexican and Greek teachers perceiving them as holding negative attitudes, and Belgian teachers tending to perceive their pupils as neither extremely positively nor negatively prejudiced. As can be seen from Table 9.13, next to no significant relationships were found between the indicators of culture teaching practice and teachers' perceptions of the direction of their pupils' attitude towards the foreign culture. This then allows the conclusion that teachers' decisions relating to culture teaching appear to be taken independently of the direction of pupils' attitudes. The fact that some teachers do not take account of their pupils' already acquired perceptions and attitudes is unfortunate, especially in view of some fundamental insights from information

Table 9.11 Teachers' familiarity with the foreign culture and the frequency with which cultural topics are touched upon in the foreign language classroom

Teachers' familiarity with different aspects of the foreign culture (left column)										*Frequency with which different aspects of culture are dealt with (right column)*
		ALL	*BEL*	*BUL*	*GRE*	*MEX*	*POL*	*SPA*	*SWE*	
History, geography, political system	Pearson	0.277$^{(**)}$	0.215$^{(**)}$	0.041	0.257	0.251	0.374$^{(**)}$	0.271	0.420$^{(**)}$	History, geography, political system
	Sig.	0.000	0.008	0.829	0.119	0.096	0.008	0.115	0.001	
	N	405	149	30	38	45	49	35	59	
Different ethnic and social groups	Pearson	0.379$^{(**)}$	0.435$^{(**)}$	0.159	0.312	0.262	0.413$^{(**)}$	0.448$^{(**)}$	0.431$^{(**)}$	Different ethnic and social groups
	Sig.	0.000	0.000	0.403	0.064	0.082	0.004	0.007	0.001	
	N	399	147	30	36	45	48	35	58	
Daily life and routines, living conditions, food and drink etc.	Pearson	0.298$^{(**)}$	0.215$^{(**)}$	0.425$^{(*)}$	0.288	0.464$^{(**)}$	0.285$^{(*)}$	0.424$^{(*)}$	0.284$^{(*)}$	Daily life and routines, living conditions, food and drink etc.
	Sig.	0.000	0.009	0.019	0.083	0.002	0.049	0.011	0.028	
	N	401	148	30	37	43	48	35	60	
Youth culture	Pearson	0.452$^{(**)}$	0.441$^{(**)}$	0.575$^{(**)}$	0.443$^{(**)}$	0.594$^{(**)}$	0.189	0.492$^{(**)}$	0.340$^{(*)}$	Youth culture
	Sig.	0.000	0.000	0.001	0.005	0.000	0.193	0.003	0.010	
	N	400	148	30	38	44	49	35	56	
Education, professional life	Pearson	0.363$^{(**)}$	0.311$^{(**)}$	0.138	0.462$^{(**)}$	0.523$^{(**)}$	0.450$^{(**)}$	0.337$^{(*)}$	0.312$^{(*)}$	Education, professional life
	Sig.	0.000	0.000	0.475	0.005	0.000	0.001	0.048	0.018	
	N	396	145	29	36	45	49	35	57	

Table 9.11 *Continued*

Traditions, folklore, tourist attractions	Pearson	0.342(**)	0.445(**)	0.392(*)	−0.025	0.243	0.414(**)	0.345(*)	0.622(**)	Traditions, folklore, tourist attractions
	Sig.	0.000	0.000	0.035	0.881	0.113	0.004	0.042	0.000	
	N	398	149	29	38	44	46	35	57	
Literature	Pearson	0.393(**)	0.477(**)	0.077	0.436(**)	0.262	0.467(**)	0.354(*)	0.303(*)	Literature
	Sig.	0.000	0.000	0.687	0.007	0.086	0.001	0.037	0.020	
	N	401	149	30	37	44	47	35	59	
Other cultural expressions (music, drama, art)	Pearson	0.404(**)	0.378(**)	0.507(**)	0.357(*)	0.529(**)	0.404(**)	0.272	0.360(**)	Other cultural expressions (music, drama, art)
	Sig.	0.000	0.000	0.006	0.028	0.000	0.005	0.114	0.006	
	N	397	148	28	38	45	46	35	57	
Values and beliefs	Pearson	0.382(**)	0.461(**)	0.496(**)	0.254	0.513(**)	0.313(*)	0.151	0.300(*)	Values and beliefs
	Sig.	0.000	0.000	0.007	0.129	0.000	0.030	0.387	0.030	
	N	387	143	28	37	44	48	35	52	
International relations (political, economic and cultural), with students' own country and other countries	Pearson	0.422(**)	0.477(**)	0.567(**)	0.275	0.617(**)	0.339(*)	0.304	0.23	International relations (political, economic and cultural) with students' own country and other countries
	Sig.	0.000	0.000	0.001	0.10	0.000	0.017	0.076	0.085	
	N	401	149	29	37	45	49	35	57	

*$p < 0.05$, **$p < 0.01$.

Table 9.12 Relationships between culture teaching practice and teachers' perceptions of their pupils' familiarity

My pupils are very knowledgeable about the culture of the foreign language I teach		***ALL***	***BEL***	***BUL***	***GRE***	***MEX***	***POL***	***SPA***	***SWE***
Frequency with which cultural elements are touched upon in the foreign language classroom	Pearson	$0.253^{(**)}$	$0.334^{(**)}$	0.216	0.262	0.255	$0.412^{(**)}$	$0.378^{(*)}$	−0.114
	Sig.	0.000	0.000	0.251	0.107	0.095	0.004	0.025	0.385
	N	404	148	30	39	44	48	35	60
Frequency with which culture teaching activities are practised	Pearson	$0.287^{(**)}$	$0.399^{(**)}$	0.298	$0.473^{(**)}$	0.142	0.244	$0.391^{(*)}$	0.047
	Sig.	0.000	0.000	0.110	0.002	0.358	0.095	0.020	0.720
	N	404	148	30	39	44	48	35	60
Distribution of teaching time over 'language teaching' and 'culture teaching'	Pearson	$0.181^{(**)}$	0.145	0.090	0.115	0.210	0.319^{*}	0.320	0.126
	Sig.	0.000	0.080	0.635	0.486	0.172	0.027	0.061	0.341
	N	401	146	30	39	44	48	35	59

$^{*}p < 0.05$, $^{**}p < 0.01$.

Table 9.13 Relationships between culture teaching practice and teachers' perceptions of their pupils' attitude towards the foreign culture

My pupils have a very positive attitude towards the people associated with the foreign language I teach		***ALL***	***BEL***	***BUL***	***GRE***	***MEX***	***POL***	***SPA***	***SWE***
Frequency with which cultural elements are touched upon in the foreign language classroom	Pearson	0.103(*)	0.125	−0.197	0.107	0.210	0.095	0.417(*)	0.176
	Sig.	0.038	0.131	0.306	0.523	0.171	0.522	0.013	0.178
	N	402	148	29	38	44	48	35	60
Frequency with which culture teaching activities are practised	Pearson	0.127(*)	0.162(*)	−0.166	0.169	0.230	0.221	0.185	0.093
	Sig.	0.011	0.049	0.390	0.310	0.134	0.132	0.287	0.478
	N	402	148	29	38	44	48	35	60
Distribution of teaching time over 'language teaching' and 'culture teaching'	Pearson	0.093	0.069	−0.001	0.132	0.124	−0.197	0.450(**)	0.107
	Sig.	0.063	0.410	0.996	0.428	0.421	0.180	0.007	0.419
	N	399	146	29	38	44	48	35	59

*$p < 0.05$, **$p < 0.01$.

processing theory. Fiske and Neuberg (1990), for example, describe the basic mechanisms of information processing as follows. Perceivers spontaneously start by categorising targets. If they are motivated, if the target is relevant to them, and if sufficient cognitive resources are available, they will pay attention to the attributes, that is, the specific characteristics of the target. Whenever possible, however, perceivers will try to confirm their initial categories. When this is not possible, they will resort to recategorisation. If the last two strategies, i.e. to retain initial categories or to recategorise, fail, and provided that sufficient motivation and cognitive resources are available, people may utilise the different bits of particular information or 'attributes' to arrive at a piecemeal integration and the construction of a new category. They will use these particular bits to attribute specific dispositions to the target, and prepare for storing it in memory. Stangor and McMillan (1992), in addition, observe that people may either be motivated to process information carefully and accurately or they may be motivated to develop and maintain a simple, coherent impression. Whereas in the first case, they are actively involved in processing inconsistent information, in the second case, they are motivated to avoid any inconsistency, either by ignoring or by distorting it. In other words, people may operate under an accuracy (in the sense of true to reality) or an impression maintenance mode. The implication of this is that, when pupils are presented with new information on a foreign culture, they may either attend to it, involve with it and process it carefully, or they may merely perceive it, not get involved with it and decide to store it in already existing categories. They may take this last option because of lack of interest: the information does not appeal to them because it is too far above or below their current level of understanding of the foreign culture and of the world. From this line of reasoning, it can be understood why it is crucial that teachers take account of pupils' already acquired categories, attitudes and motivation, since these are likely to affect the way in which pupils attend to and process information. The acquisition of new *savoirs* and, ultimately, of intercultural competence, depends on the teacher's ability to induce change in pupils' already acquired categories.

The Actual and the Envisaged Foreign Language and Intercultural Competence Teacher

We have shown that two distinct profiles of 'willingness to teach intercultural competence' can be distinguished, that teachers teach culture in a consistent way and that they take little account of their pupils' levels of familiarity with or attitude towards the foreign culture. In the final part of the chapter, we will reflect on the extent to which teachers' actual teaching profile reflects the envisaged profile of the intercultural competence teacher as we have described it in the introductory chapter to this book. There we considered the knowledge and skills an intercultural competence teachers should possess and the attitudes towards foreign cultures, peoples and intercultural issues they should display.

As regards *knowledge*, we said that foreign language teachers should be sufficiently familiar with the foreign cultures associated with the foreign language they teach, and that the contacts they have with these cultures should be both varied and frequent. We found that teachers have frequent media contacts and that teachers who appear to travel little appear to compensate for this lack of direct contact with more extensive contacts with the foreign culture at home, for example via visits to the cultural institute representing the foreign culture in their country (see Chapter 6). We found that teachers consider themselves sufficiently familiar with the foreign cultures associated with the foreign language they teach, and that the frequency with which they address cultural topics and practise culture teaching activities is a function of their degree of familiarity and the extent of their contacts. This suggests that teachers are right in their judgement regarding the extent of their familiarity. It does indeed suffice to teach about a number of different cultural topics in the foreign language classroom.

From this, one might conclude that the extent of teachers' knowledge comes up to what is expected of the FL&IC teacher, but this conclusion would be unwarranted. Today's foreign language teachers may indeed be sufficiently knowledgeable when teaching within the context of the traditional 'foreign cultural approach' (Risager, 1998). They might, however, fall short of expectations if they were to teach towards the attainment of intercultural competence, as defined in this research. From this definition (see Chapter 1), it is clear that a teacher who only possesses knowledge regarding different aspects of the foreign culture, elaborate though it may be, will not be able to adequately guide foreign language learners towards the attainment of intercultural competence in a foreign language. The demands made on teachers' knowledge go well beyond a sufficient degree of familiarity with the foreign culture. Teachers should also know their own culture well and possess culture-general knowledge that can help them to explain similarities and differences between cultures to learners. Teachers should also know both what stereotypes pupils have and how to address these in the foreign language classroom.

The findings presented in Chapter 4 have shown that teachers have some idea regarding the stereotypical ideas their pupils bring to the foreign language classroom. Whether or not the teachers participating in our research also possess a sufficient degree of culture-general knowledge and could explain different aspects of their own culture to a foreigner in a well-informed and objective way is difficult to say, since we did not collect data regarding these facets of their cultural knowledge. From the way in which teachers define the objectives of culture teaching and foreign language education, we know that teachers do not consider it important that their pupils gain a better understanding of their own cultural identity. Though we cannot conclude from this that teachers are not knowledgeable regarding their own culture, we can conclude that they do not employ the knowledge they may have in the foreign language classroom. The same is true with respect to teachers' insights regarding pupils' stereotypes. Though they may be familiar with them, they tend not to take account of them when deciding on the cultural contents of their courses.

From this, two different conclusions can be drawn. First, one could maintain that, at present, teachers may possess the knowledge needed to teach intercultural competence, but that they have not yet put that knowledge to use in the foreign language classroom, and perhaps have not yet realised that they are expected to apply it in that context. Secondly, one could conclude that teachers do not possess the required knowledge, and therefore do not teach in the way expected from the FL&IC teacher. This, of course, is not to say that teachers could not acquire the necessary insights and knowledge needed.

This then leads us to what is expected of the FL&IC teacher in terms of skills. We stated that teachers should be able to employ teaching techniques that promote the acquisition of *savoirs*, *savoir-apprendre*, *savoir-comprendre*, *savoir-faire*, *savoir-s'engager* and *savoir-être*. Teachers should be able to help pupils relate their own culture to foreign cultures, to compare cultures and to empathise with foreign cultures' points of view. They should be able to select appropriate teaching materials and to adjust these materials should they not allow the achievement of the aims of intercultural competence teaching. Next to being skilful classroom teachers, teachers should also be able to use experiential approaches to language-and-culture teaching.

From the kinds of teaching activities most frequently practised in the foreign language classroom, as described in Chapter 5, we can deduce that teachers tend to employ techniques that aim to enlarge learners' knowledge of the foreign culture, and not to encourage learners to search for information in different sources, analyse it independently and present their findings in order to discuss them with others. Though 'comparison of cultures' appears to be an activity frequently practised, other activities aiming at the acquisition of intercultural skills, such as 'reflect critically on one's sources of information', 'explore an aspect of the foreign culture', 'practise skills useful in intercultural contact situations' are not.

This allows two similar conclusions to those for knowledge regarding the extent to which teachers possess the skills needed to be able to teach intercultural competence in foreign language education. First, we could conclude that teachers may not yet be practising intercultural teaching skills because they do not realise that that is what is expected of them. A second possible conclusion could be that teachers are not practising these skills because they do not know how to go about teaching learners how to compare cultures, empathise with foreign cultures' points of view, interpret documents in appropriate ways, explore unknown aspects of foreign cultures, etc. The fact that teachers who are willing to interculturalise foreign language education are in favour of cross-curricular approaches to teaching intercultural competence and believe all teachers, not just foreign language teachers, should promote its acquisition, can be considered in this respect. Two kinds of feelings may underlie this demand for a collective effort towards the attainment of intercultural competence in learners. On the one hand, teachers may feel unable to teach intercultural competence and therefore require the assistance of other subjects and teachers. On the other hand, they may feel able to teach intercultural competence, but at the same time find that all subjects should work towards achieving this same goal if one wants to be able to achieve anything in this area.

As regards the demand that FL&IC teachers should be able to select teaching materials appropriate for intercultural competence teaching, our data suggest that teachers are definitely able to comment critically on the cultural contents of foreign language teaching materials, pointing out good and less satisfactory sides. Care has to be taken, however, not to equate this ability with the ability to assess teaching materials with respect to their potential for teaching intercultural competence. The teachers who commented on the cultural dimension of their teaching materials did so from the perspective of the traditional 'foreign cultural approach', pointing out where the information regarding the foreign culture had been faultily selected or represented. Individual teachers also point to the need to revise the textbook's approach to the teaching of culture, and to the demand for more intercultural tasks. The number of teachers doing so is very small, and does not allow the conclusion that teachers are able to assess the culture teaching approaches adopted by their textbooks from the 'intercultural approach' perspective. Neither do our data allow us to state that teachers are able to adjust the materials they use in order to enhance their potential for promoting the acquisition of intercultural competence.

Next to being skilful classroom teachers and able assessors of foreign language teaching materials, FL&IC teachers should also be able to use out-of-classroom experiential approaches to language-and-culture teaching. Our data reveal that school trips and exchange programmes tend not to be considered activities that take place in the context of foreign language education. Only a minority of the teachers devote time to preparing or following-up on this kind of activity in the foreign language classroom. It seems that most teachers are convinced school trips and exchange programmes have positive effects on learners' perceptions and attitudes regarding foreign cultures, but they also think of these activities as the responsibility of the school, of other teachers or of all teachers. Those who do devote teaching time to following-up on experiential learning activities appear to use activities which assist learners to reflect on their experiences and on cultural differences between their own and the foreign culture, and which are typical of intercultural approaches to foreign language education.

We then compared the current foreign language teachers' profile and the envisaged FL&IC teacher profile from the point of view of attitudes. With respect to attitudes, FL&IC teachers should be favourably disposed towards the integration of intercultural competence teaching in foreign language education and willing to actually work towards achieving that goal. They should define the objectives of foreign language education both in terms of language learning and intercultural competence acquisition. FC&IC teachers are willing to take account of their pupils' perceptions and attitudes regarding foreign cultures, and to start from these perceptions and attitudes when designing the learning process.

Our data reveal that a very large part of teachers are clearly willing to integrate intercultural competence teaching in foreign language education. They also reveal that this willingness is not reflected in the way in which they currently shape their teaching practice or define the objectives of foreign language education. These objectives continue to be defined mainly in linguistic terms, though teachers in some countries, notably Bulgaria and Greece, clearly give greater prominence to cultural objectives than teachers in other countries. As regards the way in which teachers attend to their pupils' perceptions and attitudes, it is clear that they take their decisions as to how to shape their culture teaching practice largely independently of their pupils' current knowledge and disposition. In this sense, they clearly do not meet the expectations of the FL&IC teacher.

To conclude, we can say that teachers are moving towards becoming FL&IC teachers, but that at present their profile does not meet all expectations of the 'foreign language and intercultural competence teacher' regarding knowledge, skills and attitudes. Individual teachers may already possess the envisaged FL&IC teacher profile. The majority of teachers in all countries participating in this research, however, either have what could be labelled 'a foreign language teacher profile', focusing primarily and almost exclusively on the acquisition of communicative competence in the foreign language, or a 'foreign language and culture teaching profile', focusing primarily on the acquisition of communicative competence in the foreign language, but also teaching culture so as to enhance pupils' familiarity with the foreign culture as well as their motivation to learn the foreign language.

In the final chapter, we discuss these findings and speculate about their implications for teacher education, educational policy and future research.

Chapter 10

The Future of Intercultural Competence in Foreign Language Education: Recommendations for Professional Development, Educational Policy and Research

LIES SERCU

Throughout this book, our focus has been on foreign language teachers' perceptions of intercultural competence teaching and on current culture-and-language teaching practices. We have found that teachers, especially those who are favourably disposed towards the teaching of intercultural competence, are moving towards becoming FL&IC teachers, but that at present their teaching profile does not meet all the expectations of the FL&IC teacher.

We believe we have, for the first time, shown the variability, but also relative consistency, of language teachers' views today in a considerable number of countries. In that sense, we consider our findings to be significant from a scientific point of view. Until now, much of the research on teachers' beliefs has focused on the areas of science and maths education or on reading (see e.g. Bell *et al.*, 2000; Prosser & Trigwell, 1999). These investigations have frequently been concerned with understanding how teacher beliefs impact on practice. Our study differs from these past studies in several ways. The focus has been on teachers of foreign languages, and more specifically on teachers' beliefs regarding the cultural dimension of foreign language education and the teaching of intercultural competence. Though some studies have investigated foreign language teachers' conceptions (for an excellent review, see Borg, 2003), far fewer have focused on foreign language teachers' perceptions of the intercultural dimension of foreign language education, with the notable exceptions of

Byram and Risager (1999), Ryan (1997; 1998) and Sercu (2001). The present study also differs from other studies of teachers' beliefs by its international character and its emphasis on commonalities in teachers' beliefs, rather than on the idiosyncrasies of individual teachers' mental processes. Though an international perspective lay at the basis of Byram and Risager's study, comparing British and Danish teachers (Byram & Risager, 1999), a far larger number of countries were involved in our study.

Our findings will be of interest to anyone wanting to find out how foreign language teachers in a number of different countries view intercultural competence and how their views currently impact on their teaching. Understanding teachers' perceptions and the reasons why they embrace or reject intercultural competence teaching is crucial for teacher educators who want to design (international) teacher education programmes which can clarify and exemplify to foreign language teachers how they can promote the acquisition of intercultural competence in their classes. Our findings highlight important differences and commonalities in teachers' perceptions. Both national and international teacher education programmes can build on these commonalities and have teachers from different countries cooperate, knowing that they all, to a certain extent, share a common body of knowledge, skills and convictions. They can also exploit differences between teachers to enhance their understanding of intercultural competence.

Our results will also help individual teachers to reflect on their own perceptions and teaching practice, on where they stand on the 'favourably disposed – unfavourably disposed' continuum in comparison with other teachers in their own country (if they live in one of the countries in the research) or compared to those who participated from other countries. The findings may serve as a starting point for discussions with colleagues, for exchange of ideas regarding the integration of an intercultural dimension in one's teaching and for initiatives to jointly reconsider existing teaching practices.

In this final chapter, we will enlarge on these different points and speculate about the implications of our findings for teacher education, educational policy and future research. We start with a discussion of what our findings mean and how they relate to previous research findings.

Discussion of Research Findings

Average foreign language and intercultural competence teaching profile

Our findings have shown that we can speak of an average FL&IC teaching profile and that this profile does not yet coincide with the envisaged FL&IC profile. The fact that an average FL&IC profile appears to exist is surprising in view of the fact that data were collected in seven different countries. These countries have different foreign language teaching traditions. In some countries, parents and pupils may be more convinced of the need to learn foreign languages than in others. Pupils' perceptions and attitudes regarding the target cultures, countries and peoples may be different, depending on the kinds of relationships that exist or existed between particular nations. For teachers and pupils in some countries, it may be easier to travel to the main target language country than in other countries. Some countries may have easier access to television channels broadcasting in the language learnt. The number of teaching periods available for learning a particular foreign language may differ across countries. In some countries, teachers are free to choose their own teaching materials, whilst in others they are not.

In spite of these differences, it was possible to profile an average FL&IC teacher. This may mean that local teaching circumstances may be less different than presupposed. The fact that teachers in all countries mention the same reasons for not getting round to culture teaching more often supports this interpretation. It may also mean that local teaching circumstances really are different, but that the respects in which they differ do not affect teachers' perceptions regarding intercultural competence teaching. Thus, though teachers do not perceive their pupils' attitudes and perceptions regarding foreign cultures in exactly the same way in the different countries, these differences do not affect their beliefs regarding intercultural competence. As a matter of fact, it appears that teachers tend to take little account of their pupils' abilities, needs and interests, and adopt teacher-centred approaches to culture teaching.

Furthermore, we want to point out here that differences between countries may be levelled out by corrective teacher behaviour. Teachers' familiarity with the foreign culture, for example, proved to be a factor affecting the extent to which they deal with different aspects of the foreign culture in their foreign language classroom. The fact that it may be more difficult for teachers in some countries to travel regularly to the foreign countries, in which the language they teach is spoken, does not mean that they are less familiar with the foreign culture. Via other kinds of contact, they manage to get to know the foreign culture to such a degree that they are able to teach about it.

Comparisons with research on teachers' beliefs

The fact that an average FL&IC profile appears to exist is also not surprising in view of the insights gained from research on teachers' beliefs.

This research tradition has shown that beliefs regarding teaching and learning tend to be well-established by the time a pupil finishes secondary education, and that they tend to persevere in a teacher's conception of teaching and learning (see e.g. Calderhead, 1996; Pajares, 1992). Once they have been formed, they are hard to change. Beliefs tend to self-perpetuate, persevering against contradiction caused by reason, time, schooling, or experience. The earlier a belief system is incorporated in the belief structure, the more difficult it is to alter. Newly acquired beliefs, by contrast, are more vulnerable to change. Woods (1996) suggests that when teachers' beliefs are very tightly connected with other beliefs, they are more difficult to change than when they are only loosely connected to a teacher's belief system. When teachers change, they may not abandon particular beliefs, but instead gradually replace them with more relevant beliefs.

Since our respondents will have been taught foreign languages with a view to the acquisition of communicative competence or perhaps only grammatical competence, not intercultural competence, it is not surprising that they define the objectives of foreign language education mainly in linguistic terms. Nor is it surprising that teachers tend to perceive culture teaching mainly in terms of the passing on of information regarding the foreign cultures associated with the foreign language they teach, for that most probably is the approach to culture teaching they have experienced themselves as learners of a foreign language. In view of the fact that the communicative approach to foreign language education has been advocated since at least the 1980s, it is not surprising that communicative conceptions of foreign language education constitute the core of teachers' views. These conceptions affect the way in which teachers teach the language and approach culture teaching, and it is against this background that they assess proposals for innovation. At present, intercultural competence teaching is perceived as an important proposal for innovation in all participating countries, but it is also viewed as peripheral to the commonly accepted linguistic goals of foreign language education. The fact that teachers in all countries are clearly willing to interculturalise foreign language education may follow from the fact that they share the same conviction that, as educators, they have to prepare learners for life in an increasingly multicultural world, in which they have to be fluent in more than one language and interculturally competent.

Though beliefs tend to persevere, this does not mean that no new beliefs can be acquired, but newly acquired beliefs are vulnerable to change. Teachers who at first welcome new ideas and believe these innovations are promising may drop them the moment they experience that an innovation does not work. Beliefs regarding what works and does not work act as filters (Carter and Doyle, 1995) and are based on teaching expertise. A large body of research on teacher thinking has been concerned with the development of teaching expertise (Berliner, 1987; Berliner 1988; Carter & Doyle, 1987; Dunkin & Precians, 1992; Kwo, 1994). Having a large network of context-specific conceptions is one of the signs of expert practice. Put the other way round, teaching experience is an important factor in the development of context-specific conceptions. A beginning teacher must make decisions based on his/her general conceptions. Going through this process, however, leads to the development of context-specific conceptions. As a teacher gets experience, teaching decisions may become more and more automated until s/he reaches the point where s/he implicitly knows what to do without having to engage in conscious thought (Berliner, 1987). This does not mean that the teacher always does things in the best possible way, only that his/her thought processes are highly automated. Our data suggest that our respondents are experienced teachers of communicative competence in a foreign language. Over the years of teaching, they will have acquired expertise regarding what works well and what does not work well with respect to teaching the grammar, vocabulary and pronunciation of the foreign language, as well as concerning how to assist pupils to integrate these different components to become more skilful readers, speakers, writers and listeners. They will have dropped particular techniques, which they found to be less successful, and acquired others, to their mind more promising and efficient ones. We can expect that a similar process will take place with respect to the teaching of intercultural competence, but we fear the developmental process towards better intercultural competence teaching may come to a halt too easily. A teacher teaching towards communicative competence may well be positively disposed towards the integration of intercultural competence, and welcome this new approach as a worthwhile and interesting innovation. Yet, this favourable disposition may be dropped the moment a teacher experiences that language and culture cannot be taught in an integrated way, and that consequently less time is available for practising communicative skills in the classroom. Our data indeed clearly point towards the fact that teachers' willingness to interculturalise foreign language education is dependent on the extent to which they believe language and culture can be taught in an integrated way. Our data, likewise, reveal that teachers' willingness to interculturalise foreign language education is also dependent on the extent to which teachers from other subjects are willing to promote the acquisition of intercultural competence. Teachers who feel a lack of support from colleagues may easily drop their favourable disposition towards the integration of intercultural competence in foreign language education. Lack of time, lack of preparation and lack of availability of suitable teaching materials were also mentioned as important contextual factors, which prevent a teacher from devoting more teaching time to intercultural competence teaching.

Research on teachers' perceptions has also revealed that their conceptions, to a large extent, shape their instructional behaviour. Prosser and Trigwell (1999) report a 'reasonably close' relation between the approaches to teaching taken and teachers' conceptions of teaching and learning. The six general conceptions of teaching which teachers may hold have been identified as (1) the transmission of the concepts of the syllabus; (2) the transmission of the teacher's knowledge; (3) helping students acquire the concepts of the syllabus; (4) helping students acquire the teacher's knowledge; (5) helping students develop concepts; and (6) helping students change concepts. These general conceptions of teaching and learning directly shape the development of context-specific conceptions, which directly lead to choice of specific teaching activities (see e.g. Gallagher & Tobin, 1987; Prosser & Trigwell, 1997, 1999; Prosser *et al.*, 1994). Our findings suggest that our respondents perceive teaching and learning culture and intercultural competence more in terms of the transmission of the teacher's knowledge than in terms of assisting learners to develop and change concepts.[1] The kinds of culture teaching activities reported most frequently in the foreign language classroom can be said to be typical of teacher-directed approaches to teaching. Teachers tend to pass on the cultural information included in the textbook, irrespective of whether or not this information is of interest to the pupils or has the potential of changing distorted pupil images. In this respect too, they appear to continue to employ the approach to culture teaching commonly used when they themselves were pupils of foreign languages. It may well be that teachers are good at perceiving pupils' linguistic abilities and difficulties; with respect to culture learning and the acquisition of intercultural competence, this appears not yet to be the case.

In the literature about teachers' beliefs, it is also stated that teachers may have conflicting conceptions, and that the link between these conflicting conceptions and teaching practices is not clear (see e.g. Lumpe *et al.*, 1998). This insight too is reflected in our findings. There appears to be a conflict between teachers' willingness to teach intercultural competence and the way in which they currently shape their teaching practice. On the one hand, they want their pupils to become proficient users of the foreign language. On the other hand, they believe their pupils should become intercultural persons. It may be the case that they are not clear in their minds as to what is meant by intercultural competence or what is expected of them as teachers of a foreign language and of intercultural competence. From the kinds of teaching activities reported most frequently in the foreign language classroom, it appears that teachers define intercultural competence primarily in terms of familiarity with the foreign culture. Other findings relating to teachers' opinions regarding different facets of intercultural competence teaching also suggest that they believe that enhancing pupils' familiarity with the foreign culture will lead to more tolerant attitudes towards that culture. This is not to say that they do not realise their approach to teaching intercultural competence may not be completely adequate. Some teachers may well realise their conception of intercultural competence is too limited in view of what is expected of them, but this realisation does not yet affect their choice of teaching activities.

Studies investigating teachers' conceptions of subject matter have also found that there is not necessarily a link between a teacher's conception of the nature of the subject taught and actual teaching behaviour. The fact that teachers teach intercultural competence in terms of the promotion of knowledge does not necessarily mean that they do not realise that intercultural competence also comprises an attitudinal and skills dimension. Furthermore, the fact that teachers appear to teach culture as a relatively unvarying and static entity made up of accumulated, classifiable, observable 'facts', does not allow the conclusion that they do not hold post-modern, dynamic views of cultures, and perceive culture in terms of cultural variations (within and across cultures). Teachers may indeed hold up-to-date views of culture, without these views affecting their teaching practice.

A final insight from research on teachers' conceptions concerns the fact that different aspects of the teaching context may affect teachers' views (Borg, 2003). These include teachers' perceptions of class size, student motivation and student ability, control over teaching methods or course content, departmental support for innovation, self-efficacy, the teaching workload, the requirements for earning tenure, and school facilities. These studies have shown that teachers' perceptions of these different aspects of the teaching context affect the way in which they teach. A student-focused approach to teaching, for example, is associated with perceptions that the workload is not too high, the class sizes are not too large, that the teacher has some control over what and how he/she teaches and that the variation in student characteristics is not too large.

In our study, we found that the reasons which teachers mentioned for not getting round to culture teaching more often were lack of time, curricular overload, lack of pupil interest in the foreign culture and lack of a basic pupil familiarity with the foreign culture. Some teachers also made reference to their own inability to teach culture or intercultural competence, or to the fact that no intercultural objectives are mentioned in the foreign language curricula.

Comparisons with research into teachers' conceptions of intercultural competence teaching

From the previous section, we can conclude that our findings are largely in line with general educational research regarding teachers' beliefs, a now well-established research discipline. In this section, the focus will be on literature regarding teachers' beliefs regarding the cultural dimension of foreign language education. Research in this area is of relatively recent date and the studies investigating this dimension do not abound. In this review, we will largely draw on Byram and Risager (1999), who report on an investigation of Danish and English teachers' perceptions of the cultural dimension of foreign language education, and on Sercu (2001), who reports on an investigation among Belgian teachers of English, French and German. Byram and Risager collected data amongst 653 Danish and 212 British teachers. All respondents completed a questionnaire. In addition, 18 British teachers and 42 Danish teachers were interviewed. Sercu collected questionnaire data amongst 78 teachers of English, 45 teachers of French and 27 teachers of German.

As regards teachers' perceptions of the aims of foreign language education, Byram and Risager (1999) found that very few teachers in Denmark or England think the cultural dimension of foreign language education is more important than the linguistic one, but that it is their responsibility to also teach about the foreign culture. Culture is typically conceived as a phenomenon, which is nationally delimited and defined, linked to a national language, and that, consequently, foreign language teachers do not spontaneously demonstrate much awareness of cultural diversity within one country nor of cultural complexity. In this respect, Danish and British teachers appear to be in accord with Flemish teachers studied by Sercu and, indeed, with the teachers in our study. From the way in which our respondents define the objectives of foreign language teaching and from the way in which they distribute their teaching time over language teaching and culture teaching, it is clear that culture teaching at present plays no more than a subsidiary role.

With regard to teachers' willingness to interculturalise foreign language education, Byram and Risager (1999) and Sercu (2001) underline that they found a growing awareness amongst their respondents of the significance of the cultural dimension as European integration proceeds, and a clear willingness to teach both language and culture. A similar tendency was found amongst the European teachers participating in our study.

As regards teachers' views on their pupils' perceptions of the foreign cultures and peoples associated with the foreign language(s) they are learning, the general impression is that Danish and British teachers, like Flemish teachers, believe that their pupils basically hold traditional stereotypes, but are gradually developing more diversified ideas, as more and more of them get the opportunity to travel to European countries. Our study too reveals that teachers hold this conviction.

Though for methodological reasons, Byram and Risager's data cannot easily be compared to Sercu's (2001) and our data,[2] we can nonetheless conclude that teachers in our study agree that daily life and routines, food and drink, history, geography, education, traditions and customs and youth culture should be dealt with in foreign language classrooms in secondary education. In all countries, teachers appear to give low priority to topics such as international relations and the country's significance for the home country, or values and norms. Comparing Sercu (2001) and Byram and Risager (1999) in somewhat more detail in this respect is revealing. Contrary to Danish and British teachers, Flemish teachers attach higher importance to tourism and travel, and to 'high' Culture. Byram and Risager observe that there were some interesting differences between Danish and English teachers. Danish respondents put more emphasis on 'history', 'ethnic relations and racism' and 'social and living conditions', and much less on 'tourism and travel' and 'working life and unemployment'. Apart from these two themes neither group includes any others that might be considered to draw upon sociological analysis: political system, gender roles and relationships, religious life and institutions, environmental issues. Both groups also omit topics from 'high' culture – literature and film, art, theatre – and give low priority to themes which might be described as relating cultures to each other or inducing reflexivity: 'the country's significance for Britain/ Denmark' and 'stereotypes'. Similar distinctions between the different teacher groups involved in our study were found with respect to individual cultural topics, but enlarging on these differences here would lead us too far. A further investigation of the reasons for these differences would be revealing. They may concern differences in teaching traditions, teaching materials, perceptions of pupils, curricular guidelines, or still other factors which a qualitative research approach might make visible (see also our discussion of our research methodology below).

With respect to culture teaching practices, Byram and Risager (1999) briefly comment on teachers' perceptions of their teaching practice. They state that teachers report using a range of activities in the classroom to work on the intercultural dimension of foreign language education. These activities include discussions, work with television programmes or other means of communication (e.g. e-mail correspondence), or inviting a foreign guest to the classroom. Teachers are convinced that direct contact is most effective in promoting change in pupils' perceptions or attitudes regarding the target people or cultures. Perhaps most notably, they state that most teachers do not have a systematic plan as to how to go about teaching intercultural competence, or how to deal with stereotypes and prejudice in the foreign language classroom. When inquiring into the details of implementing language-and-culture teaching, respondents in both Denmark and the UK consider it important to promote the acquisition of a substantial body of knowledge, since more knowledge is believed to lead to more tolerant attitudes. With respect to the way in which the foreign culture should be presented, an interesting difference exists between British and Danish teachers. Whereas British teachers think they should present a positive image of the foreign culture, Danish teachers opt for a more realistic presentation. Finally, like in the Belgian sample investigated in Sercu (2001), there is a tendency amongst respondents to give low priority to the promotion of reflection by learners on their own cultural identity, though a number of Danish teachers explicitly point out that they consider it important that pupils should become aware of their own national identity. The picture we found amongst our teachers largely coincides with the one just depicted. Our teachers employ a range of teaching activities, too, which are especially directed towards the acquisition of knowledge regarding the foreign culture and do not usually include reflection on one's own cultural identity. Though the teachers in the present study believe direct contacts, via school trips or exchange projects, have a presumably mainly positive effect on pupils, they do not usually devote time to preparing or following-up on such contacts. Contrary to Byram and Risager (1999) and Sercu (2001), we have been able to show that teachers approach culture teaching with a high degree of systematicity and consistency, even if their teaching cannot be characterised as intercultural competence teaching.

From the summary of some of the main findings presented in Byram and Risager (1999) and Sercu (2001), and from our study, we can conclude that foreign language teachers' perceptions of intercultural competence teaching and teaching practices run parallel to a large extent. Teachers are clearly willing to teach intercultural competence, yet in actual teaching appear not to move beyond a traditional information-transfer pedagogy in any of the countries, though, interestingly, different topics appear to enjoy priority in the different countries.

Discussion of Research Methodology and Recommendations for Further Research

The aim of this study was to research teachers' concepts and beliefs regarding language-and-culture teaching, and to investigate to what extent it is possible to speak of an average culture-and-language teaching profile, which is shared by teachers in a number of different countries. To achieve that aim, we chose a quantitative research design. We used an electronic questionnaire (see Appendix 1) with mainly, but not exclusively, closed questions. At relevant stages in the questionnaire, we allowed room for teachers to provide answers falling outside the closed answering categories we had designed for them on the basis of our understanding of our research questions. During data analysis, we looked for correlations between teacher characteristics and for means, without losing from sight however that teachers cannot be reduced to means. They are human beings, not variables. They have a personal history and personal reasons for making particular choices and decisions, and work within particular local contexts. We have tried to present our results as the lines of thought along which people seemingly work and have shown how these principles of mind appear to affect their teaching. We hope we have steered clear of the suggestion that these lines and principles are proof of mechanistic causal laws. Teachers are not machines, and many factors affect the connection between a principle or conviction and its actual realisation in practice. We have tried to draw all individual research results together and consider them as a totality, showing trends but also divergence.

Though some might remark that a qualitative approach to the investigation of teachers' perceptions and self-concepts would have been more appropriate, we believe our quantitative approach has proved its worth, allowing us to compare teachers in a number of different countries. We hope the findings that arose from this quantitative approach will give rise to qualitative research projects, which can inquire into teachers' deepest convictions and concerns regarding language teaching in general and intercultural competence teaching in particular. Using qualitative data collection techniques may deepen our insights regarding the personal, interpersonal or contextual factors affecting the implementation of intercultural competence teaching in day-to-day teaching practice. Investigators can then explore the types of beliefs that are more likely to cause conflict and uncertainty in a teacher's mind, the situations which give rise to conflict and perhaps incite negative feelings regarding the possibility of teaching intercultural competence as well as the processes that provide the most effective means of reconciling beliefs. Interview studies could also lead to a better understanding of teachers' present conceptions of, for example, 'cross-curricular approaches to the teaching of intercultural competence', 'the integration of language and culture teaching', 'a realistic image of the foreign culture', etc.

Valuable though qualitative research designs may be, especially where teachers' beliefs are investigated, we believe they have their limitations too. We think research will be ill-advised to suggest that particular teaching approaches and particular perceptions of teaching are wholly unique to individuals, despite the fact that teachers may voice their convictions in a highly individualistic and personalised way, as has been shown abundantly within the context of qualitative investigations. People are always also part of a community that observes its own implicit rules and displays a particular behaviour. The community has been built on the basis of experience, of what works well. Teachers may have to discover this for themselves and have to build their own frame of reference, but it would be misguided to suggest that teachers are all different and that they do not work within a community that has acquired a particular knowledge and skills' base over the course of the years. On the other hand, it is clear that teachers have the freedom to refrain from observing these rules, and follow their own paths.

A second remark we want to make regarding qualitative analyses concerns the fact that researchers within this tradition are also expected to lay bare the commonalities they have been able to distil from the highly personalised narratives they collect. The requirement in qualitative research of the absoluteness of a formulated rule or rules compensates for the fact that there are often very few cases, and that generalisation beyond these few cases is hazardous. If one concentrates on the endless diversity of life and of the data, in the end it is hard to get a hold on the phenomenon one is researching. Finally, qualitative researchers who make use of interviews or observations also always have to be aware of the fact that the way in which they phrase their questions can affect the answers they get. Interviewees may sense a desire for a particular answer and try to meet that desired answer. The view of their life, of their job may be very much guided by the themes covered in the interview. The same is of course true for survey questions, but it needs to be said here that a similar danger exists with qualitative research. Naturally occurring data would really be what one hopes to be able to collect, but with respect to teachers' beliefs this is extremely difficult.

From the above, it will be clear that different studies in the domain of teacher beliefs and teacher cognition will vary in what is considered to be evidence of cognition and cognitive change. Questionnaire responses, repertory grids, and in-depth interview responses, for example, are very different forms of data, and the extent to which these and other forms of data can capture the content, structure, and change processes of cognitive phenomena is clearly an issue for continuing methodological discussion. We hope we have been able to show that questionnaire responses have a particular value in this research domain.

Our study confined itself to describing secondary school teachers' foreign language and intercultural competence teaching profiles, which is a limitation. Studies focusing on different age groups could adduce further evidence or counter-evidence for the existence of an average FL&IC teacher profile. Studies including teachers from other nationalities than the ones included in this study could serve that same goal. We may also speculate about what might have resulted if we had made a survey among student teachers or teacher educators. Would we have found the same image? Would we have found an image that reflects a more or less outspoken desire to teach intercultural competence in foreign language education? Would these groups be more or less aware of the difficulties involved in the integration of language-and-culture teaching than the teachers we surveyed? Would they hold the same or different opinions regarding the foreign language textbooks around? Would they favour an approach to intercultural competence teaching within foreign language education, or do they rather support a cross-curricular approach?

Four-hundred and twenty-four teachers participated in our research, with Belgium having the largest sample (151) and Bulgaria the smallest (30). The respondents were not a random sample of teachers from each country. Consequently, the results may differ in some significant way from what would have been gathered from a purely random sample. The fact that in the Swedish and Bulgarian sample the respondents had all attended or were attending an in-service course devoted to intercultural competence teaching at the time of the study may mean that these teachers' responses are only to a certain extent comparable to the ordinary Swedish or Bulgarian teacher's. Enlarging the number of teachers involved in the study would have led to a higher degree of generalisability of our research findings. In the present investigation, the number of teachers per country was large enough to allow for statistical analyses, yet in most countries, it was not large enough to allow for generalizing statements regarding, say, Mexican foreign language teachers' views regarding intercultural competence teaching. On the other hand, we believe we have been able to show tendencies in the data, which are recognisable to non-participant teachers, as informal reactions to the presentation of the research findings have already shown.

We also want to speculate here about what would have happened if we had translated the questionnaire into the different mother tongues of the teachers involved in the investigation. We found that the translation of particular concepts was difficult. Either the concept did not exist in the local language, as was the case with 'intercultural competence' in many countries and a literal translation seemed awkward and did not really clarify the concept to the participants, or it covered a different reality, as was the case with for example 'intercultural education', being associated with particular societal groups only (e.g. immigrants, Roma). At the start of the project, we decided that it was preferable to offer the same English-medium questionnaire in all countries, unless an English-medium questionnaire would have meant that none of the teachers in a particular country would have participated because of insufficient knowledge of English. Teachers could answer the questions in English or in their mother tongue. In the latter case, it was up to the local researcher to translate the answers provided in the mother tongue into English so that cross-national comparisons became possible. All in all, we believe the fact that the questionnaire was English-medium did not constitute a major problem, since most of the teachers who participated were teachers of English. In Belgium, a substantial number of French and German teachers participated, which indicates that they too felt sufficiently comfortable in the English language to be able to fill out an English-medium questionnaire. In other countries, the fact that the questionnaire was English-medium will have excluded teachers of French, German or Spanish. The picture that arose from the data in Belgium indicates that teachers of English, French and Spanish differ in a number of respects, for example with respect to the cultural topics which they deal with most frequently in the foreign language classroom, but not with respect to the fundamental convictions regarding language-and-culture teaching or the teaching of intercultural competence. It would nonetheless be interesting to investigate more extensively the degree of similarity and difference between teachers of different foreign languages, coming from different teaching traditions. This would probably mean that a questionnaire would have to be drawn up in the teachers' mother tongue or else in the different languages they teach. This latter option might again raise the translation issue, which will become all the more important if this investigation is replicated with a larger variety of countries.

Because we were interested in teachers' views regarding the integration of intercultural competence teaching in foreign language education and regarding their teaching practice, we did not collect first hand information regarding teaching practice, but relied on a single source, namely a self-report questionnaire. Thus our data were not verified through other sources, such as classroom observations, lesson plans, reports from students, colleagues or administrators. Including these different sources of information into a research project would have helped to verify and contextualise our findings.

Since teachers' practices are also shaped by the social, psychological and environmental realities of the school and classroom, future research could investigate to what extent parents, principals' requirements, the school, society, curriculum mandates, classroom and school layout, school policies, colleagues, standardised tests and the available resources affect teachers' views regarding the teaching of intercultural competence in foreign language education. There is evidence to suggest that, unsurprisingly, such factors may hinder language teachers' adoption of practices which reflect their beliefs (see e.g. Burns, 1996; Johnson, 1996).

Our findings are based on a one-time moment of data collection. More longitudinal studies of language teacher cognition, both in teacher education contexts as well as in the work of practising teachers, will shed light on teachers' evolving conceptions. Further research into the processes through which language teachers' cognitions and practices are transformed as they accumulate experience is required. Much existing insight into this issue is based on comparisons of experienced and novice teachers. Longitudinal enquiries of how teachers actually change would be an important addition to the existing research here.

Though we included the perspective of the learner in our study through asking teachers to report on the perceptions and attitudes of their pupils regarding foreign cultures, countries and peoples, we did not explore the relationship between teachers' cognitions and their teaching practices on the one hand, and learning outcomes on the other. We provided a picture of the pupils through the teachers' eyes. Research focusing on learning outcomes might start with an inquiry into pupils' perceptions before the start of a particular course through working directly with the pupils, and might then investigate to what extent teachers' perceptions of their teaching and pupils appear to be related to pupils' actual learning outcomes.

Recommendations for Professional Development Sessions

One of the reasons for investigating teachers' beliefs about teaching intercultural competence in foreign language education was to be able to provide them with professional development opportunities that build on their existing beliefs and teaching practices. The findings of research on teachers' beliefs indicate that their beliefs regarding teaching and learning affect their conceptions of specific teaching situations and, ultimately, their teaching practice.

Starting from teachers' beliefs and trying to alter them, therefore, seems to hold the best promise for altering teaching practice. Professional development which engages teachers in a direct exploration of their beliefs and principles may create greater self-awareness through reflection and critical questioning as starting points for later adaptation. Teachers can monitor how their own beliefs and practices change through such activities as journal writing, case studies and other methods for reflective analysis. Opportunities to share experiences of positive change can provide a valuable source of input for in-service courses and teacher education activities. Our findings suggest for example that teachers perceive culture teaching foremost in terms of teacher-centred transmission of cultural knowledge. One way to try and change teachers' beliefs and promote reflection is to expose them to beliefs that provide alternatives for this kind of pedagogy, and that help them perceive intercultural competence not only in terms of the acquisition of cultural knowledge, but also in terms of the acquisition of intercultural skills and attitudes.

In some cases, teachers may already be convinced of the importance of assisting learners to acquire intercultural competence and yet there may still be barriers to implementing intercultural competence teaching. These can take the form of conflicts or inconsistencies in a teacher's belief system, but very often, this kind of conflicts in beliefs remains subconscious. Teacher education sessions will need to provide opportunities for them to make these conflicting beliefs explicit, to examine and discuss them.

One of the conclusions of our study is that the majority of teachers are willing to integrate intercultural competence in their teaching, and yet define the objectives of foreign language education foremost in terms of communicative competence, not intercultural communicative competence. Teachers may feel it is important that their learners become interculturally competent, and yet feel they are accountable to parents and students who think the acquisition of communicative competence in the foreign language should be the principal objective of foreign language education. This conviction that teaching time should be above all devoted to communicative competence may be reinforced by constraints related to the curriculum and to scheduling. Teachers may have to cover a full language curriculum and only be allotted a limited number of teaching periods. In addition to conflicts within a teacher's own system of beliefs, there may also be conflicts with beliefs of colleagues (e.g. a teacher would like to implement a cross-curricular approach to intercultural competence teaching but colleagues believe in language teaching within the confines of the subject) and conflicts with beliefs of students (e.g. a teacher wants his/her students to become independent explorers of cultures, but students prefer teacher-directed instruction).

Apart from building on teachers' existing beliefs, teacher development sessions should also build on their existing teaching practices and on their beliefs regarding intercultural competence teaching. The findings of our study suggest that teachers who do not believe that language and culture can be taught in an integrated way are also the ones who are not willing to integrate intercultural competence teaching in foreign language education. Providing them with examples of how language and culture teaching can be integrated may help these teachers to explore alternative ways of culture teaching and to change their negative disposition. Helping them to integrate teaching activities directed towards the acquisition of culture learning skills in day-to-day teaching may help to win over teachers who are in doubt. In view of the fact that our data reveal that textbooks play a prominent role in foreign language education and given the fact that most textbooks adopt foreign cultural approaches, not intercultural approaches, teacher training should provide opportunities for teachers to reflect on the quality of their teaching materials for promoting the acquisition of intercultural competence in their learners, and assist them to adapt existing teaching materials. Finally, teacher development programmes may help teachers realise the opportunities to enhance learners' intercultural competence inherent in experiential learning activities, such as exchange projects and school trips, and show ways to avoid possible pitfalls which can lead to reinforcement of already existing stereotypes.

Further Recommendations: Policy Issues

Apart from developers of in-service teacher training sessions, other parties involved in foreign language education may also find the results of this study of interest. We have shown that teachers try to promote an increased familiarity with the foreign culture through their teaching, but that their teaching can as yet not be characterised as promoting the acquisition of intercultural competence. The answer to the question why this is would need to make reference to many different factors at the micro, meso and macro level of teaching. We have already hinted at reasons at the micro or meso levels, pertaining to students, class sizes, the workload, the lack of support from colleagues or principals, etc. In this section, we will focus on some reasons we see at the macro level.

A first reason seems to lie in the way in which teachers in many Western European countries and Mexico, but doubtless also in many other countries, are educated. Most foreign language teachers receive both academic and pedagogical education, though the former usually dominates and focuses primarily on literature and linguistics. In some countries, literary studies are complemented by study of the country, its history and institutions but there has been a tendency to afford this only low status and reduced time allocation. The consequence is that most established and many new teachers have been formed mainly in the mould of literary studies and criticism. Their knowledge of the culture and society pertaining to the foreign language may be adequate to support their literary competence but their study of the culture and society will be at best incidental and based on limited personal, experiential learning rather than systematic description and analysis. Much of what they know about the foreign culture results from personal initiatives to read about the foreign culture, visit the foreign country or otherwise get into contact with the country, culture and people of the language they teach. Our data have shown that such experience is very variable from individual to individual. Even an extensive period abroad does not in itself guarantee acquisition of cultural knowledge and understanding. This analysis suggests therefore that those just entering a career in language teaching with an adequate knowledge of the culture and society of their language are a small minority, even if teachers consider themselves sufficiently familiar with a number of cultural topics, typically dealt with in foreign language textbooks, such as 'daily life and routines' or 'touristic highlights'. We have argued in the introduction to this book that a body of knowledge is certainly required for teachers but that intercultural communicative competence depends on other kinds of teaching as well, and that therefore, teachers also need to be skilful creators of (cross-curricular) learning environments that promote their learners' acquisition of intercultural communicative competence. They need to be able to employ teaching techniques that promote the acquisition of *savoirs* (sociocultural knowledge), *savoir-apprendre*, *savoir-comprendre* and *savoir-s'engager* (culture learning skills), *savoir-faire* and *savoir-être* (an intercultural disposition). In most cases, pre-service teacher training does not prepare teachers for this task. If we turn to the alternative source of teacher development, in-service teacher education, we find courses which offer teacher opportunities for study-visits to the country – often provided or supported by the cultural institutes of the country in question – and secondly, courses held in the home country by the usual providers of in-service education. The former are on the whole experiential in their methodology and are seen as an opportunity to gather 'authentic material'. Like the in-service training sources at home, they tend to focus on factual information and realia, renewing teachers' out-dated knowledge of country and people, though some institutes also offer courses which attempt to prepare teachers for the design of learning environments which promote the acquisition of intercultural competence in its full sense.

What changes to teacher education then do our findings suggest? Apart from promoting a high degree of familiarity with the foreign culture and one's own culture, we believe methodology courses need to include introductions to culture learning theory with specific reference to younger learners, including a knowledge of theories of 'culture shock' and experiential learning during learners' residence or visits to the foreign country for which they may be responsible. They should also demonstrate how the teaching of the foreign language and the foreign culture can be integrated and which learning environments and teaching approaches, for use inside and outside the classroom, have the potential of promoting intercultural competence. The parent disciplines for this kind of language-and-culture teaching methodology course should be anthropology and social psychology. The course should take as its focus the experience of the individual, rather than sociological study of social institutions, for example, and should promote personal development together with professional development. Teachers should come to understand better notions such as 'language and identity' or 'national identity and personal boundaries' or 'social identity and social groups'. Such a course should also grant student teachers the opportunity to study how the language embodies the concepts and values of the culture. There should be comparison, analysis of native speaker perspectives and acquisition of techniques for ethnographic investigations. Understanding their own reactions to foreign cultures and peoples will help (student) teachers to understand the psychology of reactions from learners when they find themselves in intercultural experiences which challenge their view of the world and of their own cultural and national identity.

We believe our findings are also of relevance to designers of teaching materials and textbook authors, since textbooks continue to play a central role in foreign language education, especially at beginner and intermediate levels. Our data have shown that for both the teaching of the foreign language and the promotion of learners' familiarity with the foreign culture, teachers rely heavily on textbooks, though many also use supplementary materials to a larger or lesser extent. A consequence of this is that when textbooks have only limited potential to promote the acquisition of intercultural competence in learners, either because their cultural contents or teaching approach are deficient from an intercultural competence teaching point of view, there is little hope that teachers will teach for intercultural competence. Thus, textbook authors clearly have a responsibility in helping the profession evolve towards intercultural competence teaching. This presupposes that textbook authors themselves are familiar with intercultural competence teaching methodology. Understanding how foreign language teachers currently approach teaching is essential for designing materials which build on this approach but at the same time help teachers to move one step further. Knowledge of teachers' perceptions of their pupils' attitude towards and familiarity with foreign cultures and peoples will provide a useful starting point for designing materials which can help teachers build on their pupils' current level of understanding, rectify any stereotypical perceptions they may have, increase their familiarity with the foreign culture where necessary and improve their skills to independently interpret and acquire new cultural knowledge. Finally, textbook authors may find it enlightening to read through the positive and negative comments teachers voiced regarding the foreign language textbooks they use. One recurrent remark concerns the fact that textbooks become outdated the moment they are published. To meet this comment, publishers could decide to keep a website where teachers can find up-to-date materials that can be used alongside the textbook.

Finally, our findings may help educational policy makers realise that teachers are at present not sufficiently informed about the enlarged objectives of foreign language education, and that not all teachers are favourably disposed towards intercultural competence teaching. They may realise the need to familiarise foreign language teachers with the central concepts and methods of intercultural foreign language education. We can assume that teachers' implicit theories or beliefs are affected by official policies, and that there is a certain convergence between the two. Thus, we believe that official policies, as voiced in curricular guidelines or other official documents, have an important role to play in developing teachers' implicit theories. For example, a clear statement that all pupils, not just pupils in classes with ethnic minority children, should acquire intercultural competence in a foreign language would be a clear sign to teachers that they have an obligation to teach intercultural competence, no matter which classes they teach. Building intercultural competence into the attainment targets for different pupil groups, combined with a requirement to provide proof of intercultural competence, may likewise help to convince teachers of the need to integrate intercultural competence in their teaching and assessment.

Conclusion

The inclusion of a larger number of countries in the European Union and the opening of frontiers within other parts of the world is a confirmation of the trend to mobility and migration which has been present for at least half a century. It is clear that people from different cultures will find themselves living side by side more and more often. If they are to understand each other – and not simply communicate information – language-and-culture learning has to be more complex and rich than the emphasis on communicative competence in foreign language education tends to suggest.

It follows that teachers of language-and-culture need a more complex and enriching education. In both its academic and its pedagogic dimensions, teacher education needs to provide opportunities for learning which are both cognitive and experiential. Foreign language teachers are among the most important mediators, and they need to experience a foreign culture as well as analyse it. They need to reflect upon their experience as well as carry out comparative analysis of their own and the foreign culture, and they need to understand the implications of cultural learning, both cognitive and affective, for their practices in the classroom as well as for their teaching 'in the field'. The responsibilities of the foreign language teacher for introducing learners, whether young or old, to learning which challenges and modifies their perspective on the world and their cultural identity as members of a given social and national group, are enormous. Teacher education has to face the implications and provide them with the practical and theoretical support for those responsibilities.

To influence teachers' beliefs and to assist them in reshaping their teaching practice so that it becomes better able to promote the acquisition of intercultural competence, teachers themselves need to demonstrate intercultural competence. They need to revisit their common sense notions of what it means to teach and learn a foreign language in the light of their encounter with a new philosophy, a philosophy that truly recognises the intercultural nature of all encounters between speakers originating from different cultural backgrounds.

Their belief that teaching and learning a foreign language is always an intercultural process will provide them with a firm basis for reshaping their teaching practice in such a way that it adequately prepares learners for the intercultural world in which they are living.

Notes

1. The six general conceptions of teaching which teachers may hold have been identified as (1) the transmission of the concepts of the syllabus; (2) the transmission of the teacher's knowledge; (3) helping students acquire the concepts of the syllabus; (4) helping students acquire the teacher's knowledge; (5) helping students develop conceptions; and (6) helping students change conceptions (Prosser and Trigwell, 1999).
2. Whereas we asked teachers to indicate with respect to a list of topics how frequently they touched upon each of them in the foreign language classroom, Byram and Risager (1999) asked teachers what they thought should be the topics addressed in foreign language education, offering a list of 20 themes or topics and asking the respondents to identify the ten most important ones.

References

Abbs, B. and Freebairn, I. (1989) *Blueprint Intermediate.* Harlow: Longman.

Abbs, B., Freebairn, I. and Barker, C. (2000) *Snapshot.* Harlow: Longman.

Bell, J. and Gower, R. (1995) *Intermediate Matters. Student's Book.* Harlow: Longman.

Bell, R., Lederman, N. and Abd-El-Khalick, F. (2000) Developing and acting upon one's conception of the nature of science: A follow-up study. *Journal of Research in Science Teaching* 37, 563–581.

Berliner, D.C. (1987) Ways of thinking about students and classrooms by more and less experienced teachers. In J. Calderhead (ed.) *Exploring Teachers' Thinking* (pp. 60–83). London: Cassell Educational Limited.

Berliner, D.D. (1988) Implications of studies on expertise in pedagogy for teacher education and evaluation. In J. Pfleiderer (ed.) *New Directions for Teacher Assessment (Proceedings of the 1988 ETS Invitational Conference)* (pp. 39–68). Princeton, NJ: Educational Testing Service.

Berry, J.W., Poortinga, Y.H., Segall, M.H. and Dasen, P.R. (1992) *Cross-Cultural Psychology: Research and Applications.* New York: Cambridge University Press.

Borg, S. (1998a) Teacher cognition in second language grammar teaching. PhD thesis, University of Exeter.

Borg, S. (1998b) Teachers' pedagogical systems and grammar teaching: A qualitative study. *TESOL Quarterly* 32 (1), 9–38.

Borg, S. (2003) Teacher cognition in language teaching: A review of research on what teachers think, know, believe, and do. *Language Teaching* 36, 81–109.

British Council and Teacher Training Institute Sofia (2001) *Intercultural Studies for Language Teachers. A Postgraduate Distance Learning Course.* Sofia: British Council Bulgaria.

Burns, A. (1996) Starting all over again: From teaching adults to teaching beginners. In D. Freeman and J.C. Richards (eds) *Teacher Learning in Language Teaching* (pp. 154–177). Cambridge: Cambridge University Press.

Byram, M. (1989) *Cultural Studies in Foreign Language Education.* Clevedon: Multilingual Matters.

Byram, M. (1997) *Teaching and Assessing Intercultural Communicative Competence.* Clevedon: Multilingual Matters.

Byram, M., Esarte-Sarries, V. and Taylor, S. (1991) *Cultural Studies and Language Learning. A Research Report.* Clevedon: Multilingual Matters.

Byram, M. and Risager, K. (1999) *Language Teachers, Politics and Cultures.* Clevedon: Multilingual Matters.

Byram, M. and Zarate, G. (1997) Defining and assessing intercultural competence: Some principles and proposals for the European context. *Language Teaching* 29, 239–243.

Cain, A. and Briane, C. (1994) *Comment collégiens et lycéens voient les pays dont ils apprennent la langue. Représentations et stéréotypes.* Paris: Institut National de Recherche Pédagogique.

Calderhead, J. (1996) Teachers: Beliefs and knowledge. In D. Berliner and R. Calife (eds) *Handbook of Educational Psychology* (pp. 709–725). New York: Simon & Schuster Macmillian.

Carter, K. and Doyle, W. (1987) Teachers' knowledge structures and comprehension processes. In J. Calderhead (ed.) *Exploring Teachers' Thinking* (pp. 147–160). London, Great Britain: Cassell Educational Limited.

Carter, K. and Doyle, W. (1995) Preconceptions in learning to teach. *The Educational Forum* 59, 186–195.

Christenbury, L. and Kelly, P.P. (1994) What textbooks can – and cannot – do. *English Journal* March, 76–80.

Council of Europe (2001) *Common European Framework of Reference for Languages: Learning, Teaching, Assessment.* Cambridge: Cambridge University Press.

Counts, M.C. (1999) A case study of a college physics professor's pedagogical content knowledge. Doctoral dissertation, Georgia State University, Atlanta, GA.

Creswell, J. (1994) *Research Design: Qualitative and Quantitative Approaches.* London: Sage Publications.

Davcheva, L. and Docheva, Y. (1998) *Branching Out. A Cultural Studies Syllabus.* Sofia: British Council.

Dunkin, M.J. and Precians, R.P. (1992) Award-winning university teachers' concepts of teaching. *Higher Education* 24, 483–502.

Edelhoff, C. (1993) Language teacher education for Europe. Trends and tasks for the nineties. In C. Edelhoff (ed.) *Fremde Sprachen in Europa: Schlüssel zur Kommunikation und Zusammenarbeit. Referate, Arbeitspapiere und Ergebnisse aus den Lehrgängen 91/09/001 und 92/19/001* (pp. 38–57). Fuldatal: Hessisches Institut für Lehrerfortbildung.

Evans, V. and Dooley, J. (1994) *Grammarway 3.* Newbury: Express Publishing.

Evans, V. and Dooley, J. (2000) *Enterprise 3.* Newbury: Express Publishing.

Felberbauer, M. (1997) Teacher education. In P. Doyé and A. Hurrell (eds) *Foreign Language Learning in Primary Schools* (pp. 77–85). Strasbourg: Council of Europe.

Fiske, S. and Neuberg, S.L. (1990) A continuum of impression formation from category based to individuating processes: Influences of information and motivation on attention and interpretation. In M.P. Zanna (ed.) *Advances in Experimental Social Psychology* (pp. 1–74). New York: Academic Press.

Freeman, D. and Richards, J.C. (1993) Conceptions of teaching and the education of second language teachers. *TESOL Quarterly* 27 (2), 193–216.

Gallagher, J.J. and Tobin, K. (1987) Teacher Management and student engagement in high school science. *Science Teacher Education* 71 (4), 535–555.

Green, S. (1996) The professional development of modern languages teachers. *Language Learning Journal* 14, 75–79.

Greenall, S. (1995) *Reward Intermediate. Student's Book.* Macmillan ELT.

Guilherme, M. (2002) *Critical Citizens for an Intercultural World. Foreign Language Education as Cultural Politics.* Clevedon: Multilingual Matters.

Henderson, C. (2002) Faculty conceptions about the teaching and learning of problem solving in introductory calculus-based physics. PhD thesis, University of Minnesota.

Hopkins, A., Potter, J., Naunton, J. with Hall, D., Du Vivier, M. and Marsden, B. (1995) *Look Ahead Intermediate. Student's Book.* Harlow: Longman.

Hutchinson, T. (1992) *Hotline Pre-intermediate. Student's Book.* Oxford: OUP.

Johnson, K.E. (1996) The role of theory in L2 teacher education. *TESOL Quarterly* 30 (4), 765–771.

Knowles, J.G. and Holt-Reynolds, D. (1991) Shaping pedagogies through personal histories in preservice teacher education. *Teachers College Record* 93 (1), 87–113.

Kwo, O. (1994). Learning to teach: Some theoretical propositions. In I. Carlgren, G. Handal and S. Vaage (eds) *Teachers' Minds and Actions: Research on Teachers' Thinking and Practice* (pp. 215–231). London: Falmer Press.

Lumpe, A.T., Czerniak, C.M. and Haney, J.J. (1998) Science teacher beliefs and intentions regarding the use of cooperative learning. *School Science and Mathematics* 98 (3), 123–135.

Markee, N. (1997) *Managing Curriculum Innovation.* Cambridge: Cambridge University Press.

Méndez García, M.C. (2003) *La Cultura Extranjera en los Libros de Inglés de Bachillerato.* Jaén: Servicio de Publicaciones de la Universidad de Jaén.

Merriam, S. (1998) *Qualitative Research and Case Study Applications in Education.* San Francisco: Jossey-Bass Publishers.

Nespor, J. (1987) The role of beliefs in the practice of teaching. *Journal of Curriculum Studies* 19 (4), 317–332.

Nolasco, R., Giscombe, C. and Reilly, T. (1992) *Streetwise Intermediate.* Oxford: OUP.

Pajares, M.F. (1992) Teachers' beliefs and education research: Cleaning up a messy construct. *Review of Educational Research* 63 (3), 307–332.

Prosser, M., Trigwell, K. and Taylor, P. (1994) A phenomenographic study of academics' conceptions of science learning and teaching. *Learning and Instruction* 4, 217–231.

Prosser, M. and Trigwell, K. (1997) Relations between perceptions of the teaching environment and approaches to teaching. *British Journal of Educational Psychology* 67, 25–35.

Prosser, M. and Trigwell, K. (1999) *Understanding Learning and Teaching: The Experience in Higher Education.* Great Britain: St Edmundsbury Press.

Richardson, V. (1997) *Constructivist Teacher Education: Building a World of New Understandings.* London: Falmer Press London.

Risager, K. (1998) Language teaching and the process of European integration. In M. Byram and M. Fleming (eds) *Language Learning in Intercultural Perspective. Approaches Through Drama and Ethnography* (pp. 242–254). Cambridge: Cambridge University Press.

Ryan, P. (1997) Sociolinguistic goals for foreign language teaching and teachers' metaphorical images of culture. *Foreign Language Annals* 29 (4), 571–586.

Ryan, P. (1998) Cultural knowledge and foreign language teachers: a case study of a native English speaker and a native Spanish speaker. *Language, Culture and Curriculum* 11 (2), 135–153.

Scardamalia, M. and Bereiter, C. (1991) Higher levels of agency for children in knowledge building: A challenge for the design of new knowledge media. *Journal of the Learning Sciences* 1 (1), 37–68.

Scardamalia, M. and Bereiter, C. (1994) Computer support for knowledge building communities. *Journal of the Learning Sciences* 3 (3), 265–283.

Sen Gupta, A. (2002) Changing the focus. A discussion of the dynamics of the intercultural experience. In G. Alred, M. Byram and M. Fleming (eds) *Intercultural Experience and Education* (pp. 155–178). Clevedon: Multilingual Matters.

Sercu, L. (2000a) *Acquiring Intercultural Communicative Competence from Textbooks. The Case of Flemish Adolescents Learning German.* Leuven: Leuven University Press.

Sercu, L. (2000b) Textbooks. In M. Byram (ed.) *Routledge Encyclopedia of Language Teaching and Learning* (pp. 626–628). London/New York: Routledge.

Sercu, L. (2001) La dimension interculturelle dans la vision pédagogique en langue étrangère. Analyse comparative des conceptions professionnelles des enseignants d'anglais, de français et d'allemand. In G. Zarate (ed.) *Langues, Xénophobie, Xénophilie dans une Europe Multiculturelle* (pp. 169–180). CRDP de Basse-Normandie.

Snow, D. and Byram, M. (1997) *Crossing Frontiers. The School Study Visit Abroad.* London: CILT.

Soars, J. and Soars, L. (1997) *Headway Advanced. Student's Book.* Oxford: OUP.

Stangor, C. and McMillan, D. (1992) Memory for expectancy-consistent and expectancy-inconsistent social information: A meta-analytic review of the social psychological and social developmental literatures. *Psychological Bulletin* 111, 42–61.

van Driel, J.H., Verloop, N., Werven, H.I. and Dekkers, H. (1997) Teachers' craft knowledge and curriculum innovation in higher engineering education. *Higher Education* 34, 105–122.

Viney, P. and Viney, K. (1992) *Grapevine Level 3. Student's Book.* Oxford: OUP.

Webster, D. and Worrall, C. (1997) *English Together. Student's Book.* Harlow: Longman.

Willems, G. (2000) Teacher education. In M. Byram (ed.) *Routledge Encyclopedia of Language Teaching and Learning* (pp. 603–608). London: Routledge.

Wood, D. and Wood, H. (1996) Vygotsky, tutoring and learning. *Oxford Review of Education* 22 (1), 5–10.

Woods, D. (1996) *Teacher Cognition in Language Teaching. Beliefs, Decision-Making and Classroom Practice.* Cambridge: CUP.

Appendix 1

Questionnaire

1. Survey

Section 1: Personal data

The first section of the questionnaire asks you to provide some personal data.

1.1. Are you male or a female?
Please tick the correct answer.

- ☐ Male
- ☐ Female

1.2. What year were you born?
Please enter your year of birth. You can only use numbers, not letters.

____

1.3. What degree(s) did you obtain after you finished secondary education?
Please list the degrees you obtained. You can type in the names in your native tongue.

____

____

____

____

____

1.4. What is your native tongue? Or if you consider yourself bilingual: what are your native tongues?

1.5. What is your nationality? Or, if you have more than one nationality: what are your nationalities?

1.6. What foreign language do you teach?
Or if you teach more than one foreign language: What is your main language? Of which foreign language do you teach most hours?

- ☐ German as a foreign language
- ☐ French as a foreign language
- ☐ English as a foreign language
- ☐ Spanish as a foreign language
- ☐ My native tongue as a second language
- ☐ Still other languages, namely

1.7. If you teach more than one language: What language(s) apart from your main language do you teach?
Please tick the language(s) you teach. Should you teach any other language(s) which have not been listed, please type them in the area below.

- ☐ I teach only one language
- ☐ Apart from my main language I teach German as a foreign language
- ☐ Apart from my main language I teach French as a foreign language
- ☐ Apart from my main language I teach English as a foreign language
- ☐ Apart from my main language I teach Spanish as a foreign language

- ☐ My native tongue as a first language (mother tongue teachnig)
- ☐ Apart from my main language I teach my native tongue as a second language
  (This means that you teach your mother to people residing in your country who do not speak the official language(s) of your country)
- ☐ Other language(s) not listed above. namely:

____

____

____

____

____

1.8. How long have you been teaching foreign languages?

I have been teaching foreign languages for ___________ years

2. Survey

Section 2: Your current teaching job

The questions in this section concern your current teaching job.

2.1. How many hours do you teach per week?

____

2.2. What percentage of your school's population are ethnic minority community children?
Should you be teaching in more than one school, please answer **this question and the following questions** with respect to the school where you have most hours.
Please tick the percentage that best matches your school.

- ☐ 0%
- ☐ less than 1%
- ☐ 1% – 10%
- ☐ 10% – 30%
- ☐ 30% – 50%
- ☐ more than 50%

2.3. What kind of education does your school offer?
Please tick the option(s) that match your school. Should your school offer other kinds of education, please specify them in the typing area below.

- ☐ general secondary education
- ☐ artistic secondary education
- ☐ vocational secondary education
- ☐ other kinds of education, namely:

____

____

____

____

____

2.4. What foreign languages are taught in your school?
Please tick all foreign languages taught in your school.

- ☐ Classical Latin
- ☐ Classical Greek
- ☐ French as a foreign language
- ☐ English as a foreign language
- ☐ German as a foreign language
- ☐ Spanish as a foreign language
- ☐ Others, namely:

____

____

____

____

____

2.5. Any other characteristics of your school you would like to mention
Any additional information pertinent to your school you might like to add:

____

____

____

____

____

____

Survey

Section 3: You as a teacher

You have now accessed the **third** section of the questionnaire. The questions in this section concern your perceptions of what it is that you try to achieve with your pupils.

3.1. What do you try to do as a teacher?
The following four questions ask you to make a forced choice. For every pair of statements please tick the statement that best matches your view regarding your teaching. We know it will often be difficult for you to choose, that one choice may only have a slight edge over the other.

(1)
- ☐ I want to be on good terms with my pupils.
- ☐ I want to fulfil the curricular requirements for my subject.

(2)
- ☐ I try to impart to my pupils the skills, knowledge and attitudes which they will need in life.
- ☐ I try to enthuse my pupils for my subject.

(3)
- ☐ I try to impart to my pupils the skills, knowledge and attitudes they will need to further their proficiency in the foreign language they are learning.
- ☐ I try to coach my pupils on their way to adulthood.

(4)
- ☐ I want to pass on expert knowledge regarding my subject to my pupils.
- ☐ I want to support my pupils when they have personal problems.

3.2. How do you perceive the objectives of foreign language teaching?
Below, eight possible objectives of foreign language teaching have been listed. Please rank them in order of importance through assigning each objective a number between 1.and 8. You assign the number **'1'** to the objective which you consider **most important**, '2' to the objective which you consider second in importance, and so on. You have to assign a number to each objective, and you can only assign each number once.

(1) Enthuse my pupils for learning foreign languages.
1 2 3 4 5 6 7 8

(2) Promote my pupils' familiarity with the culture, the civilisation of the countries where the language which they are learning is spoken.
1 2 3 4 5 6 7 8

(3) Assist my pupils to acquire a level of proficiency in the foreign language that will allow them to read literary works in the foreign language.
1 2 3 4 5 6 7 8

(4) Assist my pupils to acquire skills that will be useful in other subject areas and in live (such as memorise, summarise, put into words, formulate accurately, give a presentation, etc.).
1 2 3 4 5 6 7 8

(5) Promote the acquisition of an open mind and a positive disposition towards unfamiliar cultures.
1 2 3 4 5 6 7 8

(6) Promote the acquisition of learning skills that will be useful for learning other foreign languages.
1 2 3 4 5 6 7 8

(7) Promote the acquisition of a level of proficiency in the foreign language that will allow the learners to use the foreign language for practical purposes.
1 2 3 4 5 6 7 8

(8) Assist my pupils in developing a better understanding of their own identity and culture.
1 2 3 4 5 6 7 8

3.3. What do you understand by 'culture teaching' in a foreign language teaching context?

Below, nine possible objectives of culture teaching have been listed. Please rank them in order of importance through assigning each objective a number between 1.and 9. You assign the number '**1**' to the objective which you consider **most important**, '2' to the objective which you consider second in importance, and so on. As with the previous question, you have to assign a number to each objective, and you can only assign each number once.

(1) Provide information about the history, geography and political conditions of the foreign culture(s).
1 2 3 4 5 6 7 8 9

(2) Provide information about daily life and routines.
1 2 3 4 5 6 7 8 9

(3) Provide information about shared values and beliefs.
1 2 3 4 5 6 7 8 9

(4) Provide experiences with a rich variety of cultural expressions (literature, music, theatre, film, etc.).
1 2 3 4 5 6 7 8 9

(5) Develop attitudes of openness and tolerance towards other peoples and cultures.
1 2 3 4 5 6 7 8 9

(6) Promote reflection on cultural differences.
1 2 3 4 5 6 7 8 9

(7) Promote increased understanding of students' own culture.
1 2 3 4 5 6 7 8 9

(8) Promote the ability to empathise with people living in other cultures.
1 2 3 4 5 6 7 8 9

(9) Promote the ability to handle intercultural contact situations.
1 2 3 4 5 6 7 8 9

3.4. How is your teaching time distributed over 'language teaching' and 'culture teaching'?
Please tick the option that best corresponds with the average distribution of teaching time over 'language teaching' and 'culture teaching'.

- ☐ 100% language teaching–0% culture teaching
- ☐ 80% language teaching–20% culture teaching
- ☐ 60% language teaching–40% culture teaching
- ☐ 40% language teaching–60% culture teaching
- ☐ 20% language teaching–80% culture teaching
- ☐ 100% integration of language-and-culture teaching

3.5. Do you have the feeling that you would like to devote more time to 'culture teaching' during your foreign language teaching classes, but that somehowyou never get round to it?
Pleas tick the answer that best matches your opinion.

- ☐ Yes, very much so
- ☐ Yes, up to a certain extent
- ☐ No, not particularly
- ☐ No, not at all
- ☐ No opinion

3.6. If you have the feeling you would like to devote more time to 'culture teaching' but do not get round to it, what may be the reasons for that?
Please type in any reasons you see in the area below.

____

____

____

____

____

____

Survey

Section 4: Your pupils and foreign languages and cultures

The questions in this section concern your pupils. They address various aspects of their learning of foreign languages.

4.1. To what extent do you agree or disagree with the following statements? Below you find some statements regarding your pupils. Please indicate the degree to which you agree with each statement. We ask you to provide an indication of your general impression, irrespective of individual differences you may see. Please select a number ranging from 1.to 10. If you **agree completely** you assign **'10'**. If you do **not agree at all** you assign **'1'**. Of course you can also assign any of the numbers in between. If you teach more than one language, please answer the question with respect to the language you teach most hours.

(1) My pupils are very motivated to learn the foreign language I teach.
1 2 3 4 5 6 7 8 9 10

(2) My pupils think learning the foreign language I teach is very difficult.
1 2 3 4 5 6 7 8 9 10

(3) My pupils are very knowledgeable about the culture of the foreign language I teach.
1 2 3 4 5 6 7 8 9 10

(4) My pupils have a very positive attitude towards the people associated with the foreign language I teach.
1 2 3 4 5 6 7 8 9 10

4.2. What countries, cultures and peoples are usually associated with the language of which you have most hours?
Foreign languages tend to be associated with particular countries, peoples and cultures. In the area below please specify what countries, peoples and cultures are usually associated with the language you teach. As with previous questions, please answer the question with respect to the language of which you have most hours.

____

____

____

____

____

4.3. Of the countries, cultures and peoples mentioned above, which one is primarily associated with the foreign language of which you have most hours?

____

____

____

____

____

4.4. How would you describe your pupils' perceptions of and ideas regarding the country/ies and people(s) usually associated with the foreign language you teach? Please use **key words** to describe in the area below what you think your pupils associate with the country/ies, culture(s) and people(s) that are usually associated with the foreign language you teach. Please distinguish between countries, cultures and peoples when needed.

____

____

____

____

____

4.5. How frequently do you think your pupils are in contact with the foreign country primarily associated with the language you teach most hours?

(1) Travel to the foreign country (holiday with family)
Often Once in a while Never

(2) Watch one of the country's television channels.
Often Once in a while Never

(3) Read one of the country's newspapers or magazines.
Often Once in a while Never

(4) Read literature written by authors living in the foreign country or originating from the foreign country.
Often Once in a while Never

(5) Use the Internet to learn more about the foreign country.
Often Once in a while Never

____

Survey

Section 5: Your familiarity with the foreign culture(s) associated with the foreign language you teach

The questions in this section concern your familiarity with the foreign culture(s) associated with the foreign language you teach.

5.1. How familiar are you with the country, culture, people primarily associated with the foreign language of which you have most hours?

- You choose **'very familiar'** when you feel you are so familiar with that topic that it would be very easy for you to talk about it extensively in your foreign language classroom'.
- You pick **'sufficiently familiar'** when you feel you are familiar enough with a particular topic that you could say something about it during your classes.
- When you choose **'not sufficiently familiar'** you indicate that you yourself think that you are not well informed about a particular topic.
- You pick **'not familiar at all'** when you feel you don't really know anything about that particular cultural aspect.

(1) History, geography, political system

Very familiar | Sufficiently | Not sufficiently | Not familiar at all

(2) Different ethnic and social groups

Very familiar | Sufficiently | Not sufficiently | Not familiar at all

(3) Daily life and routines, living conditions, food and drink etc.

Very familiar | Sufficiently | Not sufficiently | Not familiar at all

(4) Youth culture

Very familiar | Sufficiently | Not sufficiently | Not familiar at all

(5) Education, professional life

Very familiar | Sufficiently | Not sufficiently | Not familiar at all

(6) Traditions, folklore, tourist attractions

Very familiar | Sufficiently | Not sufficiently | Not familiar at all

(7) Literature

Very familiar Sufficiently Not sufficiently Not familiar at all

(8) Other cultural expressions (music, drama, art)

Very familiar Sufficiently Not sufficiently Not familiar at all

(9) Values and beliefs

Very familiar Sufficiently Not sufficiently Not familiar at all

(10) International relations (political, economic and cultural), with students' own country and other countries

Very familiar Sufficiently Not sufficiently Not familiar at all

5.2. How frequently do you travel to the foreign country primarily associated with the foreign language of which you have most hours?

(1) Tourist stays (lasting longer than two days) in the foreign country

Often Once in a while Never

(2) Visits to relatives or friends

Often Once in a while Never

(3) Participation in a teacher training programme or a language course

Often Once in a while Never

(4) School trips (one or two days)

Often Once in a while Never

(5) Work visits, e.g. within the framework of an exchange project

Often Once in a while Never

5.3. How often do you get into contact with the foreign culture/ people/ country primarily associated with the foreign language of which you have most hours while you are at home?

(1) Media contacts (via newspapers, television, radio)

Often Once in a while Never

(2) Visits to the cultural institute representing the foreign country in my country

Often Once in a while Never

(3) Contacts with people originating from the foreign country who live in my country

Often Once in a while Never

(4) Contacts with foreign language assistants (usually natives from the foreign country) in my school

Often Once in a while Never

(5) Contacts with foreign teachers or pupils who visit my school

Often Once in a while Never

5.4. Please specify any other contacts you have in the area below.

____

____

____

____

____

Survey

Section 6: Culture in foreign language teaching

The questions in this section concern your culture teaching practice.

6.1. What kind(s) of culture teaching activities do you practise during classroom teaching time?
Below a number of possible culture teaching activities have been listed. Please indicate for each activity how often you practise it during classroom teaching time.

(1) I ask my pupils to think about the image which the media promote of the foreign country.
Often Once in a while Never

(2) I tell my pupils what I heard (or read) about the foreign country or culture.
Often Once in a while Never

(3) I tell my pupils why I find something fascinating or strange about the foreign culture(s).
Often Once in a while Never

(4) I ask my pupils to independently explore an aspect of the foreign culture.
Often Once in a while Never

(5) I use videos, CD-ROMs or the Internet to illustrate an aspect of the foreign culture.
Often Once in a while Never

(6) I ask my pupils to think about what it would be like to live in the foreign culture.
Often Once in a while Never

(7) I talk to my pupils about my own experiences in the foreign country.
Often Once in a while Never

(8) I ask my pupils about their experiences in the foreign country.
Often Once in a while Never

(9) I invite a person originating from the foreign country to my classroom.
Often Once in a while Never

(10) I ask my pupils to describe an aspect of their own culture in the foreign language.
Often Once in a while Never

(11) I bring objects originating from the foreign culture to my classroom.
Often Once in a while Never

(12) I ask my pupils to participate in role-play situations in which people from different cultures meet.
Often Once in a while Never

(13) I decorate my classroom with posters illustrating particular aspects of the foreign culture.
Often Once in a while Never

(14) I comment on the way in which the foreign culture is represented in the foreign language materials I am using in a particular class.
Often Once in a while Never

(15) I ask my pupils to compare an aspect of their own culture with that aspect in the foreign culture.
Often Once in a while Never

(16) I touch upon an aspect of the foreign culture regarding which I feel negatively disposed.
Often Once in a while Never

(17) I talk with my pupils about stereotypes regarding particular cultures and countries or regarding the inhabitants of particular countries.
Often Once in a while Never

6.2. Please specify any other activities you practise in the area below.

____

____

____

____

____

6.3. How extensively do you deal with particular cultural aspects?
Below a number of cultural aspects have been listed. Please indicate for each aspect how extensively you touch upon it in class.

(1) History, geography, political system
I deal with it extensively | I touch upon it once in a while | I never touch upon it

(2) Different ethnic and social groups
I deal with it extensively | I touch upon it once in a while | I never touch upon it

(3) Daily life and routines, living conditions, food and drink etc.
I deal with it extensively | I touch upon it once in a while | I never touch upon it

(4) Youth culture
I deal with it extensively | I touch upon it once in a while | I never touch upon it

(5) Education, professional life
I deal with it extensively | I touch upon it once in a while | I never touch upon it

(6) Traditions, folklore, tourist attractions
I deal with it extensively | I touch upon it once in a while | I never touch upon it

(7) Literature

I deal with it extensively	I touch upon it once in a while	I never touch upon it

(8) Other cultural expressions (music, drama, art)

I deal with it extensively	I touch upon it once in a while	I never touch upon it

(9) Values and beliefs

I deal with it extensively	I touch upon it once in a while	I never touch upon it

(10) International relations (political, economic and cultural) with students' own country and other countries

I deal with it extensively	I touch upon it once in a while	I never touch upon it

Survey

Section 7: Foreign language teaching materials

The questions in this section concern foreign language teaching materials.

7.1. Do you use textbooks and/or additional teaching materials?
Please select the option(s) that best match(es) your teaching practice.

- ☐ I do use textbooks. I use mainly one book per class.
  Please go to QUESTION 7.now.
- ☐ I do use textbooks. I use materials from different textbooks.
  Pleas go to QUESTION 7.now.
- ☐ I do not use textbooks. I use other materials.
  Please go to QUESTION 2.now.

7.2. If you indicated that you use other materials instead of textbooks, which are those materials?

____

____

____

____

____

7.3. If you indicated that you do not use textbooks, please explain why this is so. After you answered this question you can skip the remaining questions of this section and submit your answers right away.

____

____

____

____

____

7.4. If you indicated that together with textbooks, you also use the additional materials, please indicate which other materials you use:

☐ Video materials

☐ Audio materials

☐ Still other materials,

7.5. namely:

____

____

____

____

____

7.6. The reasons why you use additional materials together with textbooks are:

____

____

____

____

____

7.7. If you indicated that you use textbooks, which books do you use?
Please list the title(s) of the book(s) you use and the country where each book is published in the typing area below. Please quote the book you use most often first, then the one you use somewhat less often, and so on.

____

____

____

____

____

7.8. Can teachers choose their own textbooks at your school?

☐ Yes

☐ No

7.9. If you can choose your own textbook, what criteria do you observe when selecting a textbook?
Below a number of textbook characteristics that may affect your choice against or in favour of a particular textbook have been listed. Please tick the six criteria that appear most important to you.

☐ The fact that additional materials come with the book (workbook, listening materials, tests, video, etc.)

☐ The layout

☐ The price

☐ The quality of the teacher's manual

☐ The degree to which the textbook meets the curricular requirements

☐ The degree to which the book is attuned to the level and the age of my pupils.

☐ The pace of the book, the speed with which the book progresses

☐ The amount of cultural information the book offers

☐ The degree to which the book can motivate my pupils

☐ The textbook authors' nationality

☐ The degree of matching between the amount of materials offered and the number of teaching periods assigned to my subject

7.10. Please indicate in the area below any additional criteria you use when deciding on whether or not to use a particular textbook.

____

____

____

____

____

7.11. Do the cultural contents of the textbook(s) you use meet your expectations?
Please tick the answer that best matches your opinion.

☐ Yes, very much so.

☐ Yes, up to a certain extent.

☐ No, not really.

☐ No, not at all.

7.12. Please explain your choice in the typing area below.

____

____

____

____

____

____

Survey

Section 8: School trips

The questions in this section concern school trips.
School trips are short trips to the foreign country. They may last one day or longer. Exchange programmes, **which are dealt with in the next section**, also involve a shorter or longer stay in the foreign country. In addition they involve receiving the inhabitants from the other country in one's own country.

8.1. Does your school organise school trips to foreign countries?

- ☐ Yes
- ☐ No

8.2. If so, please provide the name(s) of the country/countries to which your school organises school trips in the area below.

____

____

____

____

____

8.3. What reasons do you see for organising school trips?
Below some possible reasons for organising school trips have been listed. Please rank them in order of importance. through assigning each reason a number between '1' and '5'. You assign the number '**1**' to the reason you consider **most important** and '**5**' to the reason you consider **least important**. You have to assign a number to each objective, and you can only assign each number once.

(1) Create an opportunity for pupils to practise their foreign language skills
1 2 3 4 5

(2) Enhance pupils' motivation to learn the foreign language
1 2 3 4 5

(3) Increase pupils' interest in the foreign culture
1 2 3 4 5

(4) Foster pupils' independence
1 2 3 4 5

(5) Increase pupils' familiarity with the foreign culture
1 2 3 4 5

8.4. Please provide any other reasons you see for organising school trips in the area below.

8.5. Do you consider it part of your teaching role to prepare a school trip during foreign language classes?

- ☐ Yes
- ☐ No

8.6. If your answer to the previous question was 'yes', please specify in the area below

- how much time (how many hours) on average you spend on preparing a school trip during your foreign language classes;
- what kind of preparation you offer

8.7. Do you consider it part of your teaching role to follow-up on a school trip during your foreign language classes?

- ☐ Yes
- ☐ No

8.8. If your answer to the previous question was 'yes', please specify in the area below

- how much time on average (how many hours) you spend on following-up on a school trip during your foreign language classes;
- how you follow up on a school trip

8.9. Do you believe school trips have a positive or a negative effect on the attitudes and perceptions of pupils regarding foreign country/ies, foreign culture(s), foreign people?

- ☐ Yes
- ☐ No

8.10. Please explain your answer in the area below.

____

____

____

____

____

____

Survey

Section 9: Exchanges

The questions in this section concern exchange programmes.

9.1. Does your school participate in international exchange projects?

- ☐ Yes
- ☐ No

9.2. If so, please specify the names of the country/ies involved in the exchange programme(s) in which your school participates in the area below.

____

____

____

____

____

9.3. What are the main reasons for participating in exchange projects?
Below some possible reasons for organising exchange projects have been listed. Please rank them in order of importance. through assigning each reason a number between 1.and 5. You assign the number '**1**' to the reason you consider **most important** and **5** to the reason you consider **least important** . You have to assign a number to each objective, and you can only assign each number once.

(1) Create an opportunity for pupils to practise their foreign language skills
1 2 3 4 5

(2) Enhance pupils' motivation to learn the foreign language
1 2 3 4 5

(3) Increase pupils' interest in the foreign culture
1 2 3 4 5

(4) Foster pupils' independence
1 2 3 4 5

(5) Increase pupils' familiarity with the foreign culture
1 2 3 4 5

9.4. Please provide any other reasons you see for organising exchange projects in the area below.

____

____

____

____

____

9.5. Do you consider it part of your teaching role to prepare an exchange project during foreign language classes?

☐ Yes

☐ No

9.6. If your answer to the previous question was 'yes', please specify in the area below

- how much time (how many hours) on average you spend on preparing an exchange project during your foreign language classes;
- what kind of preparation you offer

____

____

____

____

____

9.7. Do you consider it part of your teaching role to follow-up on an exchange project during your foreign language classes?

☐ Yes

☐ No

9.8. If your answer to the previous question was 'yes', please specify in the area below

- how much time on average (how many hours) you spend on following-up on an exchange project during your foreign language classes;
- how you follow up on an exchange project

____

____

____

____

____

9.9. Do you believe exchange projects have a positive or a negative effect on the attitudes and perceptions of pupils regarding foreign country/ies, foreign culture(s), foreign people?

- ☐ Yes
- ☐ No

9.10. Please explain your answer in the area below.

____

____

____

____

____

____

Survey

Section 10: (Cross-curicular) intercultural activities and projects

The questions in this section concern cross-curricular intercultural activities and projects, other than school trips or exchange projects.

10.1. Does your school organise (cross-curricular) intercultural/multicultural/ international activities?

- ☐ Yes
- ☐ No

10.2. If your answer is 'yes', please specify what other activities your school mounts in the area below.

____

____

____

____

____

10.3. Do you believe these activities have a positive effect on the attitudes and perceptions of pupils regarding foreign country/ies, foreign culture(s), foreign people?

- ☐ Yes
- ☐ No

10.4. Please explain your answer in the area below.

____

____

____

____

____

Survey

Section 11: Intercultural foreign language teaching: Your opinion

In this section, we would like you to score a number of statements on a five-point-scale, ranging from 'I agree completely' to 'I do not agree at all'. The statements concern intercultural foreign language teaching. Each time select the option that best matches your opinion.

(1) In a foreign language classroom, teaching culture is as important as teaching the foreign language.

Agree completely	Agree to a certain extent	Undecided	Disagree to a certain extent	Disagree completely

(2) Intercultural education is best undertaken cross-curricularly.

Agree completely	Agree to a certain extent	Undecided	Disagree to a certain extent	Disagree completely

(3) A foreign language teacher should present a positive image of the foreign culture and society.

Agree completely	Agree to a certain extent	Undecided	Disagree to a certain extent	Disagree completely

(4) Before you can teach culture or do anything about the intercultural dimension of foreign language teaching, pupils have to possess a sufficiently high level of proficiency in the foreign language.

Agree completely	Agree to a certain extent	Undecided	Disagree to a certain extent	Disagree completely

(5) Intercultural skills cannot be acquired at school.

Agree completely	Agree to a certain extent	Undecided	Disagree to a certain extent	Disagree completely

(6) It is impossible to teach the foreign language and the foreign culture in an integrated way.

Agree completely	Agree to a certain extent	Undecided	Disagree to a certain extent	Disagree completely

(7) I would like to promote the acquisition of intercultural skills through my teaching.

Agree completely	Agree to a certain extent	Undecided	Disagree to a certain extent	Disagree completely

(8) Intercultural education has no effect whatsoever on pupils' attitudes.

Agree completely	Agree to a certain extent	Undecided	Disagree to a certain extent	Disagree completely

(9) The more pupils know about the foreign culture, the more tolerant they are.

Agree completely	Agree to a certain extent	Undecided	Disagree to a certain extent	Disagree completely

(10) In international contacts misunderstandings arise equally often from linguistic as from cultural differences.

Agree completely	Agree to a certain extent	Undecided	Disagree to a certain extent	Disagree completely

(11) Foreign language teaching should enhance pupils' understanding of their own cultural identity.

Agree completely	Agree to a certain extent	Undecided	Disagree to a certain extent	Disagree completely

(12) All pupils should acquire intercultural competence, not only pupils in classrooms with ethnic minority community children.

Agree completely	Agree to a certain extent	Undecided	Disagree to a certain extent	Disagree completely

---

Please score the statements below in the same way as you did in the first part of this section.

(1) When you only have a limited number of teaching periods, culture teaching has to give way to language teaching.

Agree completely	Agree to a certain extent	Undecided	Disagree to a certain extent	Disagree completely

(2) Every subject, not just foreign language teaching, should promote the acquisition of intercultural skills.

Agree completely	Agree to a certain extent	Undecided	Disagree to a certain extent	Disagree completely

(3) A foreign language teacher should present a realistic image of a foreign culture, and therefore should also touch upon negative sides of the foreign culture and society.

Agree completely	Agree to a certain extent	Undecided	Disagree to a certain extent	Disagree completely

(4) If one wants to be able to achieve anything at all as regards intercultural understanding one should use texts written in the mother tongue and discuss these texts in the mother tongue, even when in a foreign language classroom.

Agree completely	Agree to a certain extent	Undecided	Disagree to a certain extent	Disagree completely

(5) In the foreign language classroom pupils can only acquire additional cultural knowledge. They cannot acquired intercultural skills.

Agree completely	Agree to a certain extent	Undecided	Disagree to a certain extent	Disagree completely

(6) Only when there are ethnic minority community pupils in your classes do you have to teach intercultural competence.

Agree completely	Agree to a certain extent	Undecided	Disagree to a certain extent	Disagree completely

(7) Language and culture cannot be taught in an integrated way. You have to separate the two.

Agree completely	Agree to a certain extent	Undecided	Disagree to a certain extent	Disagree completely

(8) I would like to teach intercultural competence through my foreign language teaching.

Agree completely	Agree to a certain extent	Undecided	Disagree to a certain extent	Disagree completely

(9) Intercultural education reinforces pupils' already existing stereotypes of other peoples and cultures.

Agree completely	Agree to a certain extent	Undecided	Disagree to a certain extent	Disagree completely

(10) Providing additional cultural information makes pupils more tolerant towards other cultures and peoples.

Agree completely	Agree to a certain extent	Undecided	Disagree to a certain extent	Disagree completely

(11) Language problems lie at the heart of misunderstandings in international contacts, not cultural differences.

Agree completely	Agree to a certain extent	Undecided	Disagree to a certain extent	Disagree completely

(12) Foreign language teaching should not only touch upon foreign cultures. It should also deepen pupils' understanding of their own culture.

Agree completely	Agree to a certain extent	Undecided	Disagree to a certain extent	Disagree completely

Appendix 2

Bonferroni Multiple Comparisons Test Results

Statistical differences between countries were identified through running the Bonferroni multiple comparisons test on the data. The test investigates which group means differ significantly from each other with respect to a particular variable through comparing all group means to each other and correcting the level of significance for the number of comparisons made. In order to ensure that the probability is no greater than 5% that something will appear to be statistically significant when there are no underlying differences, each of 'm' individual comparisons is performed at the (0.05 m) level of significance. Since the chance that the null-hypothesis is falsely rejected increases exponentially with an increase in the number of *t*-tests run on the same data, this correction has to be made.

The Bonferroni-test results are presented in a highly simplified form in the table below. The numbers in the right-hand column indicate the number of times a particular variable appeared to have been scored significantly different between two countries. The maximum number of possible differences is 42. The Bonferroni test results were interpreted as follows: we say that the seven countries participating in the research appear to be more similar than different with respect to a particular variable when the number obtained for a particular variable is below 14. We say that the countries appear to be more different than similar with respect to a particular variable when the number obtained is above 29. We say that the picture is unclear when the number obtained lies between 15 and 28.

How many hours do you teach per week?	26
What kind of education does your school offer?	26
What percentage of your school's population are minority community children?	22

My pupils have a very positive attitude towards the people associated with the foreign language I teach	22
Teacher contact at home	22
Does your school organise school trips to foreign countries?	22
What year were you born?	18
What foreign language do you teach?	18
Pupils' contact	16
How long have you been teaching foreign languages?	14
My pupils are very motivated to learn the foreign language I teach	14
In a foreign language classroom, teaching culture is as important as teaching the foreign language	14
Cultural objectives	12
My pupils think learning the foreign language I teach is very difficult	12
Does your school organise (cross-curricular) intercultural/ multicultural/international activities?	12
IC teaching involves teaching about one's own culture	12
What degree(s) did you obtain after you finished secondary education?	10
Teacher travel frequency	10
Intercultural education is best undertaken cross-curricularly	10
Language objectives	8
Do you use textbooks and/or additional teaching materials?	8
I would like to promote the acquisition of intercultural skills through my teaching	8
Foreign language teaching should enhance pupils' understanding of their own cultural identity	8
A foreign language teacher should present a realistic image of a foreign culture, and therefore should also touch upon negative sides of the foreign culture and society	8
Language and culture cannot be taught in an integrated way. You have to separate the two	8
Intercultural skills cannot be acquired at school	7
Are you male or female?	6
General objectives	6

How is your teaching time distributed over 'language teaching' and 'culture teaching'?	6
Culture elements	6
Do you consider it part of your teaching role to follow-up on a school trip during your foreign language classes?	6
L&C teaching impossible to integrate	6
Intercultural education reinforces pupils' already existing stereotypes of other peoples and cultures	6
Foreign language teaching should not only touch upon foreign cultures. It should also deepen pupils' understanding of their own culture	6
Do you consider it part of your teaching role to prepare a school trip during foreign language classes?	5
Does your school participate in international exchange projects?	4
IC skills cannot be acquired at school	4
IC teaching has no effect on pupils	4
Before you can teach culture or do anything about the intercultural dimension of foreign language teaching, pupils have to possess a sufficiently high level of proficiency in the foreign language	4
In international contacts misunderstandings arise equally often from linguistic as from cultural differences	4
All pupils should acquire intercultural competence, not only pupils in classrooms with ethnic minority community children	4
Only when there are ethnic minority community pupils in your classes do you have to teach intercultural competence	4
I would like to teach intercultural competence through my foreign language teaching	4
Preference for pupil centred teaching	2
Preference for subject centred teaching	2
Do you have the feeling that you would like to devote more time to 'culture teaching' during your foreign language teaching classes, but that somehow you never get round to it?	2
Kinds of culture teaching activities	2
Enhance pupils' motivation to learn the foreign language	2
Foster pupils' independence	2

Do you consider it part of your teaching role to follow-up on an exchange project during your foreign language classes?	2
Willingness to teach ICC	2
Misunderstandings for linguistic reasons	2
It is impossible to teach the foreign language and the foreign culture in an integrated way	2
If one wants to be able to achieve anything at all as regards intercultural understanding one should use texts written in the mother tongue and discuss these texts in the mother tongue	2
Providing additional cultural information makes pupils more tolerant towards other cultures and people	2
Language problems lie at the heart of misunderstandings in international contacts, not cultural differences	2
My pupils are very knowlegeable about the culture of the foreign language I teach	0
Teacher familiarity	0
Criteria for choosing a textbook	0
Do the cultural contents of the textbook(s) you use meet your expectations?	0
Create an opportunity for pupils to practise their foreign language skills	0
Increase pupils' interest in the foreign culture	0
Foster pupils' independence	0
Increase pupils' familiarity with the foreign culture	0
Do you believe school trips have a positive or a negative effect on the attitudes and perceptions of pupils regarding foreign country/ies?	0
Create an opportunity for pupils to practise their foreign language skills	0
Increase pupils' interest in the foreign culture	0
Increase pupils' familiarity with the foreign culture	0
Do you consider it part of your teaching role to prepare an exchange project during foreign language classes?	0
Do you believe exchange projects have a positive or negative effect on the attitudes and perceptions of pupils regarding foreign countries?	0

Do you believe these activities have a positive effect on the attitudes and perceptions of pupils regarding foreign countries?	0
Balance between language and culture teaching is required	0
Teaching IC cross-curricularly	0
Present positive image	0
Language before culture	0
More cultural information – more tolerance	0
IC only when ethnic minority	0
A foreign language teacher should present a positive image of the foreign culture and society	0
Intercultural education has no effect whatsoever on pupils' attitudes	0
The more pupils know about the foreign culture, the more tolerant they are	0
When you only have a limited number of teaching periods, culture teaching has to give way to language teaching	0
Every subject, not just foreign language teaching, should promote the acquisition of intercultural skills	0
In the foreign language classroom pupils can only acquire additional cultural knowledge. They cannot acquire intercultural skills	0